Search Engine Advertising

Buying Your Way — to the Top — to Increase Sales

CATHERINE SEDA

New Riders

1249 Eighth Street, Berkeley, California 94710

An Imprint of Pearson Education

Search Engine Advertising: Buying Your Way to the Top to Increase Sales

Copyright © 2004 by New Riders Publishing

All rights reserved. No part of this book shall be reproduced, stored in a retrieval system, or transmitted by any means—electronic, mechanical, photocopying, recording, or otherwise—without written permission from the publisher, except for the inclusion of brief quotations in a review.

International Standard Book Number: 0-7357-1399-5

Library of Congress Catalog Card Number: 2003114660

Printed in the United States of America

First printing: February, 2004

9 8 7 6 5 4

Trademarks

All terms mentioned in this book that are known to be trademarks or service marks have been appropriately capitalized. New Riders Publishing cannot attest to the accuracy of this information. Use of a term in this book should not be regarded as affecting the validity of any trademark or service mark.

Warning and Disclaimer

Every effort has been made to make this book as complete and as accurate as possible, but no warranty of fitness is implied. The information is provided on an as-is basis. The authors and New Riders Publishing shall have neither liability nor responsibility to any person or entity with respect to any loss or damages arising from the information contained in this book or from the use of the CD or programs that may accompany it.

Publisher
Stephanie Wall

Production Manager
Gina Kanouse

Executive Development Editor
Lisa Thibault

Project Editor
Michael Thurston

Copy Editor
Toni Ackley

Indexer
Cheryl Lemmens

Proofreader
Debbie Williams

Composition
Ron Wise

Manufacturing Coordinator
Dan Uhrig

Interior Designer
Kim Scott

Cover Designer
Aren Howell

Media Developer
Jay Payne

Marketing
Scott Cowlin
Tammy Detrich

Publicity Manager
Susan Nixon

WITHDRAWN

Here's what ... a)ing about S.ar. E. dvertising:

"Search engine advertising is a powerful channel for connecting with customers who are actively seeking to buy, but managing a successful search marketing campaign is anything but easy. Catherine Seda's guide helps you avoid costly mistakes that can bedevil even the most-experienced advertising veterans. The wealth of accurate, savvy information contained in this book makes it a must-read for anyone promoting products or services online. Using even a few of the tips and techniques offered in this book will boost your results significantly, paying for the book many times over."

Chris Sherman
Editor, *SearchDay*, from SearchEngineWatch.com

"*Search Engine Advertising* is an in-depth, get-your-hands-dirty book. It digs deep and provides easy-to-implement strategies and even high-level, advanced tips and techniques. The book lists the names of specific tools that help you to optimize the process, and even templates for legal letters to those who may infringe on your trademark. What most struck me about this book is that it taught me new tricks—and I have been in this space for more than eight years. I have seen Catherine speak at industry conferences since the 90's—she knows this subject matter cold, and shares her most effective strategies in these pages. This book will get the beginner off the bench and in the game, and will teach the expert new tricks, too."

Fredrick Marckini
CEO of "The Original™" Search Engine Marketing Firm: iProspect

"[Catherine's] approach is comprehensive, logical, and draws a straight line to the two most important aspects of web commerce for any business: how to maximize returns while minimizing costs. It is not simply a collection of facts, but a how-to manual of practical value."

Mike Hogan
Technology Editor, *Entrepreneur*

"So fresh and new, [Catherine] Seda is brilliant and breaking trail! She makes the seemingly impossible to understand process of #1 search engine rankings perfectly clear and with easy steps to follow. Traditional books on these topics are dry, uninteresting, and difficult to stick with. Seda's book is casual and interesting. I had no idea I had so much power to improve my business! It's comforting to know I'm on the right track, with the tools I need at my side."

Kima Hall
Owner and CEO, Ocean DIVA Jewelry & Designs

Table of Contents

Part IV Specialized Search Engines

Part V Tracking Your Return on Investment

Part VI Protecting Your Profits

About the Author

Catherine Seda is a popular speaker on the topics of search engine marketing, affiliate management, and low-cost web site promotion. She's known for sharing practical tips and tools in her dynamic sessions at leading search engine, marketing, and industry association conferences.

Since 1995, Catherine has worked with organizations in the U.S. and Europe to leverage the Internet as a marketing tool. As the marketing executive of a web agency for five years, she championed client online promotions that included search engine optimization, pay-per-click media buys, opt-in email, banner advertising, link popularity campaigns, custom sweepstakes, and ROI tracking. She also designed the search engine program, which included co-creating an affiliate trademark protection strategy, for a direct response TV agency's clients.

Through her agency, Seda Communication, Catherine offers open workshops and onsite training for search engine marketing. Additionally, she leads a team of search engine specialists in managing corporate client campaigns.

Catherine shares revenue-generating techniques in her articles as a regular columnist for *Entrepreneur* magazine, editor of the *Search Engine Sales* e-zine, and freelance writer for industry publications including *Response* magazine, *SearchDay* (Search Engine Watch), *LookSmart, Pay Per Click Analyst, FindWhat.com*, and others. She's also a contributing author of *Search Engine Positioning*.

Catherine believes in a "test before you invest" Internet marketing strategy for immediate and long-term success.

About the Technical Reviewers

These reviewers contributed their considerable hands-on expertise to the entire development process for *Search Engine Advertising*. As the book was being written, these dedicated professionals reviewed all the material for technical content, organization, and flow. Their feedback was critical to ensuring that *Search Engine Advertising* fits our readers' need for the highest-quality technical information.

Craig Fifield is a Product Manager for Microsoft bCentral, one of the largest application service providers to small business. At bCentral, Craig manages both the Submit It! search engine marketing service and their new FastCounter Pro web analytics system.

Prior to Microsoft bCentral, Craig worked as marketing manager for six years at a national building products company where he built and marketed his first web site. The success of that site led Craig to start his own Internet marketing business in 1996, where he developed and implemented online marketing strategies for a variety of businesses both large and small.

In 1997, Craig joined Submit It! as a search engine optimization consultant. Craig's knowledge of the Internet marketing field combined with his in-depth understanding of the small business consumer quickly led him to his current product management position. Submit It! is now Microsoft bCentral's most successful service.

More recently, Craig has been a speaker at Search Engine Strategies conferences and served as a technical editor for the popular book *Search Engine Visibility* by Shari Thurow. He has also written for various publications including *SearchDay*, *Traffick.com*, *MarketingProfs.com*, and Jill Whalen's *HighRankings Advisor* newsletter.

Troy D. Perkins, president of Vocal Minds, Inc. and editor-in-chief of |PPCA| *PayPerClickAnalyst.com* is at the forefront of the search engine marketing world and is a frequent participant at all of the key industry conferences. Vocal Minds, Inc. is an Internet-focused advertising and marketing firm which has been in business since 1999. Troy's clients and his company benefit from the broad reach and loyal following of the public-service web site of which Troy is editor-in-chief. Troy is a trusted advisor to many of the Pay Per Click media providers.

Jeremy Sanchez, vice president of Marketing and Product Development at Position Technologies (www.positiontech.com) has considerable experience in the online marketing business, which led him to study ways to use search engines and content as a marketing tool. Acknowledged as a search engine paid inclusion expert, he speaks and moderates search engine discussions at leading Internet conferences worldwide.

Shari Thurow is a sought-after speaker and trainer on the topics of search engine-friendly web site design, web copywriting, and link development. A popular speaker at search engine strategy, web site design, and online marketing conferences worldwide, Shari's sessions are very popular and are four-star rated.

Shari is the Webmaster and marketing director for Grantastic Designs, Inc., a full-service search engine marketing, web, and graphic design firm. She has been designing and promoting web sites since 1995 and is outsourced to many firms throughout the United States. The firm currently has a 100 percent success rate for getting client sites ranked at the top of search engine and directory queries.

She is the author of *Search Engine Visibility* (www.searchenginesbook.com), a top-selling marketing book. The book teaches web developers how to build a site, from concept through promotion, that pleases both site visitors and the search engines.

Shari has designed and successfully marketed web sites for businesses in fields such as medicine, finance, science, biotechnology, software, computers, online stores, e-commerce, real estate, manufacturing, art and design, marketing, insurance, employment, education, and law. Clients range from non-profits to Fortune 500 companies.

Shari has been featured in many publications, including *Fortune*, *Crain's Chicago Business*, *Inc.* magazine, *Internet Retailer*, *MacWorld*, *PC World*, *Wired*, Clickz.com, and ComputerUser.com. She has also received numerous design and content awards, including top site honors from Lycos, Business 2.0, and *Computer User Magazine*.

Acknowledgments

Wow. Writing this book was more intense than I had imagined. I daydreamed about writing for a few hours each day, then spent the rest of my time managing client projects, exercising, napping, learning about Feng Shui, attending culinary school, and taking up a hobby. Um, writing and client projects took center stage. Sometimes, I made it to the gym.

Tapping into nearly 10 years of my search engine experience while including today's top tools and techniques was time-consuming. But I wasn't alone in my efforts. I had a wonderfully-supportive team of statistical research and case study providers, mentors, reviewers, editors, publicists, and even cheerleaders.

I'd like to thank my first mentor in this industry, Danny Sullivan. When you spotted my postings on an online discussion list and invited me to speak at the 1999 Search Engine Strategies Conference, I was introduced to your Search Engine Watch site and a community of other search engine marketers. You created an educational hub which was, and still is, instrumental to my education. Thank you for building this extensive network of resources. And thank you for inviting me to contribute to it over the years.

A huge "thank you" goes out to my book team. Shari Thurow introduced me to New Riders Publishing and acted as my book coach. Thank you for all of your ideas, comments, and inspiration. This book was born with assistance from the New Riders staff—especially Stephanie Wall, Lisa Thibault, Michael Thurston, and Aren Howell. Stephanie, thank you for supporting my vision and walking through this process with me. Lisa, my fellow Virgo, your attention to detail and deadline reminders were much appreciated. Michael, thanks for your "hawk eyes" in perfecting page layout and content. Aren, love the cover. And many thanks to my content reviewers: Craig Fifield, Jeremy Sanchez, and Troy Perkins.

Numerous companies shared their research, tips, and experiences for this book. The search engines played a key role—especially Overture (Dina Freeman, Craig Wax, Angelin Tan) and FindWhat.com (Karen Yagnesak, Dan Ballister, Bryan Chaikin, Yvette Fernandez)—in providing additional content and recommendations. I also appreciate the case studies and information provided by the following companies: 1ShoppingCart.com (Rob Bell), Alchemist Media (Jessie Stricchiola), Baker & Hostetler (Deborah Wilcox), Bruce Clay (Bruce Clay),

Commission Junction (Nathan Fish, Lisa Riolo), Did-it.com (Kevin Lee), Osterland Enterprises (Eddie Osterland), eMarketer (David Berkowitz), Epic Sky (Tim Ash), FawnKey & Associates (Marty Fahncke), GO TOAST (Dave Carlson), Hitwise (Lizzie Babarczy), iProspect (Fredrick Marckini), Jupitermedia (David Schatsky), Microsoft (Craig Fifield, Kirk Koenigsbauer), NetIQ (Anne Lindberg, Derek Fine), Referencement.com (Sylvain Bellaiche, Cesar Henao), REVShare (Joseph Gray), Shopping.com (Krista Thomas), Urchin (Scott Crosby, Brett Crosby), WebSideStory (Erik Bratt), and Wilson Internet Services (Dr. Ralph Wilson).

Fredrick Marckini, you gave me my first taste of authorship by inviting me to write a chapter for *Search Engine Positioning*. Thank you!

The Search Engine Strategies Conference first offered, and continues to offer, me a place to share my experiences with other search engine marketers. Thanks to Karen DeWeese, Chris Elwell, Beth Ritter, Chris Sherman, and other Jupitermedia team members who make this event happen.

Great big hugs go to my mom, dad, sister, family members, and friends who cheered me on during this process. A special thanks goes to my mom, who listened to me frequently ask, "Are we there yet?" Yes, we are. And it's spa time!

Tell Us What You Think

As the reader of this book, you are the most important critic and commentator. We value your opinion and want to know what we're doing right, what we could do better, what areas you'd like to see us publish in, and any other words of wisdom you're willing to pass our way.

When you contact us, please be sure to include this book's title, ISBN, and author, as well as your name and email address. We will carefully review your comments and share them with the author and editors who worked on the book.

Email: errata@peachpit.com

Foreword

Advertisers pay millions to put their messages out on the traditional broadcast systems of television, radio, and print. These systems let advertisers reach a wide audience. The drawback, aside from the expense, is inevitably the message reaches a large number of consumers who simply aren't interested.

Search engines are also a form of broadcast, but a unique system where the normal rules are flipped around. Instead of advertisers broadcasting their messages to consumers, the "reverse broadcast network" of search engines lets millions of consumers each day tell advertisers exactly what they want. These consumers needn't be convinced to buy a particular product, such as a new car, DVD player, or washing machine. They're already in "buy mode." When they search, they're looking for someone who stands ready to fulfill their needs. As an advertiser, you simply need to know how to tune into this consumer desire. This great new book from Catherine Seda shows you how.

Catherine is a veteran of the search engine advertising industry. She spoke at our very first Search Engine Strategies Conference back in 1999 and has been coming back to educate attendees ever since. In 1999, Google had yet to become a household word, and search engine advertising was still in its infancy. Paid methods of getting top placement directly from search engines were few. But where they existed, Catherine uncovered them and got her clients successfully involved.

Search engine advertising has greatly progressed since those early days, and the wealth of information Catherine's compiled in this book is remarkable. You'll learn how to get started with search engine advertising at a very basic level, yet you'll find a full education about advanced issues available to those who want them. If you progress to a major campaign, you'll appreciate topics such as monitoring click fraud and the use of trademarks in ads.

Though search engines are a broadcast network, they don't require millions of dollars to get started. Any business can be found for a budget that involves only tens of dollars. You'll learn quickly just how powerful search engines can be, if your experience is like that of the many other advertisers who are spending enough to make search engine advertising into a multi-billion dollar industry.

So enjoy the book, then dive in and get started with search engine advertising! No other advertising medium provides such immediate, measurable results. Once you try search engine advertising, you'll wonder why it took you so long to discover it—and you'll hope your competitors never find out.

—Danny Sullivan, Editor
SearchEngineWatch.com

Introduction

Buying Your Way to the Top to Increase Sales

My experience using the Internet as a marketing tool began with a class at UC San Diego in 1994. I learned how to use email, build a web site using HTML code, and conduct research online at other university libraries. My interest in the Internet grew when I discovered how to find information by typing words into the WebCrawler search engine. How clever! The search engine's logo of a spider was the perfect visual for relating to this new experience of "crawling the web." It was fast-moving, fun, and way cool.

Search engines were key research tools in my post-college internships for a nonprofit organization in Washington, DC, and a telecommunications company in France. Although there weren't as many documents on the web as there are today, what was available saved me countless hours of contacting companies, or traveling to the library to read publications. The web also enabled these organizations to publish information on a global scale faster and more cost-effectively than ever before, by building a web site. The challenge, of course, was figuring out how to drive people to it.

When I returned to the United States, I led the online promotions division of a web agency that performed "search engine submission" as part of its monthly management program for corporate clients. This task was one of my responsibilities. The good news—often within days of submitting a web site's page (also referred to as a Uniform Resource Locator [URL]), search engines gave it a top ranking...for free. The bad news—clients didn't understand why this was important, or the growing efforts that later became required to maintain high rankings.

A lot has changed. Search engine marketing has evolved into a complex process. It's a moving target with ever-changing rules. But it's also finally gaining recognition as one of the most cost-effective online marketing methods today. Companies need a search engine strategy to grow their business.

Optimization Versus Advertising: What's the Difference?

Search engine marketing is the umbrella concept. It's also referred to as *search engine positioning* or *promotion*. Optimization and advertising are two methods within search engine marketing.

Optimization focuses on designing pages within your web site to attract search engine spiders (the automated robots that crawl the web to include documents in the search engines' databases). Web site design skills are required to optimize a site's pages properly. These days it's necessary to pay an inclusion fee to a majority of top search engines if you want specific web pages indexed. A high ranking is not guaranteed through paid inclusion, but it's a start.

To the search engines most marketers associate with advertising, your web site design has no impact on your position. You have control over your position, keyword choice, ad listing copy, and the *landing page* (the web page people arrive at when they click your link in the search engine results). Paid placement advertising guarantees instant visibility.

Because optimization and advertising require fees, both are covered in this book. But the focus here is not on the comprehensive techniques for designing a search engine-friendly web site for paid inclusion programs, although the basics are discussed. Instead, this book helps you create a cost-effective marketing strategy and choose the tools you'll need for buying your way to the top. Additionally, a few potential pitfalls and profit-enhancing tips are revealed to help experienced marketers achieve new levels of success.

Why I Wrote *Search Engine Advertising*

The most significant change in the search engine field is the shift to a "Pay-For-Placement" model. Several years ago, getting a top ranking was based solely on search engine optimization. Submitting a web site to search engines was also free. Good web site design remains key to attaining some high rankings, but now search engines allow marketers to buy specific keyword positions in addition to, or instead of, programming their way to the top.

When I talk about this opportunity with people, it's as though I've revealed the truth about the Tooth Fairy. As search engine users, they're disappointed that companies can influence their search engine positions. Some are even appalled to learn that search engines don't magically find the best sites on the web in an unbiased fashion. But, by the conclusion of the story on how search engines work, the lightbulb has turned on. "You mean I can get MY web site a #1 position?" they ask. Yes, you can. And that's why I have written a book on buying your way to the top.

All levels of business managers can participate in search engine advertising and see results…often within days. My goal is to share the common principles that are proven to work for both entrepreneurs and large corporations.

And by all means, be creative! The best (and most challenging) part about this process is that you can modify your campaigns at any time. You know your business better than anyone. By experimenting with your campaigns, you'll discover which specific techniques boost your sales and profit margins.

How This Book Is Organized

This book provides insight into buying one of the top positions on the major search engines and directories. It covers the advantages and challenges of the various types of programs. It also offers tools and resources to help you better manage the campaigns you implement. My goal is to help you increase your sales volume at the lowest cost-per-customer.

Part I, "Planning a Successful Strategy," provides an understanding of how search engines impact your business. It explains how search engine advertising supports optimization, and the relationships among the search engines. There are relevant statistics and case studies in here, but if you're not new to search engine marketing, then you can skim through Chapter 1, "Why Is Search Engine Advertising Important?"

You'll also learn in Part I the step-by-step process to creating the fundamental components in your campaigns—from keyword analysis to ad listing copywriting to converting site visitors. You'll want to refer back to this section at several stages of your advertising, because these guidelines are the foundation for running a successful campaign.

Part II, "Paid Placement Programs," reveals the two main programs that will grant you a #1 position right now: Fixed Placement and Pay-For-Placement (PFP). Often the same search engines offer both programs; one or both may fit your needs based on your resource allocation and competitive strategy.

Part III, "Paid Inclusion Programs," reviews Submit URL and Trusted Feed. You'll find mandatory web site design optimization techniques to ensure that your site is ready for an inclusion program. As in Part II, I'll address top advantages and challenges for these programs.

Part IV, "Specialized Search Engines," explores new breeds of search engines such as shopping bots and vertical market engines. If you're looking to promote your company overseas, you'll find information on the international search engines here as well.

Part V, "Tracking Your Return on Investment," is written to take your campaigns to the next level of efficiency. You may find that a tool you're already using for another online marketing application can track search engine advertising at no additional cost. This section points out software and services that have multiple uses for your business, thereby reducing your search engine advertising costs.

Part VI, "Protecting Your Profits," deals with a few key business and legal problems that cost companies a lot of money. By addressing these issues early in a campaign, you'll be spared hours and dollars trying to resolve these inefficiencies later. Many companies are already experiencing the pain of profit loss and will find resolutions they can implement right away.

This book does not address specific advertising tactics for each search engine, or the technical features within a given tool. Because the only constant in search engine advertising is change, I've created a companion web site at www.searchenginesales.com that includes greater detail on particular topics. In my free e-zine, I share tips every month responding to the latest industry developments. If you have a tool that you love (or hate), a case study you'd like to share, or questions about the material covered in this book, I welcome your email. Good luck with your search engine advertising strategy, and I'll see you at the top!

—Catherine Seda
catherine@sedacommunication.com

 **PART I**

Planning a Successful Strategy

Introduction

The key ingredient to any media campaign is the marketing strategy. Through a strategic planning process, you'll identify your messages, target audiences, and marketing goals. These foundational elements are core to search engine advertising, too. Once they've been established, you'll find it much easier to choose relevant keywords, write effective ad listings, and develop landing pages that close the sale.

As you read Part I, write down whatever creative ideas pop into your head. Plenty of tips are included to help you evaluate the market viability of your concepts. Plus, you might decide to run with them once you learn how to track your results later in this book. Let's start by uncovering the mystery of how search engines work and how they impact your business.

Chapter 1

Why Is Search Engine Advertising Important?

Web sites that lack search engine visibility are losing business. Second only to email, the most popular activity for U.S. Internet users is information search—67.3% of users perform searches, according to the U.S. Department of Commerce. And an estimated 40% of Internet users are using the web to make product or service purchases. With the popularity of online searching on the climb, eMarketer calls search engine marketing "almost a no-brainer" for companies.[1] Figure 1.1 shows the breakdown of the top five Internet activities among U.S. users.

---

[1]The eMarketer charts and quotes as provided herein have been reprinted with permission.

Figure 1.1
Product/service information search and product/service purchases are among the top five most popular Internet activities.

Top Five Activities of Americans Online, 2001 (as a % of Internet users ages 3+)

E-Mail	84.0%
Product/service information search	67.3%
News, weather, sports	61.8%
Playing games	42.1%
Product/service purchases	39.1%

Source: US Department of Commerce, February 2002

037068 ©2002 eMarketer, Inc.   www.**eMarketer**.com

These statistics suggest that if you want shoppers to buy from your web site, one way to do so is to make sure they can find you in the search engines.

With nearly all search engines moving to some form of a "pay-to-play" model, companies must proactively *advertise* on search engines. Sure, there are still a few spots to land a free link. But those opportunities of the "good ole days" are nearly extinct. Don't worry, search engines are generating profitable results for a lot of companies. Yours can be, or may already be, one of them.

It's Quick, Easy, and Inexpensive to Generate New Business

I don't know about you, but before I invest any money into a new marketing program I want to know about the potential return on investment (ROI). It helps me to hear success stories during my marketing efforts; I spot ideas to improve my results. It's also inspiring. That being said, you may be happy to know there are many examples throughout this book of how companies are achieving success from search engine advertising.

As the new media director for a direct response television agency, I witnessed immediately how profitable search engine advertising can be. A handful of the agency's clients sold "As Seen on TV" products. As soon as the latest products appeared in television commercials, I marketed them on search engines, directing shoppers to the clients' web sites.

For example, for Tristar Products' popular Flat Hose product, I bid on keyword phrases using the product trademark name, such as flat hose, flathose, tristar flat hose, as seen on tv flat hose, the flat hose, and flat garden hose. I also bid on generic terms such as hose, water hose, and garden hose. For less than $2,000 per month per client in search engine fees, several As Seen on TV companies generated an extra $10,000–$40,000 in gross sales each month. Around the 2002 holiday season, one ab fitness product generated close to $40,000 from only $800 in search engine fees. Now that's an impressive ROI.

What made this form of marketing even more exciting was that it took me less than 15 minutes to add a new product listing to a search engine. The links generally appeared during a keyword search within a few days (Google, bless them, launches listings after you've deposited money online using a credit card). Because some search engines require only a $50 deposit to start advertising, you're just $50 and a few days away from sending qualified traffic to your web site.

Expand Brand Awareness

Is driving new sales an important result of search engine marketing? Absolutely! But so is building brand awareness. Although achieving new sales immediately justifies your media expenditures, creating a strong brand continually brings you new and return customers long after your investment in a marketing campaign has ended.

According to research from The Conference Board, 60 executives from major U.S. firms cited search engine listings as their top Internet tool for enhancing their companies' brands. Figure 1.2 compares online to offline tactics for expanding brand awareness.

Important
Trademark terms identify a particular company. Generic terms, also called *related terms*, are keywords that could be relevant to more than one company.

Important
Brand refers to the collective consumer concept of a company. Elements such as names, slogans, logos, and URLs are part of brand identification, but they are not "the brand." *Brand awareness* is the expansion of a company's brand in the marketplace.

Figure 1.2
Search engine listings are
the second most-used tactic
for brand building.

Most Prevalent Online vs. Offline Brand-Building Tactics among US Companies, 2001 (as a % of respondents)

	Online	Offline
Print ads	–	71%
Search engine listings	59%	–
Event sponsorships	–	50%
Trade shows	–	48%
Referrals from online affiliate partners	48%	–
TV ads	–	46%
Banner ads	43%	–
Direct mail	–	41%
Referrals by offline partners	–	36%
Customized extranets	34%	–

Note: n=60 executives from major US firms
Source: The Conference Board, December 2001

044531 ©2002 eMarketer, Inc.   www.e**Marketer**.com

It's interesting to note that search engine listings fall behind only print ads when both forms of marketing are considered. I believe that search engine positioning is a requirement for companies doing traditional marketing, because search engines support branding efforts while providing the directions to the online store.

For example, if you're running a TV or print campaign, a percentage of people will look for your brands in the search engines, and then visit your web site to place an order. Search engines act as brand builders as well as shopping tour guides—they lead interested consumers right to your doorstep.

A Simple Way to Test New Promotions

Unlike most forms of traditional marketing, or search engine optimization, paid listings allow you to test promotional concepts quickly and inexpensively. You can buy new keywords and replace your ad listing copy every hour, day, week, or month.

It's impossible to change your print ad in a magazine during the time it's in circulation. If the ad doesn't work, you're stuck with it for a while. Even if you don't like the listing that search engines have chosen for your web page based on how it's optimized, once you redesign your page you'll wait for the search engines to re-spider it, which could take months.

What kind of promotions can you run in a paid search engine listing? Anything you want, really. Here are a few ideas:

- Unveiling of a product or service
- Change of a product or service feature, benefit, solution, or price
- Expanded geographic areas of business
- Specialized industry focus
- Limited-time discounts and offers
- Seasonal promotions or items
- Refer-a-friend or reward programs
- New partnerships or clients

Your promotion can sell a product or service. Or, it can invite the public to your site for free information, strengthening your status as an educational resource in a given field.

Advertising Complements Web Site Optimization Efforts

Just as it's a simple way to test new promotions, search engine advertising supports your optimization efforts, too. Are you hiring an optimization firm? Wait! Before you provide them with the keywords you think are important to your audience, run a paid placement campaign. You'll find out almost instantly how much traffic search engines can deliver, and what your conversion rates are for the keywords you chose.

I guarantee that you'll discover at least one surprise. A keyword you thought would perform well actually bombs, or one that you half-heartedly chose ends up being a golden winner. Now discuss these with your optimization team to better your keyword selection and web redesign objectives. And if you're going to expand your current optimization efforts, again, try paid listings before wasting resources on optimizing new pages that may get rankings but no customers.

Search Engine Alliances Show Path to Success

Right about now you're probably thinking: For which search engines do I optimize my site, and on which do I advertise? Here's where it gets messy. Each search engine can show results from its own database, as well as pull results from other search engines.

Figures 1.3 and 1.4 show a search for "used cars" on the AOL.com search engine. Not all of those links you see on the page come from AOL. Some do. At the time of this publication, the "Recommended Sites" have been selected by AOL editors. Or, it may be the official web site of a trademark name that has been searched. The "Sponsored Links" are listings of companies that have purchased Google's AdWords listings. Finally, "Matching Sites" are the web site pages that have been optimized and are appearing in top rankings under Google's listing of main search results (the ones without the "Sponsored Link" heading). (AOL provides a breakdown of its search results at http://search.aol.com/aolcom/about.jsp.)

Important

What are sponsored links or sponsored listings? They're paid advertisements.

AOL's results can also come from AOL's Yellow Pages. And before it formed a content relationship with Google, AOL had previously included results from yet another search engine, Inktomi. Confused yet? It's okay. You'll soon see a chart that shows the relationships among the search engines.

Before we get to the relationships, let's look at the search engines with the largest audience reach (see Figure 1.5). Popular ones boast a lot of traffic; it's a good idea to get your ad in front of a decent number of eyeballs. But hold on! This chart is a little misleading. Remember that search engines provide listing results to each other. For example, top Overture advertisers will also appear on Yahoo! and MSN, the top two mentioned here. So, you need to understand a bit more about the relationships among them to determine "who feeds whom?"

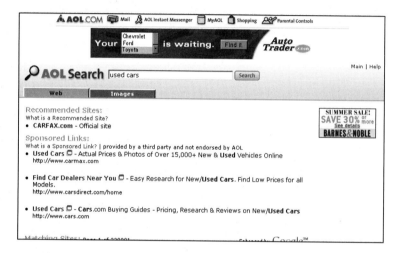

Figure 1.3

A search for "used cars" on AOL.com brings up many types of web site results.

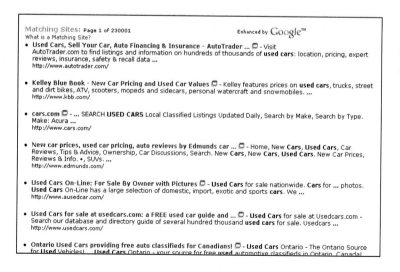

Figure 1.4

Some results are pulled from the databases of other search engines.

Figure 1.5
Who's the most popular search engine of all? Here's who has the largest audience reach.

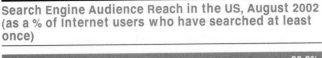

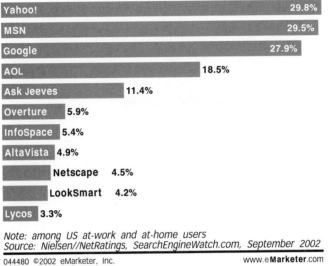

Search Engine Audience Reach in the US, August 2002 (as a % of internet users who have searched at least once)

Yahoo!	29.8%
MSN	29.5%
Google	27.9%
AOL	18.5%
Ask Jeeves	11.4%
Overture	5.9%
InfoSpace	5.4%
AltaVista	4.9%
Netscape	4.5%
LookSmart	4.2%
Lycos	3.3%

Note: among US at-work and at-home users
Source: Nielsen//NetRatings, SearchEngineWatch.com, September 2002

044480 ©2002 eMarketer, Inc.   www.eMarketer.com

Figure 1.6 shows a handy relationship chart, updated constantly by Bruce Clay, owner of a search engine optimization agency. You'll see which major U.S. players to consider for your advertising efforts. Bookmark www.bruceclay.com and download the updated chart periodically. Click the links within the chart to read more information about the search engine relationships, and to find links to the engines' inclusion or paid placement programs.

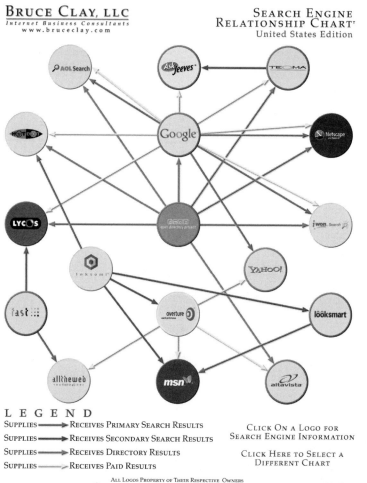

ALL LOGOS PROPERTY OF THEIR RESPECTIVE OWNERS
COPYRIGHT © 1996-2003 BRUCE CLAY, LLC. - ALL RIGHTS RESERVED   0312.1

Figure 1.6

Monitor U.S. search engine relationship changes by bookmarking sites like www.bruceclay.com.

Chapter 2

Marketing Campaign Foundation

A lot of marketers breeze through their keyword research. You might be compelled to race ahead, too. One step that makes this process much easier, though—and prepares you to write high-performing ad copy—is creating a marketing campaign foundation. You'll be setting benchmarks for measuring success before you launch your first ad listing. This is the cornerstone of your search engine advertising plan.

If you have a business plan, you've probably already outlined your marketing foundation: mission statement, target market, unique selling points, and call to action. If you haven't, take just 15 minutes, or several weeks for a more comprehensive marketing plan, to discuss the following sections with your team. Have your notes from this chapter handy because I'll be referring to your marketing foundation frequently in the upcoming chapters.

To illustrate how to apply the guidelines I'll be proposing to you, I'll reference Red Mountain Spa (www.redmountainspa.com) as an ongoing example, along with case studies from various companies. Red Mountain Spa is a fitness resort located in Utah (and home to one of my most memorable vacations!). My proposed copy for this spa is based on my personal experience with their service and their current web site (see Figure 2.1).

Figure 2.1
Red Mountain Spa, an adventure spa, is used as an example in this section. This is their home page.

Mission Statement

What's the "30-second elevator speech" you'd tell someone who asked what your company does? Include the main benefit to your customers as well as a description of your product or service.

For example, "Company A saves medical clinics millions of dollars by providing access to a centralized patient database." Or, "Company B designs flower arrangements at wholesale rates for weddings and special events." Remember, every person who receives your mission statement is a potential customer or partner. Keep your message short. Include the chief benefit your company provides that will encourage potential customers to ask for more information.

Here's a sample mission statement for Red Mountain Spa:

> Red Mountain Spa is an all-inclusive resort that offers fitness adventures and healing programs to renew your mind, body, and spirit.

Target Market

Describe your preferred buyers. To help you with this, look at your current customers (or those of your competitors, if you have a new business). Consider demographics such as sex, age, marital status, job title, and job industry, if applicable.

Also consider *psychographics*, which are the lifestyle behaviors and attitudes of your ideal customers. This information gives you an understanding of your prospects' potential buying decisions and patterns. Armed with this insight, you'll be better able to address any concerns or questions, and then guide shoppers through the purchase process. Psychographic questions include activities and purchases made in relation to business/education, health/fitness, and recreation/leisure.

Both sets of information are necessary in designing an effective advertising campaign. Your entire campaign would be dramatically different if you market a car to 16–25 year-old men who play extreme sports, as opposed to 35–45 year-old married women with children, who subscribe to parenting magazines. It's likely that you'll have multiple target markets.

The more you know about your ideal customers, the better you communicate with them and develop a relationship. Relationships are key to both initial and repeat sales.

One sample target market for Red Mountain Spa could be the following:

- Women

- 30–55 years of age

- Subscribers of *Body & Soul*, *Spa Finder*, and *Yoga International* magazines

- Working professionals in a corporate environment

- Exercise 4–5 times a week for health goals and to reduce stress

- Participate in relaxation exercise such as yoga and meditation

- Frequent patrons of day spas

Unique Selling Points

What makes your product or service different, and better, than your competitors'? Consider product, price, and distribution factors. Is your product or service of higher quality? Is your price lower than your competitors', or do you offer convenient payment terms? Do you ship your product in recyclable packaging material, which is better for the environment? Make a list of your unique selling points. Then prioritize them in order of their value to potential customers.

If one of Red Mountain Spa's customer groups subscribes to health publications and is already participating in stress-reducing fitness programs such as yoga, for example, then Red Mountain should emphasize their strength in this area, in terms of both their relaxing location and the services they offer (as shown in Figure 2.2). Considering their target market is already familiar with spas, Red Mountain needs to set themselves apart not only from other vacation resorts, but also from other spas.

Sample unique selling points for Red Mountain Spa include the following:

- **Location:** Set in picturesque and serene red mountains of the American Southwest, 90 minutes from the Las Vegas airport

- **All-inclusive resort:** Meals, health and fitness classes, healing programs, special events, and resort facilities

- **Number and diversity of fitness classes:** More than 35 weekly programs including yoga and a gentle martial arts emphasis—Yoga, YogaSpin, Pilates, Chi Ball Method, T'ai Chi

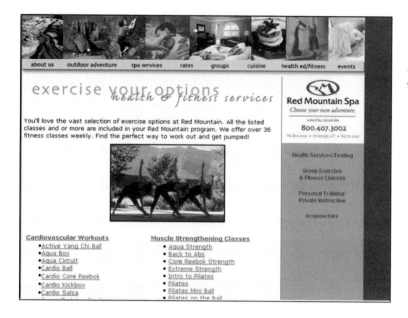

Figure 2.2
Red Mountain Spa's fitness page showcases their numerous classes—more than 35 offered per week.

Call to Action

What do you want people to do on your web site? Isolate your primary business goal to determine your top call to action; it'll more than likely be revenue-oriented, which means getting visitors to buy something.

Under your primary call to action, list secondary ones. Think about levels of visitor communication that enhance your business, even if immediate sales aren't produced. For example, consider increasing subscriptions to your online newsletter, articles in the media, new partnerships, or brochure requests as important secondary goals. These support brand awareness and strengthen relationships with your prospects and customers.

A sample call to action list for Red Mountain Spa could include:

- **Primary goal:** Increase seven-day or more vacation reservations by 10% within six months

- **Calls to action:**

  - **Primary:** Book a reservation online

  - **Secondary:** Register for email news

  - **Secondary:** Request a resort brochure

Review the designated calls to action before, during, and after you execute a keyword text link campaign on search engines. An ad listing can be created for each call to action (or you could combine a few actions into one listing). For each call to action, your keywords, ad copy, and landing pages can all be modified to continually improve your campaign performance. By tracking the performance of each ad listing, you'll be pointed to the ones you'll want to re-evaluate. Rework poor performers; mimic high-performing ones.

You can identify primary and secondary calls to action for your entire site. To achieve the best results from your online marketing efforts, however, apply this list to each major content page of your web site. There's no reason to limit your business to just one set of consumer actions.

Chapter 3

Choosing Keywords for Maximum Performance

Fortunately, choosing keywords that drive qualified leads to your site isn't rocket science. Keywords that don't produce desirable results can be deleted within hours. Variations of profitable ones can be added just as quickly.

The initial process still needs careful consideration, however. A bad set of keywords can kill your campaign if you attract browsers and not buyers. Changes in search engine user behavior, or the competitive landscape, can also alter your conversion rates. Therefore, it's a good idea to review the performance of your keyword universe at least monthly. Spending more money may dictate that you check results more frequently. Keywords fall into two main groups: branded keywords and generic keywords.

Important

A *keyword universe* is the group of words a marketer has selected to promote their business.

Branded Keywords

Start with the names of your company, products, and services. On search engines that charge a per-click fee based on the bids of other advertisers (called Pay-For-Placement [PFP]), these terms should cost only pennies[2] because there's only one brand owner...*you*. Because no other advertisers are competing for the same terms, it's no wonder that well-recognized branded keywords yield a lucrative ROI.

Hold on. Not all branded keywords are created equal. Don't buy your company or product names without doing a "popularity check" first, as discussed later in this chapter. Find out if consumers are searching for your terms. Only recognizable brand names will be searched. Once your company achieves a measurable level of brand awareness, you're ready to advertise branded keywords: trademarks, misspellings, plural forms, and domains. Following is an example:

Company: Microsoft

Branded Keywords: Microsoft, Microsoft Windows, Windows Media Player, Microsoft Internet Explorer, Microsoft PowerPoint

Trademarks

It surprises me how many companies don't bid on their trademarks. Do they assume their web site appears for these words? Sadly, this isn't always the case. Especially problematic for large corporations is that affiliates and resellers are marketing the parent company's trademarks, including the company's names or slogans. These "partners" are redirecting traffic to their own web sites. (Resolving channel competition is addressed in Part VI, "Protecting Your Profits.")

One of my contacts at Overture said that his team's most difficult sales pitches are to Fortune 500 company executives who don't believe they need search engine advertising. They think consumers find their brands with no problem. Here's a fun exercise: Type brand names into search engines and see if the parent company's site appears on the first page of results. It may not. We can't assume that we aren't facing competition for our own trademarks by a host of organizations, including competitors, affiliates, resellers, fan clubs, or the media.

---

[2]The minimum bid on major search engines is typically 5 or 10 cents per click.

Figure 3.1 shows the listings that appear in a search for "fedex" in the LookSmart directory. Although the FedEx web site is number one under Reviewed Sites, none of four Sponsored Listings belongs to the official site. This is a problem; the sponsors have better positions and theoretically are receiving the branding leads and sales.

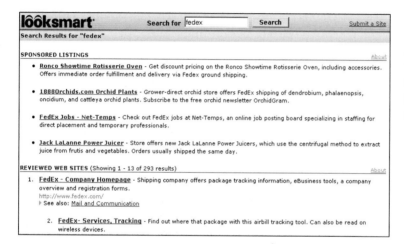

Figure 3.1

Market your own trademarks. As evidenced by a search for "fedex" in LookSmart, the Sponsored Listings are being bid on by other companies.

Misspellings, Plural Forms, and Other Variations

A fair number of companies do bid on their trademark names—but only the exact form of the trademark. Internet users type all kinds of creative variations. People spell names incorrectly, make a singular word plural, and add or delete words that belong within a trademarked phrase. Although a few search engines will automatically include misspellings of a plural form and plural forms of a keyword, not all do, and not for all keywords.

Use keyword tools to monitor the new searches people try (read the "Popularity Check" section for recommendations). Shortly after the launch of a campaign in traditional media such as TV or print, Internet users frequently add "coupon" or "discount" to the trademark, if such an offer is promoted. Then as exposure to the brand increases, shoppers narrow their search in an attempt to find more exact matches. For instance, they pair the company name with the product or service name. These are all opportunities for companies to ensure their official web site is found over others.

Company: Microsoft

Top 10 popular searches using the word "microsoft" according to the free Overture Search Term Suggestion Tool (found at www.overture.com): microsoft update, microsoft internet explorer, microsoft word, microsoft clipart, microsoft office, microsoft windows update, microsoft download, microsoft excel, microsoft outlook, microsoft publisher

Domain Names

Unfortunately, it's not always possible to buy a web site address (URL) that matches your company, product, or service name. Unless it's cost-prohibitive, register all of them in the event people type the URL directly into the browser toolbar. If you're using and promoting a different domain name, consider buying it on search engines.

We shouldn't assume that customers directly type the URL into the browser toolbar (see Figure 3.2 for the toolbar location on a browser). To this day, I'm shocked when I review client traffic reports and see how many people type the company URL into a search engine instead. A handful of your potential customers are probably doing the same thing.

For example, Telebrands advertises their domain name, www.inventionchannel.com, not www.telebrands.com, in their TV commercials. With more than 1,000 combined searches for "invention channel" and "inventionchannel" alone, the company is wise in buying the web site address they're heavily branding in other media.

Sample branded keywords for Red Mountain Spa could include:

- red mountain spa
- the adventure spa
- red mountain resort
- red mountain resort spa

- red mountain spa utah

- red mountain adventure spa

- www.redmountainspa.com

Type URL here

Figure 3.2
The toolbar on the Microsoft
Internet Explorer browser
where the web site address
(URL) should be typed.
Some people instead type a
URL into a search engine.

If you purchase multiple domain names, promote the ones that support a brand. For example, pharmaceutical companies frequently buy a different domain name for each drug they manufacture. Each of these URLs could be bid on as a keyword phrase, in case people are typing these domain names into search engines. When the ad listing is clicked, consumers are sent to a separate product web site, or simply to the page within the main pharmaceutical web site that describes that particular medication.

Generic Keywords

Figuring out your branded keywords is easy. But if consumers aren't familiar with the name of your company or products, you must rely on generic keywords to get people to your web site. Even corporations that want to expand into new markets need to promote keywords that are related to their business but aren't names of specific brands.

A good generic term list contains popular words. (There's no point in buying "underwater basket weaving" if nobody is looking for it. Although oddly enough, there were 224 searches for this phrase on the Overture network in September 2003. Go figure.) However, your list needs to be narrow enough that you won't pay for junk traffic. (If your company sells scuba gear, "water" is too broad to deliver customers cost-effectively.) The following guidelines will help you develop a list to target potential customers.

Themes

In all likelihood, your web site is about one theme, one topic. Within your site you have subthemes, or secondary themes. Assume Red Mountain Spa's overall theme is "spa." Perhaps "fitness spa" and "resort spa" are their secondary themes. All three keyword phrases are good considerations for advertising (and optimization) efforts.

When you create your keyword universe, think of words people use to refer to the same thing (a thesaurus helps). For example, Red Mountain Spa clients might associate a "spa" with resort, vacation, trip, holiday, retreat, hotel, lodge, or inn. "Fitness" to their clients may mean health, weight loss, strength, exercise, work out, training, sports, body conditioning, stress reduction, or any number of related terms. Mix and match your words to form innovative phrases.

Don't worry about trying to narrow your list yet. Brainstorm keywords that relate to your business. You'll be able to expand your keyword universe while creating more targeted phrases in subsequent steps; an initial list of 10–25 single words or phrases at this stage is fine. If you've already prepared additional ideas, great!

Popularity Check

With your basic list of keywords in hand, verify that people are actually looking for your keywords before you incorporate these into your search engine advertising (or optimization) campaigns.

Fortunately, there are several free and fee-based tools that reveal how many searches are performed for your keywords. Better yet, these tools reveal the multiple-word phrases people type along with your primary word. In each of the tools, I queried "spa" to research phrases for Red Mountain Spa.

Overture's Search Term Suggestion Tool

Overture's Search Term Suggestion Tool has been the basic tool in the search engine marketer's toolkit for years, and it's a good one that is also free. Type in your keyword(s) and see what people searched for last month using that word. Figure 3.3 shows the number of searches in September 2003 for the word "spa." These searches occurred on the Overture network, which includes searches performed on their partner sites such as Yahoo!, AltaVista, Info-Space, and MSN.

Recent changes make this tool a bit more challenging to use. Previously, Overture displayed exact searches. Now, it shows the words within a phrase in alphabetical order...some of the time. Nobody types "discount disneyland military"; people probably type "disneyland military discount." But Overture's new way of displaying the results requires that you think about how a human would run a keyword search because on most search engines you'll buy an exact phrase. And in optimization, the order of the keywords in a phrase also matters. Unfortunately, because Overture is running several databases, this format isn't always consistent, adding confusion for those of us using this tool.

Secondly, Overture has removed "filler" words such as "a" or "the" from the displayed phrases. And now it shows only the singular form of the word, even if more searches are conducted for a plural form. Because Overture no longer shows exact search results, you'll need to evaluate this data or double-check it against another keyword tool.

Important

Keep in mind that a percentage of searches come from software robots, not people. Although keyword tools generally filter these queries, some robot activity may slip by, making the numbers reported on the high side.

Figure 3.3

Overture's Search Term
Suggestion Tool shows keyword phrase that include the
word "spa," and how many
people queried those
phrases in September 2003.

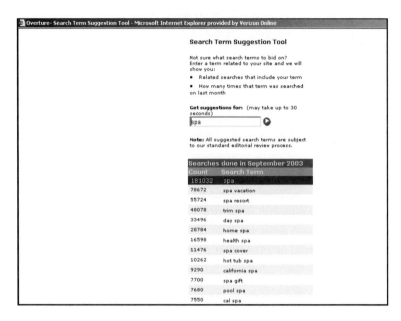

Google AdWords Keyword Suggestion

Unlike Overture, Google won't show you the number of searches
for keywords. But this tool gives you two important pieces of
information:

- It recommends similar keywords that may apply to your business. It's a computer thesaurus in that regard.

- It displays the keywords for which your ad will appear, if you
  buy the one you queried.

By default, Google's AdWords program groups other keyword
phrases that are related to the one you purchased. Google refers to
this feature as a *broad match*. This saves advertisers time setting up
listings for additional keywords. But be careful! Most of the time,
you won't want a portion of the keywords Google automatically
adds to your campaign through their broad-matching technology.
Unrelated keywords drop the profitability of your overall campaign
drastically if people click your listing but don't complete an action.
Be sure to read the Google AdWords FAQ page on keyword-matching
options. Figure 3.4 shows several keyword phrases for which the
marketer's ad will appear if "spa" is purchased in Google AdWords.

Figure 3.4
Google's AdWords Keyword Suggestion also provides keyword phrase ideas and shows you for which additional keyword phrases your listing will appear. "Spa" was used in this example.

Related or Refined Searches

Several search engines show you searches that are related to the one queried (see Figure 3.5). This not only helps web surfers who want to find more exact web site listing results, but also assists marketers who want additional keyword ideas for their ad campaigns. AltaVista, Ask Jeeves, and Yahoo! are just a few of the search engines that offer this feature. Look for the related search ideas just under the Open Search field. Or look for links entitled "related searches" or "refined search."

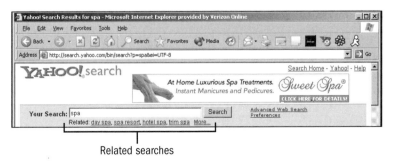

Related searches

Figure 3.5
Several search engines or directories, such as Yahoo!, offer a "related search" or "refined search" for keyword phrase ideas.

Third-Party Tools

Third-party tools are available that combine or compare the keyword activity data provided by the search engines. Good Keywords (www.goodkeywords.com) and WordTracker (www.wordtracker.com) are two such programs. The first is free software for Windows. WordTracker offers a free trial and several subscription options.

Microsoft bCentral clients who subscribe to its search engine marketing service (called Submit It!) gain access to a keyword research tool that queries activity from its own engine, MSN Search. As shown in Figure 3.6, Microsoft's tool also recommends which phrases to consider for page optimization efforts based on the ratio of searches to the number of listings competing for that phrase. Unfortunately, this feature of Submit It! doesn't reveal in which timeframe the searches occurred, so again, it's helpful to utilize more than one keyword tool for data comparison. The URL for this site is http://www.submit-it.com.

Figure 3.6

Microsoft bCentral's search engine submission service (Submit It!).

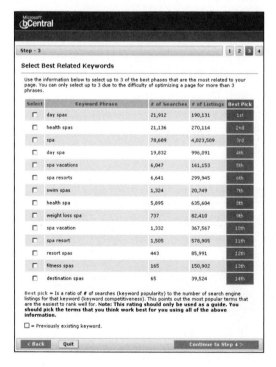

Word Stemming

Generally, *word stemming* is a topic discussed within optimization circles. It refers to the capability of a search engine to include the root stem of a keyword. For example, if a web designer optimizes a site page for "swimming," the page may get ranked for the root "swim" by search engines that support word stemming.

It's different for paid listings. Most of the time, you must buy the variations of your keyword. If you want "swimming" and "swim," you'll have to buy both of them; each can have different fees. The exception is singular versus plural forms of words. Check with each search engine you select to see if they treat this as one media buy or two. You may want one or both forms.

Web Analytics Reports

Are you using WebTrends, HitBox, Urchin, ClickTracks, or another web analytics program to evaluate your web site traffic? Most of these programs display "referral" data reports on how visitors find your site; traffic from search engines is included. Study the top keywords that drive traffic to your site. (Figure 3.7 shows a sample report from Urchin.)

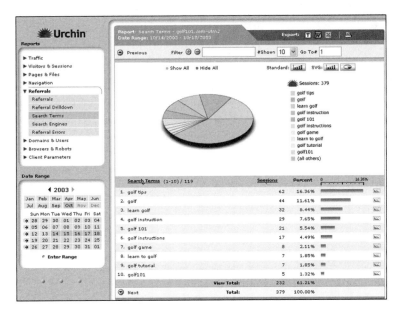

Figure 3.7
Look in the "referral" data of your web analytics reports for keywords that are already sending you traffic from organic search engine listings. This is a sample snapshot from Urchin.

Tip

If you don't host your web site in-house, ask your Internet service provider (ISP) if they offer web traffic reporting. Often ISPs have the software installed but only run reports when asked. Otherwise, the stored log files and reports take up space on their servers.

Urchin's keyword referral data includes "organic" or "natural" listings (from optimization efforts) as well as paid listings. If you're not yet buying keywords, you'll see what results your SEO efforts are generating. Depending on how much visibility your site has achieved for organic listings, consider buying these terms using paid placement programs. Gather even low-traffic terms; when purchased together the resulting boost in overall site visits is a nice surprise.

But beware—if you're not optimizing your web site, then there are a bunch of relevant keywords that won't show up in web analytics reports. That's because your most desirable words are competitive. You'll need an optimization strategy to land top rankings and capture referrals from highly-coveted keywords. A web analytics report won't reveal the critical terms that you should use, but aren't.

Profiling Your Competitors

Your competitors are great sources of keywords. There are two simple ways to observe what's working for them:

- First, browse their web site. Do any of their words relate to your business, too? Good keywords are often staring right at you!

- Second, look at meta data in their web pages: meta title, meta keywords, and meta description. Most companies place their keywords here, hoping it's the magic pill for securing a top position. Simply putting keywords in meta data without optimizing the site design won't improve a company's ranking. But your competition might not know that. Hopefully, they've included a nice list of keywords for you to evaluate.

To review your competitors' meta data, start on their web site home page. From your browser toolbar, click on "View" and then select "Source." Voilá! As in Figure 3.8, you'll spot their keywords, if they're using meta tags, near the top of the page.

What if you've launched a new business and don't know who your competitors are? Look up a generic keyword that relates to your business in Google, AlltheWeb, or another search engine. Click the web site links that aren't under a "sponsored listing" heading. These top positions aren't given to the highest bidder; these companies are optimizing their sites. Chances are, these companies have keywords in their meta data that'll apply to your web site.

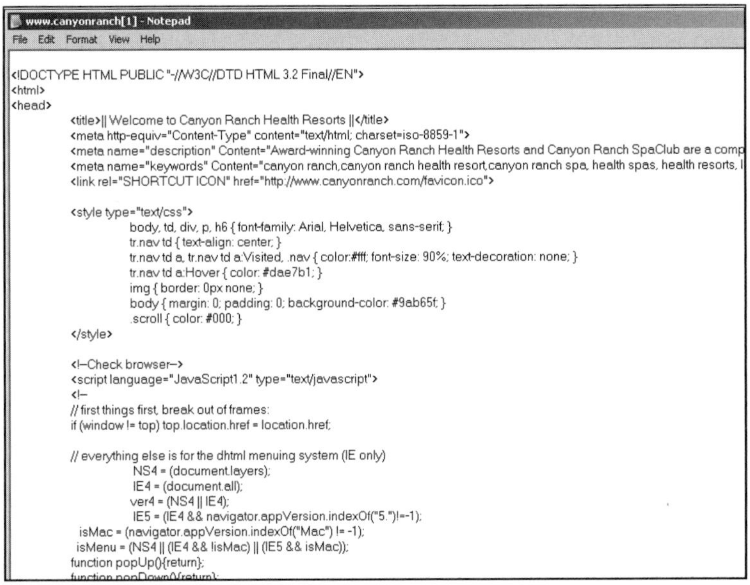
```
www.canyonranch[1] - Notepad
File Edit Format View Help

<!DOCTYPE HTML PUBLIC "-//W3C//DTD HTML 3.2 Final//EN">
<html>
<head>
        <title>|| Welcome to Canyon Ranch Health Resorts ||</title>
        <meta http-equiv="Content-Type" content="text/html; charset=iso-8859-1">
        <meta name="description" Content="Award-winning Canyon Ranch Health Resorts and Canyon Ranch SpaClub are a comp
        <meta name="keywords" Content="canyon ranch,canyon ranch health resort,canyon ranch spa, health spas, health resorts, l
        <link rel="SHORTCUT ICON" href="http://www.canyonranch.com/favicon.ico">

        <style type="text/css">
                body, td, div, p, h6 { font-family: Arial, Helvetica, sans-serif; }
                tr.nav td { text-align: center; }
                tr.nav td a, tr.nav td a:Visited, .nav { color:#fff; font-size: 90%; text-decoration: none; }
                tr.nav td a:Hover { color: #dae7b1; }
                img { border: 0px none; }
                body { margin: 0; padding: 0; background-color: #9ab65f; }
                .scroll { color: #000; }
        </style>

        <!--Check browser-->
        <script language="JavaScript1.2" type="text/javascript">
        <!--
        // first things first, break out of frames:
        if (window != top) top.location.href = location.href;

        // everything else is for the dhtml menuing system (IE only)
                NS4 = (document.layers);
                IE4 = (document.all);
                ver4 = (NS4 || IE4);
                IE5 = (IE4 && navigator.appVersion.indexOf("5.")!=-1);
          isMac = (navigator.appVersion.indexOf("Mac") != -1);
         isMenu = (NS4 || (IE4 && !isMac) || (IE5 && isMac));
        function popUp(){return};
```

Figure 3.8
View your competitors' keywords by looking at their source code. A competitor to Red Mountain Spa may be Canyon Ranch, as shown here.

Not all sites ranked for your keywords are competitors. For example, a hot tub manufacturer and a resort want their sites to appear for "spa," but they aren't direct business competitors. Industry-related sites are also good sources of keyword ideas.

Features, Benefits, and Solutions

It's time to return to the unique selling points you identified in your marketing campaign foundation. There are critical keywords hiding in your list. Realize that your future customers have a problem and want a company to provide the solution. Perhaps they don't know the product or service they need but they know what feature or benefit has to be included. Or, maybe they figure if they look for the solution, an appropriate provider will appear.

Draw three columns on a piece of paper and label them as "features," "benefits," and "solutions," as shown in Table 3.1. Brainstorm keywords for each. This exercise reveals copy ideas you can use for your web site, brochures, direct mail promotions, and other marketing materials.

Table 3.1   Example for Red Mountain Spa

Features	Benefits	Solutions
Over 35 weekly fitness classes (e.g., aqua circuit, cardio kickbox, yoga)	body conditioning gain energy improve flexibility lose weight reduce stress	fitness-focused vacation fitness activities are all-inclusive personal training option

Customer Survey

Which keywords are currently being queried by your potential customers? Ask your current ones to find out. Take an informal survey the next time you're on the phone with a client, or if your account managers maintain regular client communication, have them ask. Another option is to send out a company email to your best customers and ask them what keywords they would use to find your company on search engines.

If you haven't tracked this information before, a customer survey, however it's distributed, will shed light on the keyword journey your prospects are traveling. During one of their upcoming searches, your ad listing could appear, beckoning them to your web site.

Regional Targeting

For local companies, including a regional word as part of the keyword phrase is a must. Why promote "catering" services if your business only serves southern California cities? Many people do search for service-focused companies by a specific geographic location (see Figure 3.9). But even if you manage a national company, you can incorporate regional phrases into your media buy to really hit a narrow market. Better yet, your advertising fees will be low because they're not in high demand by other advertisers.

Industries with regional targeting potential:

- Amusement parks

- Community web sites

- Event or construction rental companies

- Florists

- Home contractors and suppliers

- Hospitals

- Hotels

- Museums

- Pet supply and service organizations

- Physicians and medical practitioners

- Real estate agents and agencies

- Religious centers

- Restaurants

- Wedding shops

Figure 3.9

Incorporate regional keywords into your phrases if applicable. Notice the cities queried with the word "catering" for this example.

A keyword search for "catering" using Overture's Search Term Suggestion Tool reveals the cities and even countries in which people request this service. The companies savvy to search engine advertising are already buying these regional keywords. As shown in Figure 3.10, on Overture there are four sponsors of "toronto catering." No doubt by the time you run a search on these phrases, the number of sponsors will have increased since I ran this search.

Figure 3.10

Regional keyword advertising is catching on. There are already four companies bidding on "toronto catering" on Overture.

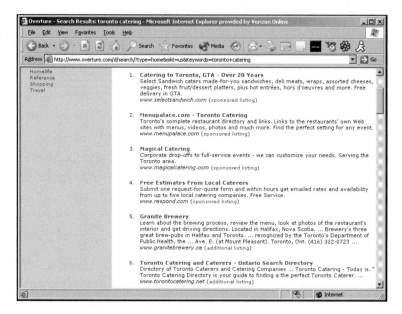

Industry Jargon

In general, don't use industry jargon in your web site copy or search engine advertising campaigns. It's easy to forget that your customers aren't working in your field. Whereas it's natural to use industry terminology with colleagues and vendors, slang may scare off potential customers who feel intimidated by their unfamiliarity with your vocabulary.

Now I'm going to contradict myself. Although you don't want to fill your ad listings with lingo that seems confusing to people outside of your industry, it's a good idea to buy these keywords. If people enter your industry jargon into a search engine, you'll be happy to reach educated prospects. These site visitors are one step closer to making a purchase—and hopefully, from your company.

Consider the case of Eddie Osterland, a Master Sommelier (someone who has passed the Master Sommelier Diploma by the Guild of Master—he's a wine expert...sounds like a dream job to me). Eddie's primary goal was to book more speaking engagements. I suggested a $50 test campaign on Overture. He bought "wine" and "speaker"-related phrases. Although it wasn't a presentation request, within four days of the campaign being live, Eddie was offered a job at $60,000–70,000 per year...from a recruiter who searched for the phrase "master sommelier" and found his web site listing. Wow, quick response! I figured that with few searches for this phrase, there wouldn't be enough traffic to produce any leads. I was wrong. This experience proved to me that obscure industry terms can be winners.

It's important to choose narrowly-focused keywords to reach your target audience. Plus, exact phrases are usually less expensive than broad, single words because fewer organizations can be associated with them. For instance, fewer companies can market themselves for "wine expert" than for "wine."

Search engine users are also becoming more sophisticated; they're using multiple-word phrases. According to a 2003 study by OneStat.com, shown in Figure 3.11, only about 25% of queries are for single words. Although I still recommend running a short-term test on very relevant single words on your list because there are always surprises, most probably won't perform well. If your primary goal is to use search engine advertising for branding purposes, however, then single keywords can deliver your message to a targeted audience, even if your click-through rate isn't very high.

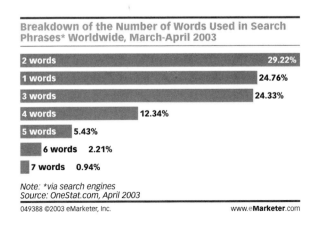

Breakdown of the Number of Words Used in Search Phrases* Worldwide, March-April 2003

2 words	29.22%
1 words	24.76%
3 words	24.33%
4 words	12.34%
5 words	5.43%
6 words	2.21%
7 words	0.94%

Note: *via search engines
Source: OneStat.com, April 2003

049388 ©2003 eMarketer, Inc.   www.e**Marketer**.com

Figure 3.11

Multiple-word phrase searches are on the rise, as indicated in OneStat.com's study. Buy phrases to reach new customers.

Following are some sample generic keywords for Red Mountain Spa:

- adventure trip
- adventure vacation
- all inclusive resort
- all inclusive vacation
- couples resort
- desert vacation
- fitness resort
- fitness resort spa
- fitness spa
- fitness spa center
- fitness spa vacation
- fitness vacation
- healing center
- healing place
- health and fitness spa
- health and healing
- health hotel spa
- health resort spa
- health spa
- las vegas spa
- meditation retreat
- mountain resort
- mountain spa resort
- national park utah
- national park vacation

- new age health spa

- saint george utah

- spa

- spa package

- spa resort

- spa vacation

- spa weekend

- spiritual retreat

- sports trip

- sports vacation

- st george utah

- travel to utah

- utah state park

- utah vacation

- vacation resort

- weight loss health spa

- yoga retreat

- yoga vacation

Based on the marketing campaign foundation set forth earlier in this book for Red Mountain Spa, a few of these keywords appear to be a perfect match: "fitness resort spa" and "mountain spa resort," for example. Some terms are a stretch, but because they relate to vacation travel, they have the potential of delivering new customers cost-effectively to Red Mountain Spa. A solid keyword universe for this resort would include an expanded list to address other target markets, as well as Red Mountain Spa's other services or products.

Your keyword list is long, right? Good. You can certainly cut words that you believe are too broad for your intended audience. But if the advertising fees are low, you may as well start with an extensive list to test the profitability of each keyword. With constant monitoring of your campaigns initially, it's easy to delete the keywords that aren't converting into sales.

Sometimes, you'll have the right keyword, but the wrong ad copy. The next chapter focuses on copywriting techniques to maximize your click-through rate among your target audience...while being surrounded by a sea of competitors.

Chapter 4

Copywriting Tips to Improve Your Click-Through Rate

You've defined your marketing campaign foundation. You've selected a keyword universe. Now that your ad listings will be in front of the right audience, what will persuade them to click on your links and visit your site? Unfortunately, you're challenged by "listing clutter," an overload of relevant search results. How can your ad shine through?

Rules for creating effective marketing messages for the web are not radically different from traditional advertising. Only on the web, ad viewers have even less patience. You need to get their attention quickly. Review your marketing campaign foundation from Chapter 2, "Marketing Campaign Foundation," follow the copywriting tips discussed in this chapter, and do a little spy work. You'll discover ways to differentiate your ad listing from your competitors'.

Keep in mind, you won't measure your paid listings entirely on click-through rates. Traffic is not your ultimate goal (unless you're selling advertising on your web site and simply need visitors). To increase your leads or sales along with profitability, write copy that'll attract qualified prospects.

Seven Ways to Attract Buyers, Not Browsers

Whereas in traditional advertising you pay for the number of people who see your ad, a majority of search engines currently sell clicks. It seems closer to a performance-based ad model because you're paying to get shoppers into your store, but watch out. Visitors who don't buy anything drain your ad budget. Fortunately, you can prequalify them somewhat by writing ad listings that grab their attention, plus describe what they'll find on your site. Use your ad listings to invite shoppers to buy, not just take a look around.

1. Appeal to Your Target Market

Your ad listing copy starts as a version of your mission statement...with a twist. Address your target audience in each ad listing. For instance, the way you address men and women could differ. Let's say your software saves customers time doing computer data entry, so instead, they can play golf or relax at a day spa with friends. Just by these two activities—golf versus spa—you can assume which appeals more to men than women. I realize that I'm stereotyping here, but my point is to create messages that consider the specific needs and wants of your target audience. This draws the "right" people to your ad. You can write a different ad listing for each keyword. Or, to save time, one ad listing can be used for a group of keywords associated with each product or service you promote. It's certainly easier to evaluate groups of terms than individual ones if your keyword universe contains thousands of them. You can always micromanage your campaigns at a per-listing level when you're ready.

2. State a Benefit or Solution

Review the benefits and solutions you outlined in Chapter 3, "Choosing Keywords for Maximum Performance." Which of these are the strongest reasons why a prospect should become your customer?

Simple reasons are the most compelling: *You save customers time and money.* Or, *you help them generate more revenue.* These are not the only influencing factors, but they're pretty high on most people's priority list.

GEICO Direct hits a home run with their ad on MSN. In Figure 4.1, GEICO's ad is located to the right of the other ads (which already gives it a visual advantage). Look at the ad copy. "Save up to 15% on your car insurance." Bam! That's a quantifiable benefit, isn't it? Compare this listing to the other Featured Sites listings. The first words in the #1 advertiser's listing are "Car insurance coverage from a quality company." Does this measure up to GEICO's offer? Nope. The next two advertisers promote their "free quote" or "compare rates" features. This is good, but including a result of their quote feature would be better. If "save hundreds of dollars" or "save up to 25% on your car insurance" applies to these companies, including this benefit in their listings would give GEICO's ad serious competition.

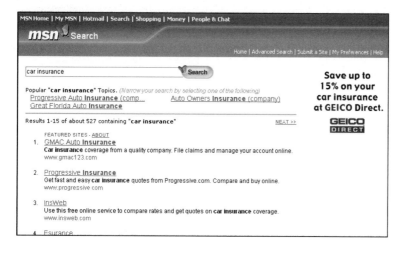

Figure 4.1

GEICO hits a home run by stating a benefit in their advertisement.

Get specific in your listings as to how you help your customers. You'll produce higher click-through and click-to-order rates. Search engine advertising isn't about attaining more traffic. With profitability as the true benchmark of your success, it's better to attract only qualified leads that are likely to become clients.

3. Offer an Incentive

Important

Discount examples:
$5 off, 25% savings

Added value example:
Buy 1 get 1 free, free gift with purchase

A discount or value-added deal mentioned in ad listings improves click-through rates. The incentive to click shouldn't far outweigh the benefit of your service (I know, this is a lot to cram into a short ad listing...especially on Google!). If it does, then you'll see low conversion rates. That's no good. An incentive should act like bait to get people to buy right now as opposed to shopping around more, or thinking they'll come back later to your listing (the problem is they don't always return).

Shoppers love "free stuff," too. And it doesn't necessarily have to be a hard good or service. Free information or a downloadable product (a special report or software, for example) costs little or no money to produce. And there are no shipping costs with electronic products. Hence, you can create a free offer without investing a lot of money.

Important

Free shipping is a significant incentive for online shoppers. Unfortunately, so many companies now offer this that it may no longer be considered the differentiation factor it once was. It's still worth a try, though, especially around the holidays.

As a note of caution, if you promote a free goodie in your listings, monitor your conversion rate where you're paying for traffic. You could end up paying for junk traffic. (Tip: Mention "free" in the description and not the title, so people have to read your listing before they notice the incentive.)

On the other hand, promoting a free offer in your ad listing is fine if your goal is to grow your lead database. This is easily done if site visitors must complete a form on your site to receive the gift. A free product sample giveaway is an excellent example of how to spark future market demand and initiate a branding campaign simultaneously.

4. Create a Sense of Urgency

With millions of searches performed on the Internet every day, how are you going to get users to stop searching and start clicking? Tell your audience why they should click on your ad listing *right now*. You can establish a sense of urgency by striking an emotional chord with them, or by limiting the timeframe of your incentive.

To connect with them on an emotional level, "feel their pain" and address how your company can stop it immediately. Are your prospects stressed from long work commutes? Are they worried about finances? What are they feeling, and why? Promise to deliver them from their painful situation, and they'll be ready to click to a solution.

Limiting your incentive to a short timeframe is a second tactic to entice web surfers to click, and buy, today. Make a sale good for "24 hours." Show a reduced price as an "introductory offer only." Or, note that your special offer is "limited to the first 50 customers." This can create the illusion that demand exceeds supply, which is very appealing.

What might shoppers' concerns be when they search for "flower delivery?" Certainly, the delivery date is a possibility. How about price? Selection? Several florists venture a guess on AOL.com, which pulls Google's Sponsored Listing results. In Figure 4.2, three of the four Sponsored Links advertisers promote same-day delivery. Two of those three address price: One promotes a 10% discount for typing the word "coupon" into the order form, while the other states that their prices start from $24.99. Which is a more compelling offer? In general, the first advertiser's click rate should be higher thanks to their special 10% discount that is assumed to be time sensitive.

5. Use a Call to Action

Ok, you identified what you want site visitors to do when they get to your site in Chapter 2; now ask them to take action.

Due to character limitations with text ad listings, saying "click here" is not an effective use of this small space. Additionally, because you want to turn your prospects into customers, the action called for in your listings should not be about getting them to your web site.

Figure 4.2
The four sponsors buying "flower delivery" promote their delivery options in different ways.

"Buy now" is a clear invitation, but on its own doesn't provide a reason to order right now. It's about offering a benefit or solution if customers take an action on your web site. As shown in Figure 4.2, Shaw Florist (www.bestflowersonline.com) offers a 10% discount on flower delivery—buying flowers is an assumption and doesn't need to be stated.

Test various calls to action to determine which are most effective for your paid listing campaigns. Here are a few examples of actions visitors can be encouraged to take:

- Buy a product or service
- Request a consultation or in-person appointment
- Request a brochure or other sales collateral
- Download a white paper, application form, or other type of document
- Subscribe to an online newsletter

- Register a product warranty

- Submit a testimonial

- Complete a survey

- Refer the site to a friend

- Send a free e-card

6. Promote Your Competitive Advantage

Relieve prospect boredom from staring at a page of content-relevant text links by standing out. Before you submit your ad listings, see what your competitors are saying. Then, say something unique (refer to your unique selling points as discussed in Chapter 2). This is quite fun. You have an opportunity to play off of your competitors' messages.

Go back to Figure 4.2 and notice that all four sponsors' ads offer flower delivery. Several address same-day delivery. But the first florist's ad offers a discount. The second advertiser reveals that they're the official company web site (important differentiator if you're competing with your own or someone else's affiliates online). The third florist's ad mentions the starting price of their flowers, $24.99, and offers a 100% satisfaction guarantee. These are all strong competitive advantages. I can't figure out why the fourth florist's ad boasts "hand delivery" and "morning delivery," which seem standard for this kind of service, not extra special.

Stay on top of your competitors' listings. If you start promoting a specific price, your competitors may announce that they can beat it. By crafting a variety of listings you'll be able to respond quickly to changes in your competitors' listings.

7. Include Your Keywords

Here's a tactic that doesn't apply to traditional marketing, but is important in search engine advertising: *Include your keywords in your ad listing*. According to Overture, advertisers' click-through rates can increase by 50% if the keyword bid on is included in the title and description of the ad. This makes sense. If shoppers search for "aromatherapy candles" they may ignore "scented candles" or "aromatic candles," even if all three phrases mean the same thing to the advertiser. Study the advertisers' listings in Figure 4.3 to see who is incorporating this tactic and who is not.

Figure 4.3

Include your keyword in your ad listing. How many of these advertisers have incorporated "aromatherapy candles" into their title or description?

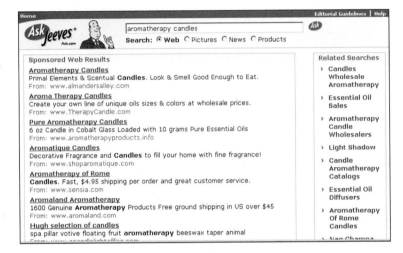

In an effort to provide more targeted results to their users, search engine editors of paid placement programs might reject your ad listing if there's no mention of the keyword you're buying in the title or description. When you submit your keywords along with your ad listing copy and landing pages (also called *destination URLs* or *target URLs*), your listings are reviewed by human editors. These editors act as the gatekeepers of the sacred positions. They'll reject or revise your submission, so it's best to appease them on the first round. Believe me, it's frustrating to submit a bunch of listings and then have to go back and edit the listings, resubmit them, and wait for another few days before they're live.

For paid inclusion programs, it's also problematic to not have the keyword in the web site page you want to rank well for that term (more about that in Part III, "Paid Inclusion Programs").

Here's sample ad listing copy for Red Mountain Spa:

Keyword: fitness spa

Title: Fitness Spa Summer Rates from $209

Description: Get in shape and re-energize through YogaSpin, Pilates, and Red Mountain Spa's 35 weekly fitness classes. Your all-inclusive adventure in the unspoiled beauty of Utah awaits your arrival.

Keyword: fitness spa

Title: $39 Summer Massages at Utah's Fitness Spa

Description: Over 35 weekly fitness programs, daily meals, resort accommodations are all included. Massage special July-August only.

Keyword: fitness spa

Title: All-Inclusive Fitness Adventure Spa

Description: Get fit with over 35 weekly fitness programs, hiking in the unspoiled red mountains, gourmet meals for healthy living—all included. 90 minutes from Las Vegas. Summer specials from $209.

Top 10 Ways to Avoid Rejection

According to Overture, about 30% of all listings submitted to them are rejected. Ouch! That's a big percentage. Although search engines' editorial policies differ on a few minor points here and there, they all generally require advertisers to adhere to the same rules. If you follow these top 10 guidelines, then your listing acceptance rate may be a perfect 100% every time.

1. No excessive capitalization: FREE, MYSITE.COM.

2. No superlatives: #1, best, largest.

3. No phone numbers or URLs in titles or descriptions.

4. Don't use symbols (&); use words instead (and).

5. Avoid exclamation points (!).

6. Avoid having pop-ups on the landing page.

7. The keyword should be mentioned once in the title or description and at least once on the landing page.

8. Content should be relevant: Product names, special, or "free" offers mentioned in the title or description must be discussed on the landing page.

9. Affiliate sites must note that they are affiliates in their title or description.

10. The links to your site must allow people to return to the search engine by clicking on the "Back" button in the browser's toolbar.

Be sure to double-check your spelling, grammar, and punctuation. This sounds like a no-brainer, but when we're in a rush we often make simple mistakes. A minor oversight can cost you a few days of waiting, plus it makes your submissions open to scrutiny and possible rewriting by the editors. This isn't good—you might be unhappy with their changes. Also, just to be safe, take an extra few minutes to test the destination URLs you assign to your listings. A broken link is absolute cause for rejection.

Really, it's not the end of the world if any of your listings are rejected; it just wastes time to go through the process again.

If you're going to launch a campaign on only one or two search engines, tailor your listings to those particular engines' policies. For example, Google allows advertisers to use an exclamation point in the description, so why not take this opportunity to make your listing as strong as possible?!

Editorial Guidelines

For the URLs of the editorial guidelines, visit www.searchenginesales.com.

Monitoring Your Competitors' Click-Through Performance

How popular are your competitors' ads? Recently developed tools grant you insight into their click-through rates. Armed with this data, you'll be able to better optimize your own ad listings.

Google Interest Bar

Run a keyword search on Google. Notice the "Sponsored Links" on the right-hand side of the page? This is Google's AdWords program. See the "Interest" bar at the bottom of each ad, as shown in Figure 4.4, for the keyword phrase "home loan service"? This bar reflects the advertisers' click-through rate. You won't actually see what the percentage is, but if you're already an advertiser and your bar doesn't look as long as the others, then your competitors are getting more clicks on their ads. First-time advertisers can compare the Interest bar of all of the current advertisers and study their ad copy for copywriting ideas.

Be careful! A Google AdWords advertiser in the #1 position does not necessarily have the best listing. Google ranks advertisers based on a combination of the advertisers' click-through rate and how much they're willing to pay per click. Unlike other Pay-For-Placement (PFP) engines, Google doesn't just reward the highest spender. Google users get a vote in who moves to number one.

Figure 4.4
Google's Interest bar under each AdWords listing indicates the click popularity of that ad.

Epic Sky's Overture Competitor Watch

Released in 2003 by Epic Sky, an Overture approved bid management company, Competitor Watch monitors the coverage, rankings, traffic, and spending of your top 10 competitors on Overture. At last check, Epic Sky will run monthly reports on a small number of keywords you're currently buying, up to more than 5,000 keywords if you're running a massive campaign. Study your competition's bidding strategy to see how you can lower your costs while increasing your traffic (see Figures 4.5 to 4.7).

Although Epic Sky's Overture Competitor Watch report reveals which of your terms has the lightest and heaviest competition, the report doesn't show what keywords your competitors are buying that you aren't. You'll have to return to your keyword research tools and start from scratch. There's no tool that I know of yet that suggests keywords to purchase based on what your chief competitors are buying. Oh well, we can dream, can't we? I guess that by not knowing this information so easily, fees won't quickly increase on those PFP engines.

Figure 4.5

Epic Sky's Overture Competitor Watch report monitors the coverage, rankings, traffic, and spending of your top 10 competitors on Overture. Here's a Spending Summary sample.

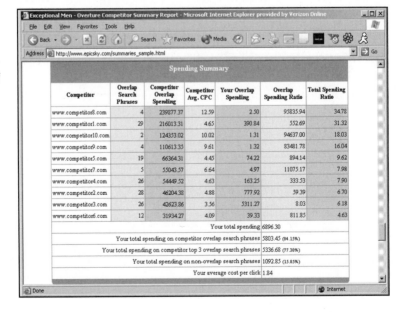

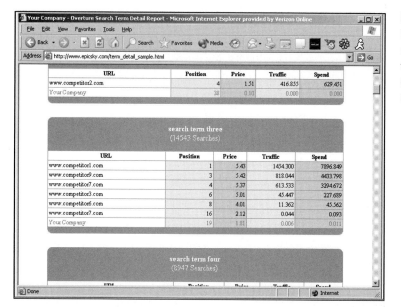

Figure 4.6
Epic Sky's Competitor Watch reveals your top 10 competitors' bidding strategies by campaign details such as keywords, as shown here.

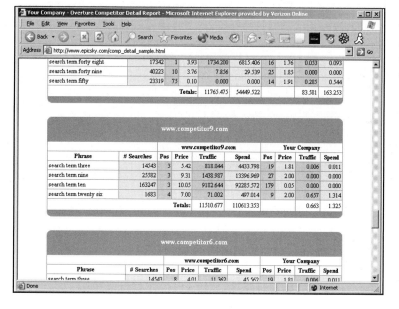

Figure 4.7
You can compare your campaign to a single Overture competitor through this report, too.

The worst thing an advertiser can do is create one listing for a keyword, or group of keywords, and just let it continually run. Ok, it's not the worst thing, but it's not making the best use of the web's advantageous marketing opportunity: *the ability for advertisers to continually change their creative.*

Pepsi doesn't show the same TV commercial year after year. The commercial storyline, featured celebrities, and music all change. This tactic improves brand awareness among repeat commercial viewers, plus draws in new TV audiences.

Likewise, your potential clients are searching for a solution provider on search engines over a week, month, or longer timeframe. If you don't intrigue them with your first ad listing, the one you display when they return may suddenly pique their interest, driving them to your web site. Then, it's up to your landing pages to persuade them to buy.

Chapter 5

Landing Pages That Convert Visitors into Buyers

Your prospects searched for a specific keyword, spotted your ad listing, and clicked on it for more information. Are they sold on your company? Not yet. But they're standing inside your online store. How do you get them to opt-in for follow-up communication from you, or buy something right now? The landing page they're visiting must sell.

This is where companies doing search engine advertising may lose the sale. A vital part of making paid listings work is not just focusing on driving additional traffic to your site or paying less money for the ads. Yes, those are important objectives, but the profitability of your campaigns will spike when you persuade a higher number of your site visitors to become customers. An effective landing page, often referred to as a destination URL or target URL, impacts your bottom line.

UNIVERSITY OF HERTFORDSHIRE LRC

Provide a Direct Path

Do not, I repeat do not, send search engine users to your home page without a very convincing reason. The home page of a web site acts as a mall directory does for an offline business. Both home page visitors and mall directory viewers are shown possible directions in which to begin their shopping experience. If online consumers use a search engine to direct them to a topic but don't see it addressed on the web page they visit, they'll abandon that site. The home page isn't a good landing page because it's too general. It's another set of directions.

Landing pages aren't necessarily part of your main web site. They can be, but it's not required. Pretend you own a flower shop. If your site currently has a page about calla lily floral arrangements, buy calla lily–related keywords and set this as the corresponding landing page. Or, you could send search engine traffic to a promotional page that's hidden on your web site. Because this might be a temporary offer, you won't want this landing page indexed by search engines; use the robots exclusion protocol. It's a text file that you place on your server that instructs search engine spiders to not index a specific area on your site. It would be embarrassing if you remove the ad listing but consumers continue to find this landing page because it appears in the natural search results.

Let's look at a search for "calla lily" on FindWhat.com (refer to Figures 5.1 to 5.5). The last four screen captures are the advertisers' landing pages. In Figure 5.2 you can see that BizRate.com does an excellent job of displaying calla lily flowers offered by online florists. Although Shopping.com (formerly DealTime, as shown in Figure 5.4) doesn't show calla lily flowers as I would have expected, they show a directory of categories where calla lily products are offered. It's relevant. However, on U.S. Southwest's landing page, I can't figure out why the company bought "calla lily" in the first place. There's no reference to this keyword in the top half of their page. Like U.S. Southwest, there's no exact match for "calla lily" on the

UNIVERSITY OF HERTFORDSHIRE LRC

top portion of the Blooming Bulb landing page either. Did the latter two fail in providing a direct path? Well, if you scroll down these landing pages you'll eventually find calla lily products. So technically, they didn't fail. But they violate one of the rules of designing a good landing page to invite the sale, which I address soon.

Figure 5.1

The top four advertisers on FindWhat.com for the keyword "calla lily" are as shown here: BizRate.com, U.S. Southwest, Shopping.com (formerly DealTime), and Blooming Bulb.

Figure 5.2

BizRate.com's landing page for "calla lily" on FindWhat.com.

Figure 5.3

U.S. Southwest's landing page for "calla lily" on FindWhat.com.

Figure 5.4

Shopping.com's (DealTime's) landing page for "calla lily" on FindWhat.com.

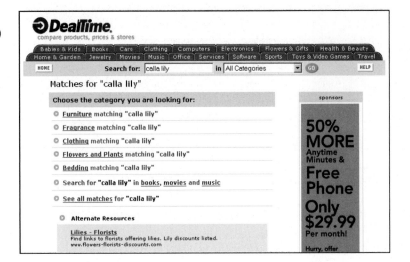

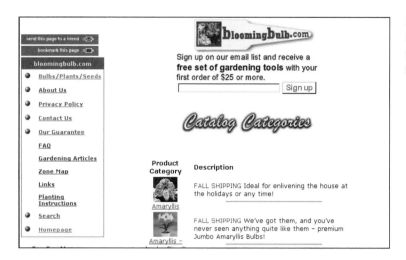

Figure 5.5
Blooming Bulb's landing
page for "calla lily" on
FindWhat.com.

If you think TV viewers are speedy clickers while channel surfing, web users exercise even less patience. Many web site design agencies believe that your visitors should get the information they're looking for within three clicks from your home page. But why make them click three more times if they already clicked your search engine listing to transport them to the requested information? Because you selected the keyword and wrote the listing, you know what visitors want. Design your landing page to show them the merchandise and then lead them to the checkout line.

Complete the Message from Your Ad Listing

I'll continue with the calla lily example. Does the content on these companies' landing pages match their ad listing copy? Let's double-check BizRate.com and Shopping.com, because they passed the first step with flying colors (refer to Figures 5.1, 5.2, and 5.4). Can shoppers compare prices and products pertaining to calla lilies on both of these companies' landing pages? Yes. Although Shopping.com gets an extra point for being more exact—they compare calla lily products, as specifically mentioned in their ad, whereas BizRate.com compares the prices of online florists, which they don't mention specifically in their ad listing.

When you lead your site visitors down the path of making a purchase, ensure your landing page follows through on the promise promoted in your ad listing. For example, if you own a flower shop that claims to deliver fresh flowers direct from the grower, then shoppers need to see this benefit featured on the landing page, so they know it exists. You begin to establish trust with your site visitors when you carry the message throughout your marketing campaign, from the ad to your landing page. Gaining consumer trust increases initial sales—plus, it's a fundamental component in developing loyal customers, instead of one-time buyers.

Design Page Layout to Invite the Sale

You're almost there. All you need to do now is ask for the sale! How your landing page is designed impacts your conversion rates. Does your current page lead shoppers down the path to a purchase, or does it let them wander aimlessly around your site? Here are some suggestions to reduce distraction while leading customers to the checkout line.

Position Critical Information Above the Fold

Product information, incentives, and the order button should all be seen on your landing page without scrolling. This section of a web page is also referred to as "above the fold." Verify that key selling information is visible on multiple computer screen resolutions. Your Webmaster may have designed your site for a 1024×768 screen resolution, without considering other sizes. Your audience members who use an 800×600 screen resolution will see a smaller portion of the web page (compare Figures 5.6 and 5.7). Can't they scroll down? Of course they can. But it's just one more step you can eliminate to let them complete their purchase a little easier and faster.

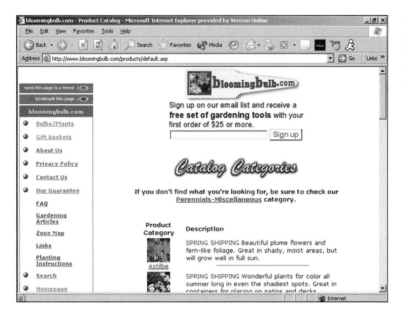

Figure 5.6

Here is Blooming Bulb's landing page for "calla lily" at an 800×600 screen resolution.

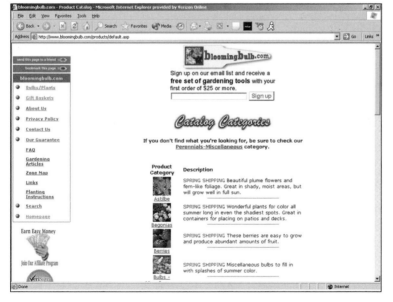

Figure 5.7

Here is Blooming Bulb's landing page for "calla lily" at a 1024×768 screen resolution.

Reduce Navigational Choices

One of the reasons why home pages don't work well as landing pages is that they have too many navigational choices. With links and buttons everywhere, picking a path can be overwhelming.

Landing pages should have fewer links on the page. Some companies completely remove their navigation bar and provide only links to information that will help them complete the sale (such as shipping information and the privacy policy).

What you allow your customers to visit when they're on your landing page is up to you. Just don't give them so many choices that they'll leave that product shelf in your store to walk around. That's almost announcing "Hey, before you buy that, do you want to take a tour?" You have a stronger chance of losing them if you distract them before they've finishing shopping. Once they complete their purchase, then you can take them to a "thank you" page that offers them site–visiting suggestions.

Use Action Words

Have you ever been ready to buy something online, and once you're on that product page thought, "Where's the buy button?" On occasion, it's only a text link, and I'm looking for a graphic image to click. Put action words like "buy" or "order" in text links and as graphics. Adding "today," "here," or "now" to these words contributes to the sense of urgency you want to foster. Hotlink the product image to your order form, too.

If you offer an option in addition to making a purchase, give that option secondary placement. For two buttons stacked on top of each other, put "Buy Now!" above "Product Details." Encourage the sale first. I was on a site recently that put "Clear Form" before "Submit Form." I must have filled that thing out twice before I hit the correct button. I'm used to seeing the "submit" button first, and the reversed order threw me...twice!

Placement of your action words on a web page matters. According to Shari Thurow, marketing director and Webmaster for Grantastic Designs, usability studies across the board report that people tend to ignore the top 60 pixels of a screen because that's the typical placement for banner ads. Consumers have developed "banner blindness." Keeping that in mind, place the buy button in a prominent area of the screen, such as the middle of the screen, and use a different color to really draw eyes to it.

Three Psychological Factors of Selling

Getting the sale isn't always about offering the lowest price or a freebie—although these help. You probably can't afford to offer a hot deal every day. It may have to be used as a seasonal sales boost. Your product or service needs to sell on its own merit. Look back at the competitive advantages you wrote down as your unique selling points. How do these speak to the emotional needs of your customers?

In addition to making your offer compelling, Dr. Ralph Wilson, web marketing and e-commerce expert, recommends using these psychological factors to sell: enhance desire, create a rationale, and build trust.

Enhance Desire

To enhance the desire for your products or services, you need to enhance your copy with words that draw your customer in emotionally. As Dr. Wilson points out in his e-book *How to Develop a Landing Page That Closes the Sale*, "Write sentences and paragraphs that paint for your prospect what it will feel like to realize those benefits."

Look at your unique selling points, or the ones I created for Red Mountain Spa as an example. Those aren't landing-page ready. Here's one:

> Number and diversity of fitness classes: over 35 weekly programs including yoga and gentle martial arts emphasis—Yoga, YogaSpin, Pilates, Chi Ball Method, T'ai Chi, Ai Chi.

That's descriptive, but does it make you feel anything? I'm guessing not. How could Red Mountain Spa emotionally sell this feature as a benefit? How about this:

> Soothe stress away through Yoga, Chi Ball, and any of Red Mountain Spa's 35 weekly health programs. Pamper your body and spirit at our all-inclusive retreat, which is surrounded by the American Southwest's natural beauty.

—or—

> Get in shape and re-energize through YogaSpin, Pilates, and any of Red Mountain Spa's 35 weekly fitness classes. Your all-inclusive adventure in rejuvenation awaits your arrival.

—or—

> Refresh your body, mind, and spirit through Yoga, Chi Ball, Pilates, or any of Red Mountain Spa's 35 health and fitness programs. Your all-inclusive vacation in relaxation and rejuvenation awaits you in the natural beauty of the American Southwest.

How will the vacation described in number one make you feel? Relaxed, less stressed, and peaceful were a few feelings I was going for. How about number two? The words set a completely different tone. These words would attract someone who wants to feel energized, challenged, and adventurous. I combined the two kinds of desires—relaxation and rejuvenation—in the third example.

This copy could be used in the ad listing as well as on the landing page. These examples don't just state the fact that Red Mountain Spa has an extensive list of fitness classes. They tap into people's desire for the benefits.

Create a Rationale

Not everyone buys on emotional appeal alone. That's where your competitive advantages come into play. For example, Red Mountain Spa even offers fitness junkies more classes than they can attend in a week. The spa's number and diversity of classes are impressive, and should be included in their landing page copy. Their program selection appeals to the logical side of people who may think "Well, out of 35 classes I'm bound to enjoy some of them. If I choose a spa that offers only a few, I'm at risk for not liking any." Sold! Combine emotional appeal with rationale and you'll connect with people through one or the other.

Build Trust

Anticipate customer concerns and proactively respond to them on the landing page. Dr. Wilson notes that credit card security, shipping costs, return policies, and email privacy are the primary concerns for doing business online. It's beneficial for any company to tackle these issues on their landing page, in addition to answering potential questions about the offer. Helping shoppers feel secure about doing business online with you is the final step before a deal is made. Although I didn't find a Red Mountain Spa listing in a search engine, they have web site material that would make a good landing page. Take a look at Figure 5.8, which is a pop-up on their home page, and 5.9, which is the landing page for the pop-up ad. Let's review how well this page does according to the landing page checklist:

Landing Page Checklist for Red Mountain Spa	YES	NO
Is a direct path provided?	X	
Is the message from the ad completed?	X	
Is critical information above the fold?	X	
Are there reduced navigational choices?		X
Are action words used?		X
Is desire enhanced?	X	
Is a rationale presented?	X	
Is trust being established?	X	

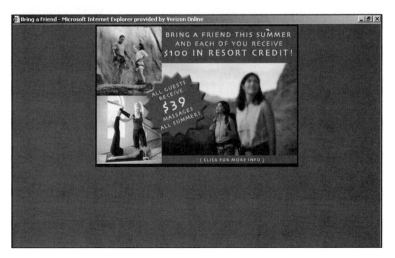

Figure 5.8

This is a pop-up ad on Red Mountain Spa's home page.

Figure 5.9

Here's the landing page once Red Mountain Spa's pop-up ad is clicked.

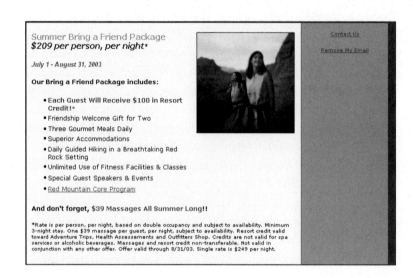

The good stuff: Red Mountain Spa's landing page highlights the special rates promoted in the pop-up ad. It also houses the relevant information inside an 800×600 screen resolution. The financial incentives appeal to visitors' logical side; the photo appeals to the visual senses by showing a peaceful location set in natural beauty.

For a few items on the checklist, Red Mountain Spa missed the mark. Because the pop-up simply sends someone to a designated spot within a web page, the main site navigation is easily found if visitors scroll up the page. Other promotional offers share the page space, too. These items provide distraction. Second, there are no action words or graphics encouraging people to book a trip today. Just a few minor edits could help drive people into their reservation form. Overall, this works pretty well as a landing page to their pop-up ad. This concept could easily be turned into a search engine ad listing.

Conclusion

A successful search engine advertising strategy begins with a plan. Being able to communicate what your company does, and for whom, provides you with the basic framework from which all of your marketing campaign components are created.

The first step in setting up a an ad paid listing campaign is to develop a keyword universe. This list should include any popular branded names you own as well as popular, yet targeted, generic terms.

Next, write ad listings that not only incorporate the keyword you've purchased, but address the needs of the target market you're are trying to reach. Think of what will invite Persuadethose prospects buyers—not browsers—to visit your web site by promoting specific benefits, incentives, and calls to action. now. Review your competitors' listings for copywriting ideas and observe the editorial guidelines of the search engines.

Finally, customize landing pages for your ad listings. Page design and copy with psychological appeal can turn your visitors into customers.

With research, creativity, and testing, you'll find the winning combinations for your campaign.

 **PART II**

Paid Placement Programs

Introduction

Paid placement advertising enables marketers to buy a specific position for each keyword. The position is guaranteed as long as the advertiser is willing to pay for it. Even better, a prime position is attained within days.

There are two types of paid placement programs: Fixed Placement and Pay-For-Placement. The main advantages described in this section will help you determine the viability of each type of program, while the identified challenges shed light on the issues you'll encounter. You're not limited to one program or the other; depending on your objectives, you may decide to participate in both.

■ Chapter 6

Fixed Placement

Just as the name suggests, Fixed Placement advertising means that your text link is locked into a set position among the other listings on a search results page. The major search engines frequently reserve a portion of the top links for their own advertisers. These advertisers can often buy logos or longer descriptions to set them apart even further from other text links. Each search engine varies slightly in their offering, so I've included a questionnaire at the end of this section to assist you in your media planning efforts.

As an example of a Fixed Placement program, let's look at Microsoft's consumer information and entertainment site, MSN. Figure 6.1 shows the results for "home loans" on the MSN Search service. The Featured Sites are MSN advertisers, affiliates, partners, sponsors, or editors' recommendations. Up to three advertisers are accepted per keyword, although additional web site listings may appear under this heading. The MSN editorial team works with advertisers to determine which keywords and associated landing pages provide the best possible return on investment.

Figure 6.1
Microsoft's Featured Sites listings, which appear on the results page of their MSN Search service, are an example of a Fixed Placement program.

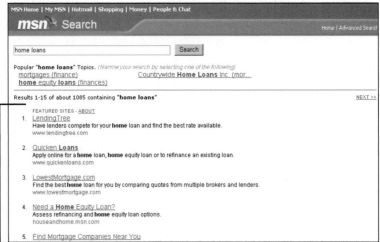

Featured Sites ——

The Advantages of Using Fixed Placement

Fixed placement advertising is less time-consuming to manage than other types of search engine advertising programs because your position is guaranteed and your costs are fixed. This program offers several competitive advantages to advertisers, as described in the following sections.

Lock In Rates

It's easy to forecast your cost for a Fixed Placement program because you'll establish a rate before you start advertising. You'll usually contact a media representative and negotiate a contract for the keywords you wish to buy. (To contact a media rep, look for an "Advertise" link on the search engine's home page or after you run a keyword search, as shown in Figure 6.2.)

The media rep will tell you how many estimated searches there are for your terms based on the previous month's search volume. Your fee is based on the traffic estimates for the month(s) in which you'd like to advertise.

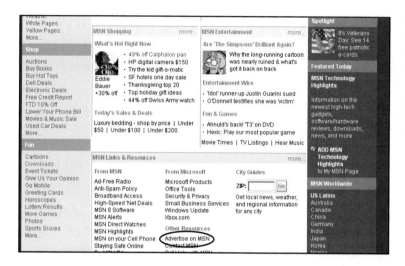

Figure 6.2
To find an MSN media representative, run a keyword search and look for the "Advertise on MSN" link under the "Other Resources" heading at the bottom of the results page.

Generally, you can sign a 30-day, a multiple-month, or an annual contract. Generally, the longer your contract term, the lower your keyword rate. Keywords are priced on a cost per thousand (CPM) impressions, cost-per-click (CPC), or cost-per-acquisition (CPA) basis.

- CPM refers to the number of times your ad listing appears during a search for the keywords you've purchased.

- CPC is the fee required for each click on your ad listing.

- CPA can define either a lead or a sale that you receive from your ad listing.

CPA is a marketer's dream. And unlike several years ago, today this pricing option is easier to secure by advertisers who are willing to spend big bucks every month. But hold on! CPA sounds like the most cost-effective option, but it isn't always. Companies with a strong brand identity, for example, could find that paying a per-impression or per-click rate yields a lower per-customer cost because their conversion rates can be high. (I'll discuss tracking solutions that help you monitor your profitability in Part V.) Why agree to pay a search engine $10 per order if instead you can pay them pennies to deliver traffic that ends up producing new customers at $7.50 per order?

Whichever type of rate and fee you negotiate, it'll remain the same during your advertising term. Your set cost buys you guaranteed visibility, traffic, leads, or sales.

Check your agreement for the delivery terms. If you pay for 5,000 clicks in one month, but only receive 4,000, does the search engine run the campaign until your minimum is met, refund the difference to you, or give you additional freebies? If these specifications aren't in the contract, you'll have a hard time collecting any option after the fact. Therefore, ask for it "in writing" before you sign.

Today, search engines are typically writing into their contracts that their reports, not yours, are used for billing purposes. Even if this restriction is in your contract, I advise double-checking their reports against yours. My clients' internal reports have been off 10–30% of what search engines, or search engine tracking vendors, report. This can represent a frighteningly big discrepancy that warrants investigation.

Lock Out Competitors from Top Positions

Arguably, the chief benefit of buying a Fixed Placement keyword position is the ability to block your competitors from prime visibility. Search engines sell a limited number of listings. If you occupy one of these spots and the others have already been sold, then your competitors can't outbid you for a higher position, or design their site to outrank yours. Competitor "lock-out" is yours during the length of your contract (as long as the other advertisers renew theirs, or a spot could open up).

Important

Set up an advertising calendar to note renewal dates in case your contract expires but you aren't notified. Evaluate the campaign performance ahead of time to determine any contract changes before you renew the same campaign.

You'll also have "first right of renewal." At the end of your advertising campaign, you can renew the agreement for another specified length of time, continuing your hold on these positions.

Ask search engine media reps about keyword exclusivity. Because companies can buy a specific number of impressions or clicks, a competitor might buy the excess inventory. For example, if you buy 10,000 impressions for the phrase "home health care," and next month the traffic doubles, your competitor could be next in line to buy this traffic. Which is more important to you: Spend more money that month buying the extra inventory to block your competitors, or keep your set monthly cost and hope that your competitors don't ask about new impressions? Discuss your needs with your media representatives to avoid surprises when this opportunity arises.

Deals Are Negotiable

Unlike other types of search engine advertising programs, Fixed Placement deals leave room for negotiation. And fortunately, with the Dot Com boom behind us, it's an advertiser's market once again. Amen! Highly-coveted keywords are in demand by competing advertisers, but a large portion of keyword inventory goes unsold. Try your hand in structuring a more profitable deal by using the negotiation secrets in the following sections.

Ask for a Frequency Discount

In your initial discussions with media representatives, ask for costs based on a 30-day campaign. Give them this short timeframe even if you'll commit to a one-year agreement (I've received a 5–10% frequency discount on 3 to 12-month campaigns, and so can you). If you reveal that you're interested in an annual program too soon, then this discount might not be extended to you.

Ask for Bonus Ads

Search engines sell more than just keyword text links. They offer banner ads, content sponsorships, and opt-in email. As a way to increase the overall profitability of that search engine's campaign, ask for additional advertising opportunities at no additional cost. With so much ad space available, a media rep who is on the ball will conduct a little research and propose ideas for your consideration.

Keep in mind, however, that this free offer must be targeted or it'll kill your profit margins, unless you simply view this as a branding bonus. When I purchased search engine ads for clients I didn't accept run-of-site banner ads or text links because I knew they wouldn't perform. I negotiated free generic or branded keywords with a low search volume because these were still highly targeted, even if there weren't a lot of people searching for them. Because low-traffic terms

Important

Track main media buys and free bonus ads as two separate campaigns to ensure that the former performs on its own merit without the freebie.

aren't in high demand by other advertisers, media reps are able to bundle these into contracts fairly easily.

Accept the Cost, Ask for a Reduced Rate

Search engines have contract cost minimums that average a couple thousand dollars per month. There's no point in asking for a reduced contract cost. However, you'll more than likely be quoted retail rates for keywords. As long as the search engines receive a minimum payment from you, they're generally happy. If you get more for your dollar, then you'll be happy too.

Pretend a search engine proposes $3,000 a month for 100,000 impressions, which is $0.03 per impression. Accept the $3,000 cost; then ask for 150,000 impressions to close the deal, which brings the rate down to $0.02 per impression.

Important

Don't ask media reps for keyword recommendations and associated quotes if you have no intention of participating in their programs. Use keyword tools instead.

Whether you're already running search engine campaigns or this is your first one, a Fixed Placement program will give you new keyword ideas. Submit a keyword universe to your media representatives and ask them to propose an expanded list. They'll tap into their keyword inventory database and tools to help you with your research. Consider these keywords for other ad programs and optimization efforts.

Better-Positioned Real Estate

It's fair to assume that search engines put their own advertisers in optimal positions. These listings are above the fold and close to the search box. Fixed Placement advertisers' listings can be set apart from other listings with logos, longer descriptions, or multiple links to different web pages of the advertiser's site.

Just look how much real estate Mortgage Expo.com has on Excite for the keyword "mortgage" (see Figure 6.3). This advertiser is lucky; Excite appears to sell just one ad position under their fixed position program. Did you notice how many text links Mortgage Expo.com has in this sponsored area? Excite allows the advertiser to connect with their target audience through a variety of marketing messages, which probably helps their overall click-through rate.

Unfortunately, Mortgage Expo.com is not fully utilizing this perk to their advantage—all of the links dump visitors onto their home page. Sigh…they own a prime piece of the advertising landscape and it would be so easy to link to the appropriate landing pages. That would mean one less click to the information their potential clients seek. When you buy the best lot on any search engine, invite the neighbors inside your house for a visit—don't leave them standing at the front door.

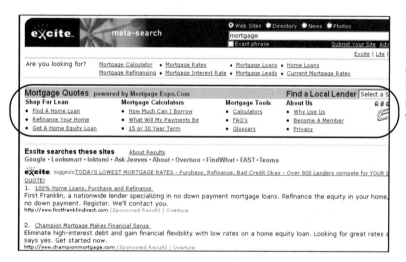

Figure 6.3

Fixed Placement advertisers receive well-positioned ad space, as demonstrated by Mortgage Expo.com's multiple listings on Excite.com for the keyword "mortgage."

The Challenges of Fixed Placement

The challenges with Fixed Placement advertising tend to prevent small businesses from investing in this program. Contract minimums can be cost-prohibitive. Furthermore, campaign management is confusing or downright frustrating to entrepreneurs who need to modify their campaigns quickly but don't have the time or technology to do so. Review the following challenges to see how well equipped your company is to address these issues before initiating a Fixed Placement program.

Contract Length and Cost Minimum

To get price breaks on Fixed Placement ads, you'll need to commit to long-term contracts. This is risky. What if your campaign bombs within a few weeks and you've signed up for a one-year campaign? A cancellation clause allows you to pull the parachute cord and jump out of your ad agreement with written notification, but search engines began eliminating these a few years ago (still ask for it anyway). As part of a "test before you invest" strategy, run a 30-day campaign and then draft a long-term agreement based on the results. This isn't a guarantee of long-term performance, but it'll give you an idea of what to expect.

The cost minimum of Fixed Placement far exceeds that of Pay-For-Placement (which we'll be getting to in the next chapter), so this can't be a first advertising step for small business owners. It doesn't make good sense to learn from a $2,000 campaign when you can test a $50 one instead.

Keyword Replacement Restrictions

Keep in mind that you're committed to the keywords you select for the entire length of the contract. With several other types of paid advertising programs you can immediately delete the nonperforming keywords. Not so with Fixed Placement.

If you notice that certain keywords are hurting your entire campaign, ask for a contract revision to replace those with other terms. Although keyword replacement isn't a guaranteed option, it's worth asking about if you wind up in this situation.

Ad Listing Limitations

Throughout your campaign, you'll be editing your ad copy, and probably destination URLs, continuously. This task is a piece of cake through self-service, Pay-For-Placement programs. Unfortunately, changes to your Fixed Placement campaign dictate that you work with the search engines' technical support people or systems. Modifications to your listings can take longer. Worse, there could be limits on the number of modifications permitted each month without incurring a fee. Check your agreement or ask your media rep how ad listing updates are handled.

Invoice Reconciliation Hassles

Generally, your cost is broken down into a monthly schedule of fixed, equal payments. Therefore, budgeting for Fixed Placement campaigns is effortless because your cost is a known figure. Keep in mind that you're paying for *estimated* visibility, traffic, and sales. So unless you've purchased a set number of these deliverables each month, you won't know what is actually delivered until you check your tracking reports. Absolutely, positively review search engine invoices each month. I've witnessed how a couple of search engines' bills were based on estimated deliverables instead of actual ones. If this happens to you, don't panic. Check with your media representative to ensure they'll deliver what was guaranteed in your contract by the end of the term. It's just something you'll need to monitor with Fixed Placement.

The second headache with regard to payment is multiple invoice reconciliation. As inventory becomes available for the keywords you've purchased, you'll sign new agreements. An invoice is issued for each contract. Several years ago, I managed keyword banner and text link campaigns on over 15 search engines for one client. For AOL.com alone, I reviewed about 10 invoices each month because the client continued to buy new impressions for a core set of keywords. Ugh. Luckily, most search engine campaigns now allow you to add and delete keywords without this extra paperwork.

Creating a Fixed Placement Questionnaire

Fixed placement is alive and well when it comes to keyword banner ads. However, due in large part to the demand for Pay-For-Placement pricing by advertisers, search engines are replacing their Fixed Placement advertising program with a Pay-For-Placement model when it comes to keyword text links. There's certainly no harm in requesting Fixed Placement for keyword listings if the advantages appear to outweigh the challenges for your company. The right amount of cash always opens doors that don't appear visible from the outside, or in this case, in the online media kit.

And where one door closes, another opens. Vertical market content sites are tapping into the demand for text link advertising, and a great number are starting with Fixed Placement programs. CPM, CPC, and CPA are all fair game pricing models for negotiation on content sites. Vertical content sites are targeted because they're focused around keyword themes. Search engines connect consumers to content sites, so why not advertise at the end destination?

Whether you're interested in Fixed Placement on search engines or content sites, there are many questions whose answers will help you better evaluate each venue's program. The following are based on the advantages and challenges reviewed in this chapter, so you can return here once you have collected the data. The questions require slight modification if you use them for content sites because the "keyword" part won't likely apply; you'll be considering specific content pages instead.

1. What is the name of your keyword text link advertising programs (if applicable)?

2. Where is the ad listing located on a search results page?

3. What are the ad specifications (number of lines, character length of each line, and so on)?

4. Will my ad listing appear on any of your partner web sites? If so, describe.

5. How many ad positions are available?

6. What is your contract length minimum?

7. What is your contract cost minimum?

8. What are your keyword rates (CPM, CPC, CPA)?

9. Have you offered keyword advertising on a CPA basis, and if so, at what monthly spending level?

10. What are your cancellation terms?

11. Do you offer keyword exclusivity? If so, define exclusivity.

12. What percentage of your monthly keyword inventory is available for purchase?

13. What happens if there are impressions or clicks available over what I've purchased?

14. Do you have a limit on the number of listing modifications per month? If so, describe.

After you've collected this information, you can assess the deliverables and risks of each venue. When you're ready to narrow your list to a few main players, then put on your negotiator's hat and ask for those deal-making incentives I mentioned earlier. This gives you final data to select the winning vendors.

Agencies that manage Fixed Placement campaigns on behalf of clients sometimes receive a commission from the search engines. If you represent an agency, ask your media rep if the quoted rates are gross or net. An average gross rate includes a 15% markup that search engines won't rebate back to an advertiser, but will offer to an agency as an incentive to bring them multiple clients. A net rate means there's no markup, so an agency needs to determine how they'll get paid for their efforts (online media agencies may charge a 15–30% media commission for campaign setup, management, and reporting).

Not quite sure if Fixed Placement is the best start for your company? There's an easier and less expensive way to jump into the search engine advertising game. Along with a myriad of companies, you can get your feet wet with Pay-For-Placement campaigns.

Chapter 7

Pay-For-Placement

Pay-For-Placement (PFP) programs allow you to outbid competing advertisers to attain higher keyword positions. It's an ongoing auction where your competitors, not the search engines, set the going keyword rate. This paid placement program is easy and affordable for small businesses to start driving traffic to their web sites almost immediately. But both entrepreneurs and corporate advertisers need to be aware of the challenges to manage their campaigns effectively.

As an example of PFP, I ran a search for "pet supplies" in FindWhat.com (shown in Figure 7.1). You can see the per-click fee each advertiser is willing to pay for its position. FindWhat.com advertisers open an account online for $25 using a credit card, and start bidding on keywords (FindWhat.com's minimum bid is $.05 per click). An advertiser's account is debited when someone clicks the ad listing. Of course, for competitive terms, the fees will be much higher than the minimum required. Keyword tools, as discussed in Part I, "Planning a Successful Strategy," help you find less competitive phrases that are still mere pennies per click.

Figure 7.1

FindWhat.com is a PFP search engine that allows advertisers to outbid each other for specified keyword positions. Bids are based on per-click fees set by competing advertisers.

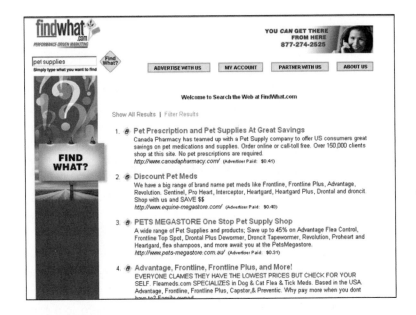

The Advantages of Pay-For-Placement

Pay-For-Placement is the fastest and easiest way for advertisers to achieve a #1 position on leading search engines. Within days, your web site listing will appear on the PFP search engine you purchase clicks from, as well as on their distribution partner sites.

When PFP search engines hit the marketing scene with cost-per-click (CPC) pricing, they introduced businesses to the precursor of performance-based marketing. Today, most marketers still can't negotiate cost-per-acquisition (CPA) deals due to the high antici-pated sales volume required, so to all levels of advertisers, PFP engines guarantee the next best deliverable: traffic.

Reaching a Large Audience Is Convenient

Many Internet users have never used PFP search engines such as FindWhat.com, Overture, or Kanoodle. However, a lot of these people use AltaVista, Yahoo!, or MSN Search. Herein lies a valuable secret:

Buying top listings on Pay-For-Placement search engines gives advertisers high placement instantly on other well-recognized search engines and content sites.

For instance, Kanoodle's advertisers appear as sponsored listings on Dogpile, MetaCrawler, WebCrawler, c/net, and Search.com, as well as 2,500 other search-enabled web sites. Advertisers pay click fees to Kanoodle, regardless of which Kanoodle partner sites deliver the traffic.

The attractiveness of PFP engines is in the search distribution partnerships they keep. In some cases, you can bypass marketing on the first-tier search engines by advertising through their sponsored listing suppliers. Bid for a top position on Overture, and your paid listing will be on Yahoo! (Figures 7.2 and 7.3). Buy text links through Google's AdWords program, and your ad will appear on AOL.com and the AOL network. These relationships change constantly, which is why it's important to advertise on multiple search engines and use a variety of programs. You never know where your listing will appear next.

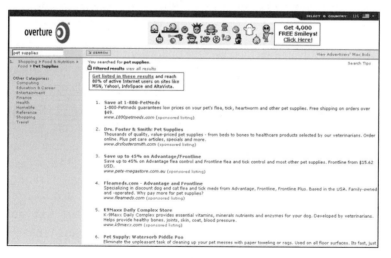

Figure 7.2

Notice the advertisers' positions on Overture for the phrase "pet supplies."

Figure 7.3

Overture's advertisers are listed in the same positions under Yahoo!'s Sponsored Results, for the same phrase, because Yahoo! is one of Overture's search distribution partners.

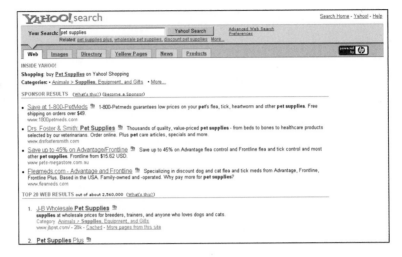

Optional Visibility Through Contextual Advertising

As mentioned, PFP engines offer their search results to distribution partners. This means your ad listing appears on partner sites when a search is performed for the keyword you've bid on at the PFP engine.

Contextual advertising increases the opportunities for your ad listing to appear on partner sites. A keyword search isn't actually performed on a partner site; rather your ad listing will appear if the PFP engine technology determines that the partner's web page content is relevant to your ad listing. Figure 7.4 shows where PetPlace.com allows Google to serve ad listings on their home page. PetPlace.com earns money when their site visitors click on Google's ads.

This is a great revenue opportunity for contextual ad distribution partners, such as PetPlace.com, that generate significant web site traffic. Google calls this their AdSense program; Overture refers to it as Content Match; Kanoodle recently launched Context Target; and FindWhat.com and others were testing contextual advertising at the time of this publication. If you're interested, contact them about hosting contextual ads on your web site as a revenue-sharing opportunity.

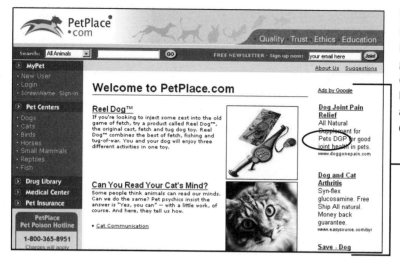

Figure 7.4
PetPlace.com is participating
in Google's AdSense pro-
gram, where companies that
display Google's AdWords
listings on their web sites
are paid for resulting clicks
on those ads.

—— Google ads

PFP advertisers, on the other hand, should be wary about participating in a contextual ad program. Sure, it's greater visibility because
your ad listings are displayed on a higher number of web sites and
more often. However, with search-based advertising, your listings
appear for the keywords you've specifically selected. With contextual
advertising, your ads can appear on sites that aren't as relevant as
you want. And watch out—you may be automatically enrolled in the
PFP engine's contextual ad program by being a keyword advertiser.

To determine if contextual advertising hurts or helps your business,
track resulting sales from your contextual ad listings separately
from your keyword search listings. The easiest way to do this is to
set up two separate campaigns or entire accounts, depending on
what the PFP engine allows. In one campaign or account, disable the
contextual ad listings. In the other, disable keyword search ad listings. Figure 7.5 shows how to do this on Overture. Check the PFP
search engine's Frequently Asked Questions page for instructions on
how to disable either program.

Important

Overture and Google
advertisers are automati-
cally opted-in to their
contextual ad programs. If
you don't want to participate, look for the instructions on disabling this
option within their ad
management center; on
the other hand, Kanoodle
offers search and contex-
tual advertising as two
separate programs.

Figure 7.5
Overture advertisers can isolate search from contextual advertising. "Overture Results" includes both, and is the default option.

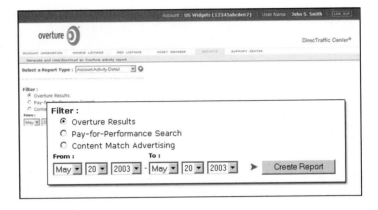

Inexpensive Costs

Inexpensive setup fees and a pay-as-you-get-traffic fee structure make a Pay-For-Placement campaign affordable to initiate. You'll open an account for $5–$50 using your credit card. Each time there's a click on your listing, the click fee is debited from your account. The lowest starting bid is $.01–$.10 per click, depending on the PFP engine. One penny more than an advertiser above you bumps your listing above his. Don't get too excited yet; competitive terms are much higher than the minimum bid. However, for terms that are pennies per click, this is far less expensive than paying pennies per impression, which was the only option for paid placement several years ago.

> **Important**
>
> Competitive keywords are pricey. For example, at the time I wrote this section, the #1 advertiser's maximum bid for "mesothelioma" on Overture was $60.02 per click.

Easy Campaign Setup and Management

Ready to launch an ad campaign today? Well, you can with Pay-For-Placement. Start on the PFP search engine's home page and look for an "Advertise" link. You'll be directed to a series of forms through the web. Within minutes you can submit the following information:

- Company information
- Billing information
- Selected keywords
- Title for each keyword
- Description for each keyword

- Destination URL (landing page) for each keyword

- Bid price for each keyword

You might need a few minutes, or a few hours, to write the title and description for each keyword you wish to bid on. Plus, you'll need to determine the landing page for each keyword, or a group of words. Before you start the sign-up process, research your keywords on that PFP engine to determine what bid price you'll need to pay to get the position you want.

Type all of this campaign information into a spreadsheet so you can copy and paste it into the account forms. The new account enrollment process requires a few forms, and if you stay on one form too long, it could be rendered inactive and you'll have to start all over.

Important

Several search engines offer keyword research and listing assistance for a fee.

Immediate Launch of Campaigns

Whereas search engine optimization takes months to witness any improvement in your site rankings, paid placement sidesteps the waiting game. Pay-For-Placement is the fastest way to achieve a #1 position.

As soon as you submit your information on Google, for example, you'll be sent a confirmation email asking you to activate your campaign by clicking on the link provided within the email. Once your credit card information has been entered, your listings are live within minutes. Other PFP engines launch your listings within days, once they're approved by their listing editors.

Ability to Optimize Your Ad Copy

With search engine advertising, you control the copy in your ad listing. The self-service functionality of Pay-For-Placement makes it convenient to edit your listings to enhance performance. Modify your titles and descriptions daily, weekly, or monthly. Although it usually takes a few days for new listings to be approved by PFP editors once you submit them, you're able to delete nonperforming ad listings within minutes.

Google is a winner in this arena because they allow for an unlimited number of ad listings to be rotated for each keyword. Copywriters can become nearly obsessed with testing multiple listings to maximize ad copy performance. In late November, Google released an Auto-Optimization feature that automatically optimizes advertiser campaigns to improve the experience of both advertisers and users. When there are multiple ads in an Ad Group, the ad with the highest click-through rate (CTR) is shown more often.

Control Over Daypart Targeting

If you've got the time and interest, you can advertise your PFP ad listings during the most profitable times of each 24-hour period. This is referred to as *daypart marketing*. TV advertisers have been doing this for years; they buy commercial airtime based on the time of day they believe their target audience is watching. You can do this with PFP advertising, too.

Start by analyzing your online sales data to determine the days and hours your conversion rates are at their highest and lowest points. If you don't have this data accessible, you can use web analytics reports such as HitBox or WebTrends to at least discover the peaks and valleys of your site traffic, although this data could be misleading in defining a daypart strategy because your ultimate goal is sales, not traffic.

Jump into top positions by increasing your bids. Remember to check the minimum position you can be in to ensure your listing appears on that PFP's distribution partner sites. In periods of low site conversions, lower your PFP positions to reduce the flow of traffic to your web site. This tactic increases the profit margins of your overall campaign.

Manually making these changes across multiple search engines is time-consuming. Luckily, a few bid management services, provided by GO TOAST or Did-it.com, for example, allow you to set timed bids. Both of these services are reviewed in greater detail in Part V, "Tracking Your Return on Investment."

The Challenges of Pay-For-Placement

Ok, with so many advantages to PFP advertising, you're ready to sign up and watch your listings go live this weekend, right? Yes, there are a lot of benefits for first-time search engine advertisers and experienced marketers. But with this instant traffic delivery system and the increase in advertisers using it, there are several ways to quickly bleed time and money. Understand what challenges await you and get ready to respond to obstacles.

The Battle with Editors for Ad Approval

Because it's painless for companies to bid for thousands of premium keyword positions, there's the potential of companies bidding on nonrelevant terms. What happens if web users see what they consider to be junk results on a PFP engine, or one of their partner sites? You got it; they'll stop using that search engine. Therefore, as a way of maintaining the integrity of their search results, PFP editors are tough when it comes to approving sponsors' ad listings.

Editors reject ad listing submissions that will frustrate their users: those containing broken destination URLs, for instance. Rejection is certainly frustrating for advertisers. One of my client's listings was declined for the keyword "white sewing machine" because the word "white" wasn't on the landing page copy. Um, the sewing machine in the photo was white. There were no other color options on the order form either. Needless to say, I was irked that I had to resubmit the listing. Due to that experience, I began verifying that keywords were in the landing page copy, not just as an obvious match to images on the page.

Overture shared that up to 30% of listings submitted to them are rejected, which means a lot of advertisers are unhappily modifying and resubmitting listings. Hopefully, by following each search engine's editorial guidelines, you'll avoid this fate. (Revisit the submission guidelines in Chapter 4, "Copywriting Tips to Improve Your Click-Through Rate.")

Only Top Spots Win Traffic

Unlike Fixed Placement, with PFP you can bid for a #1 position, but you won't be king of the keyword for long. Every hour competitors could outbid you for the highest position. Once your listing is knocked below a Top 5 or Top 10 position, you're generally no longer getting visibility on a majority of Pay-For-Placement partner sites. A significant amount of PFP traffic comes from their partners. Therefore, it's paramount to maintain a top position to continue a strong flow of traffic to your site.

Let's review the "pet meds" example again by looking at Find-What.com's partner sites running this keyword search. Figures 7.6 and 7.7 show the part of the search results page on Excite and Dog-pile where FindWhat.com's advertisers are displayed. It's interesting to see how Excite integrates the results from the PFP engines on their page, while Dogpile sorts the results by PFP engine. You may not always easily identify which search engine is providing the results, as you can in these examples, but look for a "Sponsored Listing" type of header and you'll know that they are paid listings.

Figure 7.6

Excite integrates FindWhat.com's sponsored listings among results from other search engines, including Overture, Inktomi, Ask Jeeves, Google, and Sprinks.

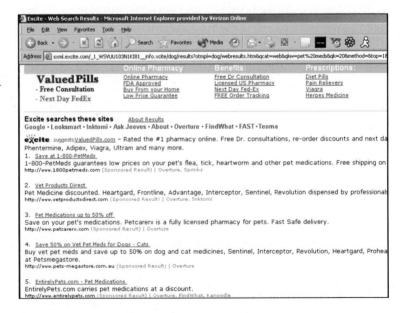

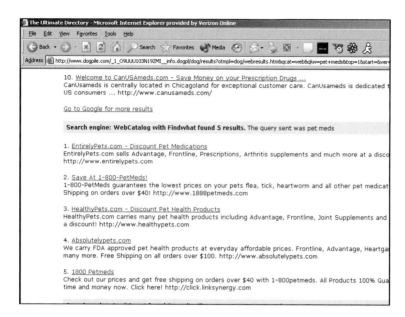

Figure 7.7
Dogpile sorts results by
Pay-For-Placement search
engine.

Be Hot or Be Dropped

Search engine representatives want their technology to provide relevant results for a better user experience. They also want to maximize revenue from their advertisers. As a way of serving both objectives, some PFP engines now contain a click popularity feature that penalizes advertisers who are receiving a low click-through rate; unpopular listings are deleted.

Unfortunately, this hurts advertisers whose conversion rates make their PFP campaign profitable, but because their click-through rates fall below the acceptable minimums, those listings are dropped. If this happens, you should receive a notice via email with the listings that will be yanked. Modify them ASAP in an attempt to boost your click rate, or they'll be deleted.

The Threat of Increased Competition

Search engine advertising is finally receiving publicity in mainstream media for being one of the most effective marketing methods available today. Tools now exist to make search engine advertising easier to monitor. Unfortunately, with greater awareness of this hot topic, competition on the Pay-For-Placement field is skyrocketing.

It's harder to find keywords without advertisers, which means it's challenging to land minimum $.01, $.05, or $.10 per-click bids.

Companies also are either using management tools or outsourcing these efforts to search engine marketing professionals. Battles over keywords continue to escalate, and newer competitors are outfitted with sophisticated weapons for the fight. Arm yourself with the research, management, and tracking tools described in this book to not simply beat your competitors, but guarantee that you're refining your campaigns based on ROI goals and not on maintaining a #1 position.

Bid Gaps Drain Extra Profits

To climb into a higher position with Pay-For-Placement engines, you must increase your per-click bid. For a penny over what a competitor is paying, your listing will jump above his. Bids are generally updated hourly, which means the lineup of advertisers is in a constant state of flux. Advertisers not only add keywords and raise their bids, but also delete keywords and lower bids. Suddenly, you're in a #1 spot paying $2 per click while advertiser #2 is paying only $.50 per click. This difference is known as a *bid gap*. To continue being #1 you'd only need to pay $.51 per click. Even though a few pennies come between you and the next advertiser, this amount adds up quickly and drains the profits on your campaigns. Spend the bare minimum to maintain your desired position.

Fortunately, tools exist to solve this time-consuming problem. As previously mentioned, Did-it.com and GO TOAST offer services that include bid gap management. There are also inexpensive bidding tools that won't manage your campaigns based on return on investment targets, but will maintain your bids and positions for you, in addition to adjusting bid gaps. A good list of vendors to consider are those already approved by Overture for the North American marketplace, which at the time of this writing included:

- BidRank
- Did-it.com
- Dynamic Keyword Bid Maximizer (Apex Pacific)
- Epic Sky
- GO TOAST

- PPC BidTracker (Trellian)

- PPC Pro (PPC Management)

- Send Traffic

- Sure Hits

A few PFP search engines, including Overture, have integrated an automated bid gap adjustment feature. Whew...you won't have to worry about wasting money because all bids are reduced to the lowest possible bid. That's a relief...almost.

You should know one important feature about Overture's Max Bid, or you could be the victim of a "punish your competitor" attack. (I've heard about this being done and it's not pretty.) On Overture, advertisers set the maximum bid they're willing to pay for a keyword. The Auto Bid feature reduces each advertiser's bid to one penny above the bid beneath him, which becomes the actual fee paid by the advertisers. For example, if the #1 advertiser sets his max bid at $1 and the next highest bid is $.20, then #1 will actually pay $.21 per click. This works out well unless the #2 advertiser forces the #1 advertiser to pay his max bid. In this same scenario, if advertiser #2 bids $.99, then the #1 advertiser will pay $1 because that's a penny above #2's bid. The tables below illustrate these two possibilities (the lowest-positioned bidder pays $.10 because that is Overture's minimum bid; this scenario assumes there are only three advertisers).

Option One
Max Bids Set on Overture

Advertiser #1 = $1.00 per click
Advertiser #2 = $.20 per click
Advertiser #3 = $.15 per click

Overture's Auto Bid Feature (advertisers' actual fees)

Advertiser #1 = $.21 per click
Advertiser #2 = $.16 per click
Advertiser #3 = $.10 per click

continues

continued

Option Two

"Punish the #1 Advertiser on Overture" Scenario

Advertiser #1 = $1.00 per click
Advertiser #2 = $.99 per click
Advertiser #3 = $.15 per click

Overture's Auto Bid Feature (advertisers' actual fees)

Advertiser #1 = $1.00 per click
Advertiser #2 = $.16 per click
Advertiser #3 = $.10 per click

According to an Overture representative, this isn't a common problem for their advertisers. Even with that reassurance, the moral of this story is: *Don't set a maximum bid that you don't really want to pay.*

Constant Monitoring Is Required

Of course, it's important to monitor the results of any search engine advertising campaign. But with Fixed Placement you'll know your estimated cost because you've negotiated the media buy. Although over-delivery is infrequent with Fixed Placement, if it does happen it can be a free bonus because your cost would exceed the commitment you approved in the contract (ask your media rep about this to be sure). With Pay-For-Placement, you can estimate the number of clicks to your site, but your actual delivered traffic could be substantially higher than you had expected. When you set up a campaign on PFP engines, you might not want to choose the "unlimited traffic" payment option, to avoid surprise surges. Approve a specified amount and you'll receive an email notification when your account runs low and needs a refill.

Click fraud is a quiet yet expensive problem on Pay-For-Placement search engines. Essentially, this is junk traffic for which you're being charged. Click fraud is caused by your competitors or by unethical behavior by a few distribution partners of PFP engines. Search engines do have click fraud protection mechanisms in place, but not all of it is caught, and it's costing a few companies significant dollars. We'll look more at how to protect your campaigns from click fraud in Part VI, "Protecting Your Profits." Just be aware that click fraud is another issue that demands your attention if you're running decent-sized PFP campaigns.

No Control Over Search Distribution Partners

Very few search engines are "pure." They don't offer entire search results from only their own database of web site links (Google and Teoma do, however). Not only do search engines tap into each other's databases for web site links, but when their relationships change they use other vendors as their sources. Furthermore, search engines redesign their sites so the location and content of the ad listings always shift. Subsequently, marketers need to engage in optimization and advertising efforts, as well as a myriad of advertising programs.

When changes in partnerships occur, these impact Pay-For-Placement advertisers the most because the core benefit of PFP engines rests in their distribution partner network. Suddenly, your traffic levels could spike, or die off. The partnerships influence the quality of traffic, too. To remain abreast of the latest dance partners in the PFP space, subscribe to online newsletters such as those recommended in the Resources section of this book.

Pay-For-Placement Questionnaire

The nature of Pay-For-Placement advertising necessitates a very different set of questions from Fixed Placement. Most of this information can be found on each PFP web site. If you call the sales departments of these search engines you'll probably be referred to their web site. It's a good idea to start there, and if you can't find all of the information you need, by all means give them a call.

1. What is the name of the program (if applicable)?

2. How many search results distribution partners do you have?

3. Who are your major distribution partners (search engines first, then content sites)?

4. Which positions must advertisers secure to appear on your major partner sites?

5. What's the minimum amount required to open an account?

6. What's the minimum and maximum per-click bid?

7. Is there a monthly spending minimum?

8. How many days does approval of new campaigns and new listings take?

9. At what spending level is monthly invoicing possible?

10. Who are your approved bid management tool vendors?

11. Are bid gaps automatically adjusted?

12. How many times per day can bids be changed?

13. How many different ad listings can run per keyword? How are these served?

14. Are single and plural forms of a word one or two media buys?

15. Do you offer a free or fee-based ROI tracking system?

16. Does your system penalize listings for falling below a specified click rate? If so, describe.

Obviously, fees are net, and there is no agency commission given. An outside firm that manages your campaign may charge a flat monthly fee, an hourly rate, or a percentage of the media buy. If you use affiliates to run your search engine marketing for you, you'll only have to pay a cost-per-acquisition rate. But affiliates represent an interesting dilemma that poses a threat to your profit margins. This quandary is addressed in Part VI.

Conclusion

Paid placement campaigns, both Fixed Placement and Pay-For-Placement, can be done without optimizing your web site for keywords. This isn't to say that web page design doesn't matter in terms of getting approval from the search engine editors or converting your visitors into buyers. It does. But through paid placement, you can secure a #1 position regardless of your site architecture. Within days, your ad listings will appear in the positions, and for the keywords, you choose.

Visit www.searchenginesales.com for updates and links to many of the resources mentioned in this book.

PART III

Paid Inclusion Programs

Introduction

Paid inclusion does not guarantee marketers a top ranking for specific keywords. However, to achieve high visibility in the "organic" (also called "natural") area of search results, most search engines require an inclusion fee for each web site page you'd like indexed. Long-term, paid inclusion is less expensive than paid placement if you can achieve similar positions and number of searches for your keywords.

There are two types of paid inclusion programs: Submit URL and Trusted Feed. The advantages and challenges of each program are more similar than they are different. But unlike with paid placement, the paid inclusion program you choose is not determined by your marketing goals, but rather the architecture of your web site.

Chapter 8

Submit URL

After reading Part II, you now know that some search results are actually ads from search engines that sell paid placement programs to companies. You also know that other listings are "organic" (or "natural"), which means a search engine spider has crawled the web and retrieved site pages for its database (or index). When a web surfer performs a keyword search, a crawler-based (or algorithm-based) search engine ranks the pages within its database based on keyword relevancy.

To get your web site's pages into the organic area of search results, you have one of two options:

- Pray, then wait for months or years hoping that spiders find your site pages

- Pay a "come hither" fee, which guarantees spider visits to each page you submit

If your web site has less than 500 pages, then you'll use *Submit URL* to tell the search engine spiders which pages to visit and include in their databases. This program is sometimes referred to as Add URL, Direct Submit, or Site Submit. It's recommended that you submit your home page and site pages that have good content for your human visitors.

Rankings achieved through paid inclusion programs aren't marked as sponsored ads. They're often called "Web pages" or "Results." Look at MSN Search in Figure 8.1 as an example. In a query for "welding services," the organic listings begin at position #6 (first page) and are entitled "Web Pages." Keep in mind that both Submit URL and Trusted Feed inclusion programs (discussed in the next chapter), as with Pay-Per-Placement (PPP), provide search results to distribution partners including MSN Search.

Figure 8.1

Organic rankings achieved in MSN Search through paid inclusion are listed under the "Web Pages" heading.

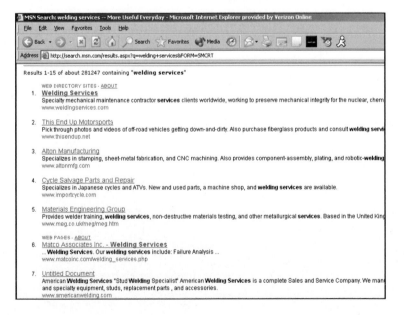

The Advantages of Submit URL

Submit URL is without a doubt the least expensive search engine advertising program long term, outscoring Fixed Placement and PFP programs. Submit URL shares a majority of its advantages with its sister paid inclusion program, Trusted Feed. But you'll choose one paid inclusion, not both. If you have less than 500 web site pages to submit, here are a few advantages you'll receive by participating in Submit URL.

Appears as an Organic Search Result, Not an Advertisement

In the beginning of search engine time, text links were organic search results. Or, a few were editors' web site recommendations. If marketers wanted to buy keywords, banner ads were their only option. Banner ads were an obvious form of advertising. Web site listings in search results were not. While consumers learned to develop "banner blindness" when performing keyword queries on search engines, savvy marketers were already promoting their web sites in the search results. Simple search engine optimization (SEO) techniques coupled with the URL submission process achieved top rankings fairly easily. Only then, Submit URL wasn't considered paid inclusion because for nearly all search engines it was free.

Today, marketers can buy their way to the top through paid placement or paid inclusion. Due to recent pressure from the U.S. Federal Trade Commission, search engines that offer paid placement are labeling this form of sponsorship. Perhaps a portion of consumers who spot a "Sponsored Listing" heading skip over these as they do banner ads. This is important to consider because Submit URL (or Trusted Feed) enables marketers to appear in the natural search results. Consumers might assume that these are unbiased site matches to their query. Paid inclusion marketers continue to draw the attention of consumers who intentionally skip what they consider to be advertisements.

This is an interesting assumption because natural search results aren't all that pure. Paying an inclusion fee improves marketers' odds of getting into the search engines. Then implementing a solid

SEO strategy definitely influences page rankings. Many companies opt to outsource these efforts to professional firms, so again they're paying a fee. Therefore, isn't all search engine marketing advertising to a degree? Yes. But as long as consumers believe there's a difference, there's value to being visible in the area they consider to contain unbiased search results.

Score Additional Rankings for Relevant Keywords

With paid placement, you specify the keywords you want to buy. Through paid inclusion, when you optimize your site design for primary keywords you'll often score rankings for relevant secondary keywords at no extra charge.

Content is central to achieving high rankings; search engine spiders need to determine what each site page is about and how it compares to other pages with similar content. Look at the relevant content on the Matco Associates Inc. welding page (see Figures 8.2 and 8.3). It's no wonder that this company ranks first under "Web Pages" on MSN Search for "welding services."

Figure 8.2

The Matco Associates Inc. welding page ranks first under MSN Search's organic listings (see "Web Pages" heading) for the phrase "welding services."

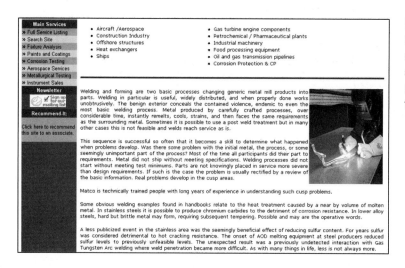

Figure 8.3

Look how much relevant content search engines can scan on Matco's welding page and consider for additional keyword rankings.

Matco makes the copy people-friendly by using a client testimonial, bullets to highlight their services, plus in-depth copy explaining the welding process. Potential customers are offered pretty extensive educational information about the topic. Search engines love this approach too, and fortunately, often reward sites following this model.

The search engines, or their authorized resellers, that offer a Submit URL service often provide reports. These usually include the keywords that send traffic to your site or to specific pages. Figure 8.4 is a sample Inktomi report from Position Technologies, a Submit URL and Trusted Feed reseller.

Continual Re-indexing of Site Pages

Marketers who aren't using a paid inclusion program wait indefinitely for search engine spiders to make return visits to their sites. Sure, a couple of search engines and directories offer a free Add URL form (AltaVista, Lycos, Google, Open Directory Project/dmoz.org). But, if there's significant competition for your keywords, don't rely on the chance that perhaps this year a spider travels your way. (Top SEO firms can achieve success with free submissions because they're experts at site optimization.) Furthermore, when you update your content or add site pages, you'll want to invite the search engines to swing by for a closer look immediately. The sooner they evaluate your pages, the sooner they'll include them in their databases. I recommend using their fee-based service, if available.

Figure 8.4

A Submit URL report generally reveals the keywords that send traffic to your site. Paid inclusion resellers such as Position Technologies provide one account login for you to review reports for multiple programs. This is their sample Inktomi Submit URL report.

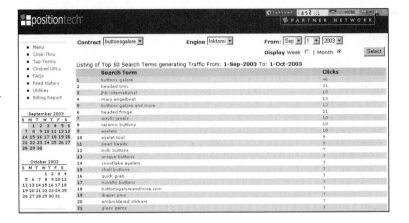

Important

A web site page can't achieve an organic ranking without being in the search engine's database. Once included in the database, a top ranking is earned, not guaranteed.

Once you've paid the fee, first-time inclusion generally occurs within 72 hours, as it does with Inktomi. Inktomi provides 48-hour refreshes for their Submit URL programs. You're only a few days away from initial and repeat spider visits. No praying to the spider gods and checking web analytics reports to spot their visits. It's an automated process.

Getting listed by search engines is similar to being last in a pathetically long line at an over-the-top trendy restaurant. A little cash catches the host's attention and voilá, you're in. In this case, that cash incentive guarantees that a waiter will actually serve you. Now it's up to your astonishingly-beautiful attire and electric personality to win VIP treatment. Back in the online world, paying the inclusion fee instantly opens the doors to the search engine database. Then it's up to your web site design and content to earn you prominent visibility.

Least Expensive Traffic Generator Long-Term

The aforementioned advantages apply to both Submit URL and Trusted Feed inclusion programs. This benefit, however, is owned completely by Submit URL. It's the only search engine advertising program where you pay an annual or semi-annual fee for unlimited traffic.

Table 8.1 shows sample pricing for two search engines that offer Submit URL. (Remember that the same search engine often sells both types of paid placement and paid inclusion programs as well.)

Table 8.1 Sample Submit URL pricing structure for two search engines through Position Technologies.

Search Engine	First URL Fee	Additional URL Fee
Ask Jeeves/Teoma	$30/year	$18/year
Inktomi	$39/year	$25/year

As an example, if you submit 10 web site pages to Ask Jeeves, you'll pay $192 for the year (1st URL = $30, 9 additional URLs = $162). On Pay-For-Placement (PFP) search engines, $192 buys you 3,840 clicks—if the keywords you want are only $.05 each. For competitive terms, you won't pay the minimum bid amount. Maybe your keywords are $1 per click; you'll receive 192 clicks. High bids on PFP engines make Submit URL a more profitable option for companies with highly competitive keywords. Even if clicks to the advertiser's site cost roughly the same amount, conversion rates could be higher through Submit URL. You'll have to review your tracking reports to make that determination.

Important

With the popularity of cost-per-click pricing on the rise, don't be surprised if their pricing model moves into the Submit URL program space too.

The risk with Submit URL is that neither rankings nor clicks are guaranteed. Therefore, submit site pages with customer-focused content that have been optimized for a group of keywords. You'll increase the likelihood of driving traffic to those pages through a variety of search terms, which will lower your per-visitor cost. The home page and main products or services pages are good candidates for Submit URL. A contact page is not. Start with 10–20 pages at a time as a test run.

Stable Positions in Directories

Directories typically fall under Submit URL because an annual or semi-annual submission fee is generally required, and a particular position is not guaranteed. Unlike crawler-based search engines, a directory is composed of human editors who determine if a web site will be included in the directory, and under which category it will be placed.

Yahoo! is a good example of a directory. Scroll down Yahoo!'s home page to find the category options (Figure 8.5). Click through the categories until you find a subcategory that relates to your business. Once on that subcategory page, click on the "Suggest a Site" link on the upper-right side to begin the submission process (Figure 8.6). Yahoo! charges $299 for a site submission, which guarantees site *review* but not *inclusion*. Once accepted as a "Site Listing," web sites are ranked in alphabetical order by company name. The $299 fee covers a one-year listing, which must be renewed annually.

Are you noticing differences between directory inclusion and crawler-based inclusion? Although each directory and search engine's Submit URL program is unique, Table 8.2 shows a few highlights to keep in mind.

Important

Nonprofit organizations may submit their web site to Yahoo! for free. The free option generally appears once you click the "Suggest a Site" link from within a nonprofit category. Timely site review is not guaranteed with this option.

Figure 8.5
To find which category to submit your web site to in Yahoo!, click through the directory.

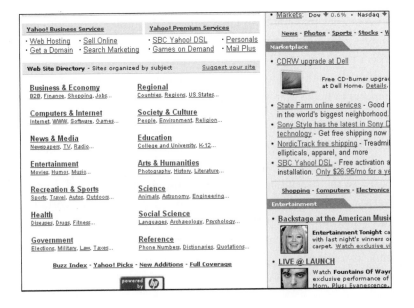

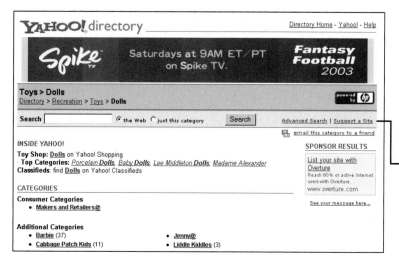

Figure 8.6
Once you've identified a category match for your site, click on the "Suggest a Site" link in the upper-right side of this page.

Suggest a site by clicking here

Table 8.2 Submit URL inclusion general comparisons.

Crawler-Based Search Engine	Directory
Fee per web page submitted	Fee per web site submitted
First review within 72 hours	First review within 7 days or longer
Technology evaluates site pages	Humans evaluate site pages
Database inclusion guaranteed	Category inclusion not guaranteed
Rankings not guaranteed	Position guaranteed (alphabetized) if accepted
Multiple web pages listed	Home page listed in one or two categories

Open Directory Project/dmoz.org and Zeal are volunteer-based directories. Anyone can become an editor. The great news here is if you can get through to the sites (ODP's site is frequently down or really slow), and get a volunteer to review your site, the listing is free! Directories can be a good source of qualified leads. Furthermore, a directory listing boosts your link popularity, which crawler-based search engines consider in determining your ranking within their index. The number and quality of inbound links to your site matter. (Link popularity is discussed in Chapter 10, "Web Site Optimization.")

The Challenges of Submit URL

Although Submit URL has plenty of benefits, it often doesn't provide enough qualified site traffic. This is due in large part because Submit URL (and Trusted Feed) rely on search distribution partners to display their results. And currently, PFP ad listings are filling these spots. Many web site owners find they need to use the Submit URL programs in conjunction with other forms of search engine advertising. The uncertainty of your results using Submit URL, as described in the following sections, pose the biggest challenges to marketers.

Top Positions Are Not Guaranteed

With either type of paid placement program, you pay an exact fee for the position you want. Not so with paid inclusion. In fact, it's possible to pay for every page of a web site using Submit URL, yet *none* of them break into the Top 10 results. At least through Trusted Feed you'll only pay a cost-per-click fee. No traffic, no fee. With Submit URL, you're stuck paying the bill regardless of performance.

Paid inclusion allows you to buy your way in. It's your web site design, copywriting, and link popularity that determine your ability to outrank your competitors for popular keywords, and climb to the top. In Chapter 10, I'll cover optimization basics to help you prepare your web site for an inclusion program, and for beating your competition. Before you learn about those specific techniques, consider following these five simple steps for each web page you plan on registering via Submit URL.

Step 1: Evaluate Your Keywords

Your web site has an overall theme. To support that theme, your site pages should contain secondary or subthemes. Look primarily at the page copy to identify your current keyword groupings. If they're not there, now's the time to refer back to Chapter 3, "Choosing Keywords for Maximum Performance," and brainstorm keywords for every page you want to rank well in search engines.

Step 2: Run a Ranking Report

You'll be able to benchmark improvements in your rankings by finding out where your pages rank right now. Perform a query for each keyword in your keyword universe and study the sites in top positions. Or, you could use ranking report software. Do not use automated ranking programs too often (like daily), because search engines will penalize sites abusing such programs. Google's Webmaster Guidelines, however, warn Webmasters against using unauthorized computer programs at all.

Step 3: Study Your Competitors

Your entire web site isn't fighting for a top position among other sites. Each web page has a unique cluster of competitors. This is where themed pages improve your rankings. Include a variety of relevant keywords within the same site page and you could outrank a competing page that is optimized for one term.

Step 4: Edit Your Content

You knew I'd say this, right? Well, by the time you get through Steps 1, 2, and 3 you'll see where your page content could use an infusion of the keywords you want positions for! Using keywords in the page body copy is the not-so-secret yet often-missed ingredient for successful optimization. Show these keywords to consumers, and search engines will take notice.

Step 5: Tweak Your Site Design

Why is this last? Because it's going to be difficult to change design elements of each web page without doing a total site facelift. For instance, hyperlinking keywords in one page to other pages can be done for just a few pages. But if this is not a site-wide modification, the inconsistencies won't sit well with your primary target audience: potential customers. However, if minor tweaks ready your pages for submission without impacting your brand or navigation, then go for it.

Organic Listings Are Positioned Below Paid Sponsors

Have you seen where natural results are posted? Almost always, they're well beneath sponsored listings and graphical ads. To see an example of this, return to MSN Search to run your own query. MSN's "Featured Sites" (Fixed Placement) and "Sponsored Sites" (PFP) are positioned above organic listings.

Yes, a percentage of consumers who prefer avoiding ads will skip sponsored listings and scroll down the page to find organic ones. Yet, how many people know that keyword text links can be purchased? How many of them who know really care?

Even a top ranking in organic search results might not deliver the traffic volume paid placement listings can.

Granular Tracking Is Tedious

It's easier to track details of a paid placement campaign than paid inclusion. Through unique tracking code, marketers can easily monitor sales under one report by each campaign component: search engine venue, keyword, ad listing, or landing page.

A few search engines that offer paid inclusion, including Ask Jeeves/Teoma, track clicks to the page submitted (refer to Figure 8.7 for Ask Jeeves' sample Submit URL report). Unfortunately, you can forget about tracking sales because you won't know which search engine or content site click produced the sale (assuming that you submit the same page to multiple search engines and negotiate inbound links from other content sites to that page as well, which is recommended for a comprehensive marketing campaign).

Figure 8.7

Ask Jeeves/Teoma offers click tracking for their Site Submit program. Advertisers have to set up their own order tracking for Submit URL programs.

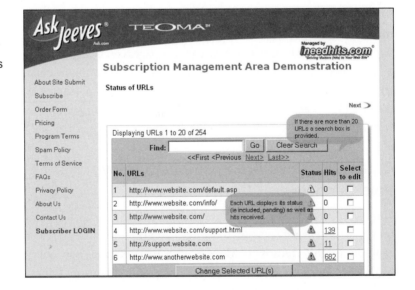

You might not discover which keywords drive traffic to that page either without going to a web analytics report, such as HitBox or WebTrends. But there, the data is generally combined, so you'll see which keywords and search engines refer traffic to your entire site, not a breakdown of each by specific pages. It's not impossible to find out; however, it's not worth the time to find out your ROI on a few hundred dollars. If you're a big picture kind of marketer, this won't really matter to you as long as your overall return rate is healthy. If you like detail, the lack of easy access to deep data will drive you nuts.

Hindered by Sites with "Deadly Design Elements"

Got Flash? Is your site in frames? Does your e-commerce solution produce dynamic pages? These are the usual culprits of search engine spider killers. A handful of today's popular design elements seriously impede your chance of getting included in a search engine's database, let alone triumphing over competing pages. These include:

- Dynamic web pages
- Forms
- Frames
- Graphics, Flash, or multimedia files
- Image maps
- JavaScript
- Session IDs

Important

Because this book does not focus on web site design and optimization, I don't address the workarounds for these complex issues. Shari Thurow goes into this in great detail in her book, *Search Engine Visibility*, by New Riders Publishing. (Bonus content from her book is included at the end of this book.)

Be aware that the way you're using these design elements likely requires workarounds before you spend money submitting pages that can't outrank sites without them. Then again, if you have over 500 web pages to submit to search engines, you can turn to a Trusted Feed program.

Chapter 9

Trusted Feed

If you have more than 500 site pages to submit to search engines, then *Trusted Feed* is the paid inclusion program for you. Your page listings are given the same opportunity to rank among the organic links as those registered by Submit URL.

Whereas in Submit URL you pay for each page you register, with Trusted Feed, you pay a set fee for each click your listings receive. Rankings are still not guaranteed, but at least payment is required only if there's traffic. Trusted Feed is also referred to as Direct, Data, or XML Feed.

The Advantages of Trusted Feed

Trusted Feed shares several advantages with Submit URL. Both appear as organic listings not ads, score additional keyword rankings, and are continually re-indexed. However, there are a few distinct advantages you can look forward to if your site qualifies for a Trusted Feed program.

Works for Deep and Dynamic Content

For content-rich sites, the pages worthy of top rankings are buried within a web site. A majority of search engine spiders won't crawl that deep into a site, certainly not without marketers at least paying a Submit URL fee, which can become expensive when adding hundreds or thousands of pages.

A secondary problem exists for sites that are database driven. If you sell products on your site and you're managing the products with an e-commerce solution, it's likely that your product data is stored inside a database. Search engines have difficulty indexing dynamic web pages that contain multiple parameters (Google can index dynamic URLs with a single parameter without a problem). Dynamic web pages are usually created with Active Server Pages (.asp), ColdFusion (.cfm), Hypertext PreProcessor (.php), and Java Server Pages (.jsp).

Are your dynamic pages spider killers? Look at your URLs. If they contain more than one stop symbol such as ?, &, $, =, +, or %, then the answer is yes. The following examples illustrate degrees of indexing difficulty for search engine spiders:

- Dynamic web page with multiple variables (bad):
  www.company.com/products.asp?product_no=1&product_sortorder=asc&product_color=red

- Dynamic web page with one variable (better):
  www.company.com/products.asp?product_no=1

- Dynamic web page with no variables (best):
  www.company.com/products.asp

■ Static web page (best):

www.company.com/products.html

Fortunately, Trusted Feed resolves the issue of indexing deep and dynamic content because it allows the content of these pages to be directly fed to search engine databases. Usually in an Excel file, you'll enter the URL, title, meta description, meta keywords, and body content, which will then be converted into an XML feed. Another option is to ask a search engine or their inclusion partner to crawl your URLs to extract page content from your site, then customize ad listing information for those pages. In either case, with Trusted Feed it's easier than with Submit URL to control what content gets indexed and how your listings appear for the pages you submit.

You can work directly with each search engine, or go through an inclusion partner who'll prepare one data feed for multiple engines. Inktomi, for example, forges direct client relationships for sites with more than 1,000 URLs. Otherwise, they refer advertisers to the partners listed in Table 9.1. You'll notice that inclusion partners often work with more than one search engine, as in the case of Position Technologies. Resellers, such as Position Technologies, sell Trusted Feed programs on behalf of multiple search engines.

Table 9.1 Search engines, such as Inktomi, allow multiple resellers to sell their Trusted Feed programs.

Inktomi's Resellers		Position Technologies Is a Trusted Feed Reseller For:
Marketleap		AlltheWeb/FAST
Referencement.com		AltaVista
Position Technologies	>	Ask Jeeves
Decide Interactive		Inktomi
TrafficLeader		

Refer to http://www.inktomi.com/products/web_search/connect.html and http://www.positiontech.com/tf_overview.htm.

An in-house programmer can force dynamic pages to appear static by using mod_rewrite for Apache or Port80 Software for an IIS server. This process helps get content into search engines via Submit URL instead of Trusted Feed, if the first paid inclusion program is needed or preferred. However, most programmers are already too overwhelmed with their current workload to take on another task. Additionally, simply generating static pages won't impact rankings through Submit URL unless pages are optimized with relevant keywords and are void of spider-repelling elements such as frames or Flash.

There are various manual methods, tools, and outsourcing options for optimizing a dynamic site. Each company needs to evaluate their internal resources to devise a plan that is cost-effective for them. You can always ask a search engine optimization (SEO) professional to analyze your site and recommend a few options for you to consider.

Third-Party E-Commerce Pages Can Be Submitted

Here's where plenty of companies run into a roadblock. A significant number of online retailers lease their e-commerce solution. These pages are preconfigured templates that can't be customized, which means they can't be properly optimized. Search engine spiders won't index the content hosted on other people's sites and give original content owners rankings for them either.

A Yahoo! Store is a perfect example. You can usually identify a Yahoo! Store retailer because their URL switches over to Yahoo!'s somewhere within the web site. Look at Figures 9.1 and 9.2, which show Oakville Grocery's home page and Gift Baskets page. Notice the home page domain is http://www.oakvillegrocery.com, but the URL then switches over to http://store.yahoo.com/oakvillegrocery/giftbaskets1.html when you click the Gift Baskets link. The web pages you optimize need to be part of your web site.

Leasing an e-commerce solution is extremely cost-effective for small to medium-sized companies. A Yahoo! Store includes powerful e-marketing features at no additional cost, including a tool that can be used to track paid placement search engines listings. (Yahoo! Small business merchant solutions are reviewed in Part V, "Tracking

Your Return on Investment.") If you're renting an online store from a vendor, you can build flat product pages on your site, and then link over to a third-party site for the final transaction. The product pages hosted on your site can be submitted to search engines via Submit URL or Trusted Feed.

Figure 9.1
The home page of Oakville Grocery.

Figure 9.2
Notice how their URL switches over to a Yahoo! e-commerce solution. Third-party content may not be indexed by search engines.

The Herrington web site is attractive to shoppers and spiders alike (see Figures 9.3 to 9.5). It uses a Yahoo! e-commerce solution, but notice that not until a product is added to the shopping cart is the customer transferred to Yahoo!'s site. This enables Herrington to host and optimize the content of each product page.

Figure 9.3

The Herrington Catalog home page.

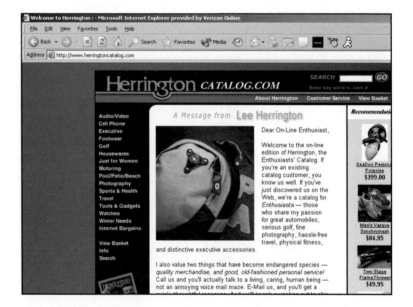

Figure 9.4

A product page from the Herrington site.

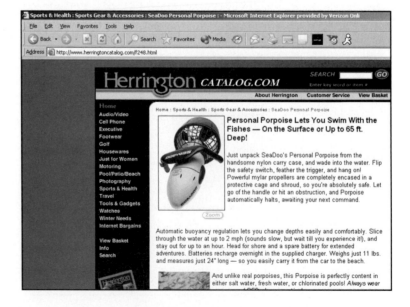

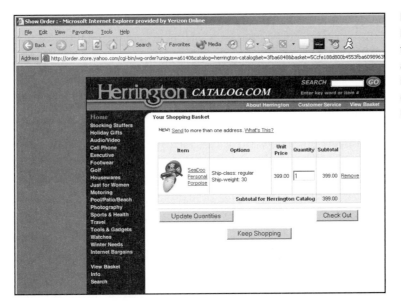

Figure 9.5
Herrington sends customers to their Yahoo! Store once a product is added to Herrington's shopping cart (notice the change of the URL).

Are too many of your product pages already in a third-party database to consider making them static? Don't worry, a Trusted Feed program can deliver this data to search engines for you. Remember that you prepare a document with page data that is fed to the search engines. You don't have to alter the pages that sit in a Yahoo! Store. You'll simply describe the content of each page there. The link that is displayed during a related keyword query will take shoppers to that exact page location.

Low Click Fees Are Guaranteed for Competitive Keywords

What do Pay-For-Placement (PFP) and Trusted Feed programs have in common? Both are based on cost-per-click (CPC) pricing. PFP click fees for each keyword are constantly fluctuating, however, because advertisers continually modify their bids. With Trusted Feed, you'll negotiate one fixed CPC rate with the search engines, or with their inclusion partners.

For example, inclusion resellers Position Technologies and Marketleap's Trusted Feed programs average $.25 per click. Take a look at your PFP campaigns. On the more popular PFP engines, including

Google and Overture, your CPC rate is probably much higher than $.25 across a majority of keywords, right? A low and nonfluctuating CPC rate makes Trusted Feed a very attractive marketing option for corporate clients. As click rates on PFP search engines continue to rise, the Trusted Feed set fee structure becomes an even bigger advantage.

Keep an eye on changes in the paid inclusion space. On which search engines or content sites are paid inclusion results offered? Who becomes a new or dismissed authorized reseller of paid inclusion? Expect price hikes among certain players as stronger search empires are formed. In March 2003, Yahoo! acquired Inktomi, while in April 2003, Overture acquired AltaVista. Both Inktomi and AltaVista offer Trusted Feed programs. Then, in October 2003, Yahoo! acquired Overture. Price changes are inevitable. The consolidation of key players will likely result in an increase, not a decrease. If you can sign a long-term agreement to lock in rates soon, it may be a good idea.

Third-Party Tracking URLs Are Supported

Many companies utilize a third-party ad tracking system to monitor sales produced by other Internet marketing efforts, such as email or banner ads. A tracking URL that is generated redirects consumers from the ad to the tracking company's server, then over to the advertiser's web site. Third-party tracking solutions easily enable nontechnical search engine marketers to monitor sales by multiple components of an advertising campaign, such as by search engine, keyword, ad listing, and landing page.

Trusted Feed supports use of third-party tracking URLs for each search engine and corresponding landing pages. Companies can breathe easier knowing that their Fixed Placement, PFP, and Trusted Feed campaigns can be monitored under one third-party system, along with their other e-marketing programs.

Search engine spiders hate redirects, so third-party tracking URLs can't be provided through a Submit URL program. You're stuck submitting the same site URL to various search engines. (You don't want to create different landing pages for each search engine based on the same copy or you'll get dropped for duplicated content.) At least you'll get traffic flow data from a couple of inclusion programs and your web analytics reports. But you won't be able to track sales separately by venue, keyword, and landing page.

Site Pages Can Be Removed Quickly from the Index

A major concern for product retailers is inventory management. What if a national auto parts manufacturer runs out of a product, or stops making it altogether? This company doesn't want that product page sitting out in the search engines continuing to bring in frustrated prospects.

Well, both Submit URL and Trusted Feed programs allow advertisers to remove site pages from their databases. However, because Trusted Feed supports tracking URLs, which marketers can monitor for real-time sales performance, companies can react faster and delete particular product pages. Furthermore, if a landing page receives clicks but no orders from a specific venue, marketers can turn off the page listing only in that search engine.

The Challenges of Trusted Feed

Trusted Feed shares a few disadvantages with Submit URL, too. Top rankings are not guaranteed, and any positions achieved are located far below those of sponsored ads.

Fortunately, Trusted Feed helps web sites with complex architectures get indexed, which isn't easily done with Submit URL. Unfortunately, there's a price that comes with managing large-scale, sophisticated sites. You can probably guess that time is an issue. Furthermore, although the CPC model is enticing to a variety of marketers, only big players with big bucks can play.

Time-Consuming to Prepare Data

Preparing your data for a Trusted Feed doesn't end once your URLs are crawled and the content is extracted. Someone needs to write

Warning

Be prepared; even with data-feed assistance, review the final copy. Search engines and Trusted Feed partners know how to please indexing spiders, and you know your business and your target audience. This program demands your attention, even if you have outside support.

compelling titles and descriptions for each page. Decisions need to be made as to whether a manufacturer's name and product code number should be incorporated into that ad listing, for example.

Who on your team will be responsible for optimizing marketing copy for hundreds or thousands of pages? Outsourcing Trusted Feed is a very good idea. Or, if your site qualifies for a direct relationship with the search engines, find out how much they'll help you optimize your pages (usually not much, but this additional service may soon be offered).

Slow Time to Market

Following the former point, it usually takes longer to see your listings in search engines through Trusted Feed than through any other program.

A programmer can export the page data to a document within minutes. It's a simple process. Realistically, though, because it's not the top priority for most companies, it takes weeks or months for this task to be completed. Add in a person's time to write the ad listing information, or allow up to a week for an inclusion partner to do this work. Finally, once this data is fed to the search engines you have another 5–10 days before you'll see any rankings, according to Position Technologies.

This is an assignment issue. A marketer may sit down to create the components of a PFP campaign in one day. Once this information is entered into a PFP engine, the ad listings are live within three to five business days, if not sooner. Trusted Feed preparation normally involves an IT team member whose priority is not marketing. Unless the company servers are on fire and require an IT person's attention, I recommend that marketers shower the person with pizza, beer, or another incentive to get that data prepared. The hold-up with Trusted Feed isn't search engines—it's the people who need to prepare the data.

Not an Option for Small Sites

You might be thinking, "I want CPC pricing! I want to do a Trusted Feed program." Unfortunately, you're out of luck if you manage a small web site (less than 500 unique content pages to submit). Preparing an XML feed requires too much effort on the part of the search engines or their inclusion partners. Understandably, they need to make a living, too. At $.25 per click or another negotiated rate, assurance that a site will receive substantial traffic is required. If your site borders on the minimum number of URLs and receives approval, consider it strong faith in your traffic potential.

Constant Monitoring Is Required

Trusted Feed shares this challenge with PFP. Although companies investing in Trusted Feed don't have to worry about a click-fee spike because they have a fixed rate, marketers still need to monitor campaign profitability. Otherwise, it's comparable to not paying attention while playing casino slot machines. Before you know it, you've spent all of your money but see less in your winnings tray. A continuous flow of visitors from Trusted Feed listings can suddenly start producing fewer customers. When you're paying for store visitors, periodically check your cash registers.

Whether you're submitting a site to the search engines via Trusted Feed or Submit URL, optimize your site pages for a shot at premium rankings. Although each search engine uses slightly different criteria for giving a site a #1 position, they all adhere to the same basic principles. By utilizing the techniques described in Chapter 10, "Web Site Optimization," you'll create an effective foundation in search engine optimization. The presence of deadly design elements, as mentioned in Chapter 8, "Submit URL," requires specific workarounds. But for niche web sites with few technical barriers, the tips in the next chapter will help you secure high visibility for narrowly-targeted keywords.

Web Site Optimization

In the Submit URL and Trusted Feed chapters, I mention that web page design is a vital component of paid inclusion. There's no point paying inclusion fees if your site pages will never rank high enough to be seen by new customers.

A search engine optimization (SEO) firm or inclusion partner (if you've chosen Trusted Feed) can optimize your pages. However, if hiring a third party isn't an option for you, your Webmaster can create a basic foundation. Even if you do outsource these efforts, you'll be better equipped to provide the information specialists will request.

What Do Search Engines Want?

Search engines love simple web site designs. Fancy "bells and whistles," such as Flash, hinder a site's ability to score a premium position in the natural search results. What's assumed to be alluring to consumers is opposite of what search engines want.

Have you ever browsed the sites that rank well for a keyword and thought, *"That's the UGLIEST site in the world. Why is it #1?"* Unfortunately, ugly can often equal good rankings. Ugly to consumers usually means text-heavy web pages that seem to scroll down forever and are absent of ample images or multimedia. These are a perfectly delicious meal for search engine spiders; they don't have to sift through lengthy lines of complex code to find keywords. There's no code clutter.

Does this mean you're committed to an ugly site? Not at all, thank goodness! Watch your use of sophisticated design elements and place keywords in the locations described in this chapter. These are merely the basic components of an SEO foundation, but when used in unison they unquestionably influence rankings. I've prioritized them from the easiest to the most difficult to implement in an existing site. To illustrate several of these elements, I've referenced International Crystal Manufacturing Co, Inc. (http://www.icmfg.com), a company that provides crystals, oscillators, and filters for the military.

Link Popularity

This task makes your Webmaster happy; no web site design modifications are necessary to increase your link popularity. Well, the traditional definition of it anyway.

Important

An *inbound link* points from another web site to yours. An *outbound link* is one on your site that hyperlinks to another site.

Link popularity generally refers to the number and quality of content-relevant web sites that link to yours. Search engines place a heavy evaluation emphasis on inbound links because it's assumed that if other sites link to yours, you offer valuable content to web users. An inbound link therefore appears as an online testimonial to search engine spiders. Popular sites score major ranking points.

Google offers a downloadable toolbar for Internet Explorer that indicates a site's link popularity (http://www.google.com/options).

One of the toolbar's beneficial features is PageRank, which shows Google's ranking of a current page based in large part on link popularity. After you download the toolbar, visit a web site page and mouse over the PageRank bar to reveal the score. As you can see in Figure 10.1, International Crystal Manufacturing's home page has a PageRank score of 4 out of a possible 10 points.

PageRank button

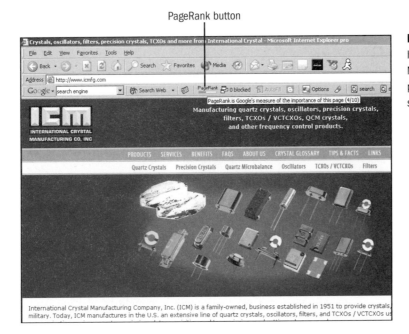

Figure 10.1
International Crystal Manufacturing's home page has a PageRank score of 4/10.

Four simple steps pave the pathway to your popularity, as described in the following sections.

Step 1: Identify High-Ranked Sites

Avoid web rings that only link from one site to another site in a circular pattern. Don't place links to your site in guestbooks, classified ads, or forums either. These tactics are considered "spam" by the search engines because the sole purpose of these methods is to trick search engines into thinking your site is popular based on the number of inbound links. Once your site is banned from a search engine's database, even an SEO firm might not be able to get you back in without considerable time, energy, and money.

Tip

Plan a few weeks to execute a link campaign. It doesn't have to be a full-time job, but it typically takes a few weeks to complete the communication with your link partners.

Instead, run a search for your primary keywords to request a link from fewer, but content-relevant, web sites. For instance, a link from a military or government web site would be a stronger link for International Crystal Manufacturing than one from "Bob's" personal site.

Step 2: Request an Inbound Link

The most efficient way of asking for a site link is to email the Webmaster or marketing director. (I've received a 10–50% acceptance rate for clients using this method.) It's imperative to customize each email to get a response and, more importantly, avoid being mislabeled as a spammer. Here are a few tips:

- These days, it's best to use the personal email address of the marketing director (call, or surf the site for this information), not a generic address listed on the site. Address the person by his or her name in your message.

- Avoid generic subject lines and "spammy" words such as "free." Although "link request" is accurate, it could nowadays be viewed as spam, without a little more information. "I'm interested in marketing opportunities on <site name>" should at least get your email opened.

- Be upfront about requesting a link to your site. Include reasons why visitors to their site would benefit by visiting yours.

- Prove that you've reviewed their site by mentioning something specific about it. Comment on a recent accomplishment discussed in a press release, for example. A generic "I liked your site" or "We're a good match" message sounds like spam and may be deleted.

- If you're willing to link to their site in exchange, or have already done so, state the URL where their link will be displayed on your site.

Important

Request a free link first, and then consider asking about advertising opportunities if you don't get a response. A paid link from a site that complements yours can improve your link popularity score, plus send new prospects your way.

Step 3: Hyperlink Keywords in Your Description

Hopefully, you'll negotiate a listing that contains a brief description of your site, in addition to a company name and link. Include one of your keyword phrases in your description. This phrase should be hyperlinked to your web site.

Here's a sample site description using the keyword "precision crystals" that International Crystal Manufacturing could submit in a link request:

> International Crystal Manufacturing manufactures a broad line of custom <u>precision crystals</u> (link to: http://www.icmfg.com/precisioncrystals.html) for use in military applications, communications, microwave transmission, data acquisition and transmission, and cutting edge research.

Step 4: Use Relevant Landing Pages

Divide your inbound links among secondary theme pages; don't send them all to the home page. Your home page has its own master theme. Because each site page should be optimized for a different but related group of keywords, each page needs its own inbound links. Remember that individual site pages, not entire sites, compete for rankings. As a follow-up to the example given in Step 3, Figure 10.2 shows the site page International Crystal Manufacturing would want to link to for the keyword "precision crystals."

Important

Researching sites is the most time-consuming portion of a link campaign. Want a little extra help? Hire an intern to surf the web looking for relevant content sites. Instead of or in addition to hiring an intern, you can use a link-building tool such as Zeus, developed by Cyber-Robotics (http://www.cyber-robotics.com).

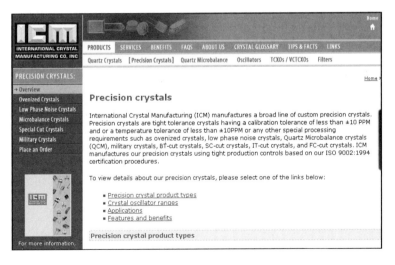

Figure 10.2
Direct your inbound link to the landing page that relates to the keyword you hyperlinked. For "precision crystals," International Crystal Manufacturing should link to this page.

Meta Data

Meta data, or *meta tags*, provides information about the content of a web page. It's an HTML tag that doesn't impact page layout but contains data attributes.

In the early days of SEO, simply placing keywords in these tags influenced page rankings significantly. Today, numerous search engine marketers proclaim, "Meta tags are dead!" Are they dead? As a sole tactic to boost rankings—yes. As a way to enhance the copy of your listings in search results—no.

When search engines pull a title and description for your web site listing, a majority will display the meta data you provide. Without meta data, search engines typically grab the first text lines from the page. Ever see listings in search results with a date, copyright information, or other useless text? Yuck. Not appealing to potential customers. Use meta data as a way to control your web site listings and prevent search engines from randomly selecting irrelevant copy from your site. There are three meta tags to use:

- Title
- Description
- Keywords

Look at the meta data for International Crystal Manufacturing's page on precision crystals as an example (Figure 10.3). Write custom copy for the meta data of each web page you want to rank well in the search engines. You can also review your competitors' HTML code for ideas. (To view the meta data of your competitors' pages, click on Edit, View Source in the browser toolbar.)

Headings

Headings are generally phrases placed above the first paragraph of page content, acting as a headline. Visitors are encouraged to read headings first, as are search engine spiders. Therefore, it's a great place to include keywords that describe the overall theme of that page.

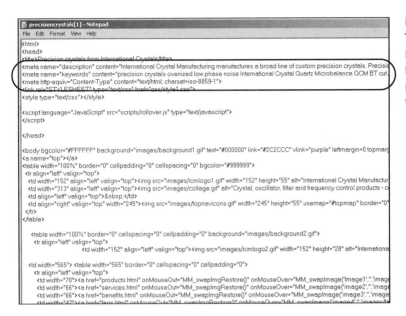

Figure 10.3
The meta data for
International Crystal
Manufacturing's page on
precision crystals is at the
top of the source code.

Webmasters need to incorporate an <h1> to an <h6> tag. The International Crystal's Precision Page uses an <h1> tag, and the HTML code looks like this:

<h1>Precision Crystals</h1>

Page Copy

Your web site copy makes or breaks your rankings. Rankings are all about relevancy. Where do search engines look for keywords when evaluating web sites? The words on each page. If you display keywords to visitors, then your pages are indeed relevant for these terms.

Unfortunately, numerous companies incorporate their existing marketing material into their sites. This copy won't contain all of the relevant keywords you now know that your target audience is looking for in search engines.

You'll also need to study your competitors' pages that rank well to see how many total words they're using and how many times that keyword is mentioned. Analyze their average word usage as a formula for your own web site.

Tip

Companies still make the mistake of hotlinking "click here" in their site content. Yikes. Nobody types this phrase into a search engine. It's a wasted link. Hyperlink a keyword phrase instead.

Hypertext Links

As you're editing the copy on one page, incorporate keywords from your other web pages. Then hotlink the keywords to the corresponding pages within your site. Even though cross-links are not weighed the same as inbound links from other sites, if they can help, place keywords in your own hypertext links.

You should be careful of a few elements when working with hyperlinks to prevent being flagged as a spammer by search engines:

- Don't hide links. This includes placing links in areas of your code other than visible body copy. It won't help your rankings, and if caught your site pages could suffer spam penalties.

- Check your link-to-copy ratio. This is problematic for e-commerce sites that exclusively pair product photos with links to an order form. Where are the product descriptions? Again, because search engines reward sites with valuable information, if 80% of a site page is full of hyperlinks, this won't outrank a content-rich page. Think content before commerce.

Alternative Text

Your site probably has at least a couple of images, or perhaps graphics-based navigation. You can place keywords inside the alternative text in the HTML code for these images. When you roll over an image you'll see the alternative text appear in a box, if the web designer set this up.

International Crystal Manufacturing mentions "precision crystals" in a few graphic images. Check out all of the keywords, however, in the company's logo. Although you don't want to repeat the same set of keywords in every <alt> tag, it's appropriate (as shown in Figure 10.4) to include more than one in a prime location, such as a logo.

The HTML code for the alternative text highlighted in Figure 10.4 looks like this:

```
<img src="images/icmlogo1.gif" width="152" height="55"
alt="International Crystal Manufacturing (ICM) offers a broad range of
quartz crystals, precision crystals, oscillators, filters, TCXO / VCTCXOs,
and Quartz Microbalance products.">
```

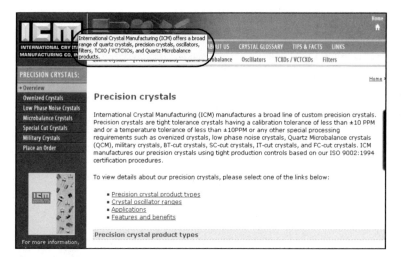

Figure 10.4
Place alternative text inside
your site's graphic images.
Use a keyword phrase relevant to that page. The <alt>
tag for ICM's logo has
several keywords.

URL/File Names

Search engine marketers argue over the importance of keywords in
the URL or file names. International Crystal Manufacturing's web
site is:

    http://www.icmfg.com

The company could have used its full name, which would have given
them the words "crystal" and "crystal manufacturing":

    http://www.internationalcrystalmanufacturing.com/

Of course, that's a hideously long URL for anyone to type into a
browser toolbar. Avoid frustrating your prospects who see your
URL on business cards, brochures, or print ads and then go to the
web to type it. Don't use numerous characters in your URL if possible. Remember: search engines, important. Customers, more
important.

Some search engine marketers would argue to keep ICM's full name
as the domain because of the keywords that are included. A shorter
version of the URL could be used in the company's marketing

materials. ICM has included keywords in the site's directory file names. Refer back to Figure 10.4 and notice the URL of their precision crystal page:

http://www.icmfg.com/precisioncrystals.html

Keywords could be grouped together, as shown here. Or they could be separated by an underscore or hyphen, as illustrated next. Marketers don't agree on one format of the three either. Some believe that keywords in URLs make no difference whatsoever.

Tip

It may be a good idea to group keywords together in the file name instead of separating them with underscores or hyphens. The latter two are becoming associated with spam tactics, and if continually used by spammers could eventually jeopardize your page rankings.

http://www.icmfg.com/precision_crystals.html

http://www.icmfg.com/precision-crystals.html

Search engine marketers do agree on one thing: The use of keywords in domains or file names on a site lacking solid content will get banned. In early 2003, I spotted a bunch of these keyword-based domains in the insurance industry. The web pages had no valuable content, and apparently one company owned multiple domains and simply linked them all together. The web ring issue was probably the biggest red flag to search engines, but even so, a few months later these organic listings started to disappear out of the Top 10 rankings. The search engines had obviously caught on.

Keyword Density and Rankings

Outranking competing pages isn't limited to where you place keywords on your page; it's also about how many times those terms are used. The relationship of a keyword phrase to the total number of words on a page equals a keyword density number.

Don't assume that a higher keyword density is always better. A page that uses all 500 words of copy to repeat "crystals" over and over again will be penalized. A 100% keyword density for one phrase is useless to a human visitor; search engines notice this, too.

Some search engine marketers spend hours on keyword density analysis; others spend none. Luckily for the marketers who want to focus on this detail, there are programs that instantly reveal the ideal formula for your pages, without spending hours of manual analysis time.

The Keyword Density Analyzer, part of Bruce Clay's SEOToolSet, analyzes the competitors of your choosing for a specific keyword or phrase. Looking at the top competing pages for "precision crystals," Figure 10.5 shows the recommended configuration based on how the competitors are currently ranked. I think this kind of tool is similar to being Superman with x-ray vision—only here, you're seeing into your competitors' web pages.

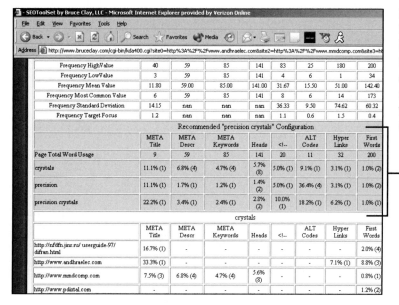

Figure 10.5

Bruce Clay's Keyword Density Analyzer tool within the SEOToolSet shows marketers an ideal page configuration for keywords based on well-ranked, competing web pages.

Recommended "precision crystal" Configuration

Mimic the average configuration of top-ranked pages. Scale your configuration to match pages on the higher end of the spectrum once you study how far the average configuration takes yours. As with other optimization tactics, there's a tipping point to this scale, and adding too much density won't catapult you to #1, but instead will drop you out of a premier ranking.

One tool isn't necessarily enough. Each evaluates keyword density using different criteria. Results can vary wildly. Consider using more than one tool; Keyword Count (http://www.keywordcount.com) and Keyword Density & Prominence (http://www.jimworld.com/tools/keyword-analyzer) are both free.

Search engines evaluate sites using a range of criteria, including site architecture and link popularity, which have nothing to do with the number of keywords on your site. Keyword density is merely one influential factor. Therefore, remember to balance your time among other search engine marketing tasks.

Search Engine Submission Checklist

This chapter provides an overview of basic keyword optimization. Growing competition in the search engine space will soon necessitate, if it hasn't already, that your site resolve any deadly design elements prior to submission using either inclusion program. As a way to prepare you for the next level of optimization, review the following checklist that Shari Thurow recommends in her book, *Search Engine Visibility*.

❏Yes	❏No	Are you creating web pages with content your target audience is genuinely interested in reading?
❏Yes	❏No	Does your content contain highly focused keyword phrases rather than phrases that are too general and competitive?
❏Yes	❏No	Are you optimizing your web pages for at least three to five keywords at a time?
❏Yes	❏No	Are you using regionally specific keywords, when applicable?
❏Yes	❏No	Are you using the most commonly used variations of your keywords, based on your keyword research?
❏Yes	❏No	Does each optimized page contain a unique title?
❏Yes	❏No	Are you using multiple keywords in your title tags (using the power combo strategy) when appropriate?
❏Yes	❏No	Are your most important keywords appearing above the fold and throughout each optimized page?
❏Yes	❏No	Are you using keywords in hypertext links, whenever possible?

❑Yes	❑No	Does each optimized page have at least one call to action?
❑Yes	❑No	Does each optimized page contain a unique meta-tag description?
❑Yes	❑No	Do your meta-tag descriptions contain both targeted keyword phrases and a call to action?
❑Yes	❑No	Does each optimized page contain a unique meta-tag keyword list?
❑Yes	❑No	Does each set of meta-tag keywords contain words and phrases that you actually use within the visible body text?
❑Yes	❑No	Do you place common misspellings of your keywords within your meta-tag keywords?
❑Yes	❑No	Do your graphic images contain descriptive keywords within the alternative text attribute, when appropriate?
❑Yes	❑No	Do you provide at least two means of navigating your site: one for your visitors and one for the search engines?
❑Yes	❑No	Does your site have a site map, to assist both your visitors and the search engine spiders?
❑Yes	❑No	If your site uses frames, is your site navigable with and without the frameset?
❑Yes	❑No	If you are using JavaScript on your site, did you place the JavaScript in an external .js file and place the Robots Exclusion Protocol on that file?
❑Yes	❑No	If you are using Cascading Style Sheets (CSS) on your site, did you place the style sheets in an external .css file?
❑Yes	❑No	Do you have any redirects on your site? If so, have you placed the Robots Exclusion Protocol on pages that use redirects?
❑Yes	❑No	Are your optimized pages placed in the root directory (along with your home page) on your web server?

❏Yes ❏No Is your robots.txt file placed in the root directory on your web server? Did you remember to transfer your robots.txt file before you transferred any other web pages to your server?

❏Yes ❏No Are you using subdomains instead of subdirectories if you find that your subdomains contain unique and substantial content?

❏Yes ❏No If you are submitting pages to non-U.S. search engines, are you writing your pages in the appropriate language?

❏Yes ❏No If it is within your budget, did you submit your optimized pages to pay-for-inclusion (PFI) programs?

❏Yes ❏No If you use Pay-For-Placement (PFP) advertising, are your purchases based on detailed keyword research and selection?

❏Yes ❏No If you use PFP advertising, do you carefully monitor your bids to get the best search engine visibility at the most reasonable cost?

❏Yes ❏No Did you name your web pages something that your target audience can remember and spell easily, using keywords whenever possible?

❏Yes ❏No Did you design or select a series of landing pages for your PFP advertising? If the landing pages do not contain substantially unique content, did you place the Robots Exclusion Protocol on those pages?

❏Yes ❏No Do the search engines and your site visitors view the same page? (The only exception to this rule is sites that participate in XML-feed programs.)

❏Yes ❏No Do you submit the maximum allowable number of pages per day for each of the major search engines?

❏Yes ❏No Do you avoid submitting the same pages twice within a 24-hour period?

❏Yes ❏No Do you resubmit to a search engine only if a page has dropped from the index or if a page's content has changed significantly?

Part III

Conclusion

Paid inclusion programs, either Submit URL
or Trusted Feed, ensure that your site pages are
included in the search engine databases. The number
of pages you submit determines which program you'll
choose. Then, the optimization of your page content
and design will determine the ranking you'll achieve.
Fortunately, a range of tools and service providers exist
today to serve companies that pursue either program.

Visit www.searchenginesales.com for updates and
links to many of the resources mentioned in this book.

 **PART IV**

Specialized Search Engines

Part IV

Introduction

Specialized search engines are the best-kept secret of this industry. They're not well-guarded treasure; rather, the media is too busy unraveling the mysteries of the "traditional" search engines to address these new players. The notion of buying keywords is foreign to a lot of people. Learning about the various programs, ad listing copywriting, and tracking takes time.

However, companies that are experimenting with comparison shopping, vertical markets, and international search engines are tapping into a new customer base right now. Many are still finding little competition and low prices, which together yield high profit margins.

Chapter 11

Comparison Shopping Engines

Move over, Google and Overture. There's a new breed of search engine in town—one that exclusively caters to customers and their buying experience. Think online shopping mall plus search functionality. What's the result? You've guessed it: comparison shopping engines.

Welcome to a marketplace where consumers compare products in the same category by multiple purchasing factors; price is a popular one. Having shopping information and tools in one central location helps consumers shop more efficiently, according to a ForeSee Results December 2002 survey on why online consumers use shopping engines (see Figure 11.1).

Figure 11.1

Shopping engines offer pur-
chasing-specific benefits to
consumers.

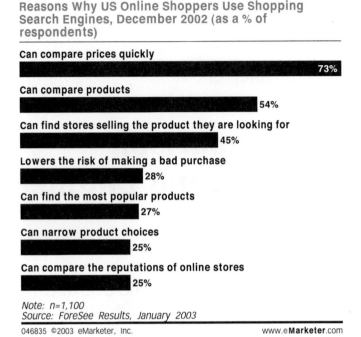

Reasons Why US Online Shoppers Use Shopping
Search Engines, December 2002 (as a % of
respondents)

Can compare prices quickly

73%

Can compare products

54%

Can find stores selling the product they are looking for

45%

Lowers the risk of making a bad purchase

28%

Can find the most popular products

27%

Can narrow product choices

25%

Can compare the reputations of online stores

25%

Note: n=1,100
Source: ForeSee Results, January 2003

046835 ©2003 eMarketer, Inc.   www.e**Marketer**.com

Although not all products are good matches for a shopping engine
merchant program, if general search engines are advancing your
product sales, then be sure to look into this opportunity.

Preparing for a Shopping Engine Program

The first thing you need to know is: *Which sites are shopping
engines?* See Figure 11.2 for the list of popular shopping engines
compiled by Hitwise, an online competitive intelligence company.
Review the programs of sites that drive significant traffic to their
sites. It's the same concept as with general search engines; you need
a decent level of site traffic to achieve a minimum sales volume to
make it worth your management time. If you choose a small general
or shopping search engine for a test campaign, you might not collect enough data to accurately determine how to improve sales from
that campaign, or others.

Web Site	Market Share of Visits
Yahoo! Shopping	36.28%
Shopping.com	22.36%
MSN Shopping	9.46%
BizRate Shopping	8.33%
NexTag	8.18%
PriceGrabber	8.06%
MySimon	3.47%
PriceWatch	2.75%
PriceScan	0.56%
Froogle	0.55%

Figure 11.2

The most popular shopping engines, as visited by U.S. Internet users for October 2003 (based on visits), according to Hitwise. All sites listed include aggregations of related sites to provide an overall market share of visits.

Now I have to amend my first sentence in this chapter, about Google and Overture. Which shopping engine is #1 in the Hitwise chart? That's right, Yahoo! Shopping. Which giant portal acquired Overture? Right again, Yahoo! So, although Overture is not directly playing in the shopping engine space, their new parent company, Yahoo!, is. Regarding Google, in December 2002 the company launched Froogle, a search engine that identifies web pages with only products for sale. At the time of this publication, companies can become Froogle merchants and submit a data feed for free. What?! There's something free in the search engine space? Yes, but once Froogle is no longer in beta testing this opportunity may disappear. Act quickly.

Speaking of free, some shopping engines allow merchants to submit their products for free and then take a transaction fee. Merchants who want to enhance their listing position within a category can often buy advertising, generally on a cost-per-click basis.

As is to be expected, certain groups of products sell better than others. In interviews with shopping engines PriceGrabber.com and Shopping.com (formerly DealTime), top-selling items include computers, electronics (such as digital cameras and DVD players), video games, movies, books, music, apparel, jewelry, and photography. Your items don't fit into these categories? That's not necessarily bad. Perhaps you'll win a higher percentage of shoppers if your products fall into less-competitive categories.

Important

Competition is fierce in certain product categories on comparison shopping engines. Because similar items sold by different merchants are placed side-by-side, consider creating a special promotion for shopping engine campaigns to draw a higher number of clicks and subsequent orders for your products.

Questionnaire for Prospective Merchants

Each shopping engine has different requirements for its merchant partners. Use this basic questionnaire as a guide in your initial conversations with a merchant account representative. Check their web sites, because many post extensive information about their merchant programs online.

1. What are the fees involved (setup, sales commission, ad listing enhancements)?

2. Do I have to maintain monthly minimums to continue being a merchant?

3. Can I set a maximum spending limit?

4. At what volume of item listings, or transaction levels, do you offer merchant discounts?

5. How do you handle the merchandise transactions and what do you need from me?

6. Do you have a shipping policy for merchants?

7. How can I remove listings for products that are not available or no longer offered? How quickly is the listing removed?

8. How is product information submitted (do I provide it as a data feed, or do you crawl my web site)?

9. What information do you need in the data feed, or what will you extract from my site?

10. How long will it take for my product listings to appear?

11. Will my product listings appear on any of your partner sites, and if so, which ones?

12. How do I manage my merchandise?

13. Do you offer customer testimonials on your site?

14. Do you offer any type of performance reporting?

15. Will you sign an agreement to not market my trademark names in the search engines? (Read Part VI, "Protecting Your Profits," to determine if this is a concern for your company.)

Live or Die by Customer Testimonials

Customer reviews on shopping engines make or break merchants. ForeSee Results discovered that 25% of shopping engine users want to compare the reputation of online stores, according to a January 2003 survey conducted for Shopping.com. Because many merchants are resellers of big brands, consumers are frequently hesitant about working with a third-party source. What better way to convey integrity and develop trust than by way of happy customer testimonials (Figures 11.3 and 11.4)?

Merchants who receive excellent customer ratings often link to the reviews from their own web sites. A customer testimonial on the merchant's own web site could be construed as contrived, whereas a customer feedback posted on a third-party shopping site is given a higher degree of credibility. Including these reviews on your site with a link to the shopping site is a double winner: You get great site content, plus these testimonials appear as unbiased endorsements.

How can merchants avoid poor customer reviews? Proving excellent customer service is the chief influencing factor. As indicated in the following list from Shopping.com merchant recommendations, customer service starts with the order and ends with the follow-up communication after the product is received.

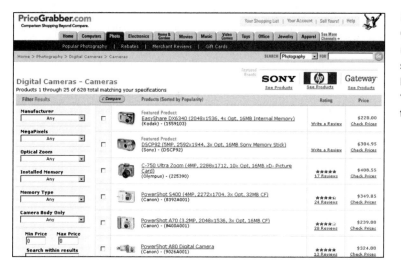

Figure 11.3
Customers can rate merchants on comparison shopping engines. On PriceGrabber.com, click the "reviews" link under products to read customer comments.

Figure 11.4

In the reviews, customers share their experiences with the merchant and the merchandise.

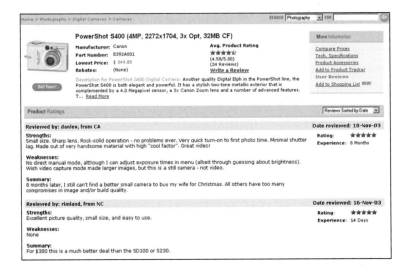

- Don't hide additional fees or do a "bait and switch," such as lowering the sticker price only to artificially inflate shipping costs to compensate.

- Deliver quality goods and excellent service.

- Update your product listings frequently, while removing out-of-stock items immediately.

- Play an active role in responding to unhappy customers immediately.

- Leverage merchant rebuttal systems on shopping engines to resolve customer concerns and show that you offer "make goods" (which also discredits any fraudulent reviewers).

- Inspire good reviews by offering merchant surveys, providing links in shipping confirmation emails that point to the shopping site, and sending "thank you" emails that invite customers to provide feedback about your store and the products they purchased.

Consumers are not using comparison shopping engines as often as general search engines and directories to locate products, as reported by a Jupiter/Ipsos-Insight Retail Survey (Figure 11.5). Yet, I'm not worried. Jupiter Research notes that although shopping engines currently attract a smaller audience, consumers are highly qualified and intend to make a purchase. Plus, as a greater number of companies become shopping site merchants, consumers gain a wider selection of products and will tell their friends. Shopping engines will draw more visitors with their own promotional efforts, too; Shopping.com launched its first TV campaign in November 2003. Expect to hear more about shopping engines across a myriad of marketing channels.

How Frequently Do You Use the Following Types of Sites to Help You Find Products?

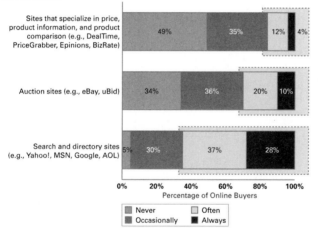

Figure 11.5

Consumers are not yet using comparison shopping engines to find products as frequently as they use general search engines, but Jupiter Research points out that shopping engine users are highly targeted consumers who intend to buy a product.

Source: Jupiter/Ipsos-Insight Retail Survey, n = 1,952 (online buyers, US only)
© 2003 Jupiter Research, a division of Jupitermedia Corporation

As pointed out earlier in this chapter, comparison shopping engines prove to be valuable tools in helping consumers make a purchasing decision. I predict that growth in usage, and subsequent sales, is on the horizon.

Chapter 12

Vertical Market Search Engines

General search engines, such as Google, connect consumers to relevant information sites. Many of these destination sites are beginning to sell paid listings in their own site search results; a comparison shopping site is a perfect example. It's an online hub for shoppers who search for products by category, or a keyword query. But on shopping engines, merchants *are* the content. These merchants can participate further by purchasing enhanced search results listings.

On content sites where information (not sponsors) forms the bulk of web site material, keyword advertising may now exist. These topic-oriented sites can act as vertical market search engines for advertisers, according to Fredrick Marckini, CEO of iProspect, a search engine marketing firm. Why not reach your target audience once they've landed at their favorite destination site?

Vertical market shopping engines are everywhere. Amazon.com is best known as a marketplace for book lovers. eBay is a hot spot for buyers and sellers to transact with each other. The National Gardening Association educates and inspires gardeners. Today's marketers are lucky. Niche topic sites such as these continue to launch while a growing number of them sell search-based keyword advertising. How can marketers get involved? Let's look at eBay as an example.

In June 2003, eBay released their *Keywords on eBay* program, in partnership with AdMarketplace, to eBay sellers and select partners. By purchasing keyword banner ads, eBay sellers drive buyers to their merchandise (see Figure 12.1).

Figure 12.1

eBay merchants can drive traffic to their merchandise listings through keyword banner ads on eBay. Here's a relevant banner that appeared in a search for "women's shoes."

Banner ad

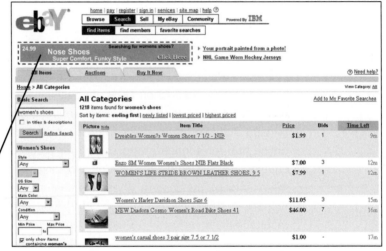

To get started, eBay sellers start at https://ebay.admarketplace.net and complete these steps:

1. Select relevant keywords.

2. Create a free banner ad, or use one of yours.

3. Set your price and budget.

Not surprisingly, the eBay seller who agrees to pay the most for a click earns higher preference in the rotation and higher frequency with which their banner is shown (obviously, higher ad revenue for eBay, too). This is an opportunity for eBay sellers to cut through the marketplace clutter and reach a highly targeted audience through keyword advertising.

Go to Your Target Market

Amazon.com, eBay, and The National Gardening Association represent a miniscule portion of the vertical market search engines available. Marketers have hundreds, if not thousands, of content-relevant sites to research for advertising partnerships. Want a way to reduce your research time finding them?

Hitwise, an online competitive intelligence company, monitors how over 25 million global Internet users interact with more than 450,000 businesses online. Their competitive reports include traffic data of these major businesses, which fall into one of 160+ industry categories (see Figure 12.2). You can use Hitwise reports to profile your competitors as well as identify potential marketing partners. Web sites with substantial traffic for a topic relevant to your business are strong initial matches.

With a little effort, budget-conscious marketers can forgo research fees by doing the work themselves. Click through the categories within Yahoo! or Open Directory Project (www.dmoz.org) and compile a list of vertical market sites that are relevant to your organization. You won't get the site traffic data Hitwise provides. That's ok. Using a free directory won't save you time, but it'll save you money while you're looking for marketing opportunities.

Of course, browse the sites that hold top positions in general search engines for your keywords. Perhaps it's no longer cost-effective for a garden tool manufacturer to buy "gardening" on Google's AdWords. As you'll notice in Figure 12.3, the National Gardening Association has already scored a #1 organic ranking on Google for this keyword (out of more than 7 million web pages!). At the time of this publication, advertisers can buy up to 10 keywords in the National Gardening's Online Buyer's Guide section for only $299 per year (http://www.garden.org/b2b/ADinfo.ASP; see Figures 12.4 and 12.5). Therefore, a garden tool manufacturer could buy "gardening" on this site instead of, or in addition to, Google AdWords. More than likely, a $299 budget on Google AdWords for garden keywords won't last an entire year. This opportunity should scream "WHAT A DEAL!" to garden-related companies.

Figure 12.2
Hitwise offers traffic reports on top web sites within 160 industry categories. Contact the sites within your category about a keyword advertising program.

Hitwise
category list

Hitwise reports on over 450,000 websites across 160 industry categories—providing clients with an instant overview of key competitors. A summary of the Hitwise industry categories is as follows.

All Categories

Automotive
- Classifieds
- Dealerships
- Manufacturers
- Motorcycling
- Motorsport
- Recreation

Aviation
- Commercial Airlines

Business and Finance
- Accountancy
- Agricultural
- Banks and Financial Institutions
- Book Publishers
- Building and Construction
- Business Information
- Consultancies
- Employment
- Freight and Couriers
- IT and Internet
- Insurance
- Legal
- Manufacturing/Industrial
- Marketing
- Primary Industry/Resources
- Professional Associations
- Real Estate
- Stocks and Shares
- Telecommunications
- Utilities

Community
- Humanitarian
- Organizations

Computers and Internet
- E-Greetings
- Electronics
- Email Services
- Graphics and Clip Art
- Hardware
- Hosting and Domain Registration
- Internet Advertising
- Net Communities and Chat
- Paid to surf
- Search Engines/Directories
- Software
- Web Development
- Webcams

Education & Reference
- Institutions
- Reference

Entertainment
- Animation and Comics
- Art
- Books and Writing
- Competitions
- Gambling
- Games
- Humor
- Mobile Phones
- Movies
- Multimedia
- Nightlife
- Performing Arts
- Personalities
- Photography
- Radio
- Television
- Wrestling

Food and Beverage
- Brands & Manufacturers
- Lifestyle & Reference
- Restaurants & Catering

Government
- County, City and Town
- Federal
- State

Health and Medical
- Alternative
- Health Insurance
- Hospitals
- Information
- Organizations
- Paramedical and Ancillary
- Pharmaceutical & Medical Products
- Pharmacies
- Primary and Specialist
- Research
- Wellbeing

Lifestyle
- Beauty
- Children's Sites
- Dating
- Environment
- Family
- Fashion
- Gay and Lesbian
- Hobbies and Crafts
- House and Garden
- Men's Sites
- New Age
- Personal Websites
- Pets and Animals
- Politics
- Religion
- Weddings
- Women's Sites

Music
- Bands and Artists
- Companies

News and Media
- Broadcast Media
- Community Directories and Guides
- IT Media
- Print

Shopping & Classifieds
- Apparel & Accessories
- Appliances & Electronics
- Auctions
- Automotive
- Books
- Classifieds
- Computers
- Department Stores
- Flowers & Gifts
- Grocery & Alcohol
- Health & Beauty
- House & Garden
- Music
- Office Supplies
- Rewards and Directories
- Sport & Fitness
- Toys & Hobbies
- Video & Games
- Wholesale & Relationship Sales

Sport
- Baseball
- Basketball
- Boxing
- Brands
- College
- Cycling
- Fantasy
- Football
- Fishing
- Golf
- Hockey
- Horse Racing
- Motorsport
- Skateboarding/In Line Skating
- Snow Sports
- Soccer
- Tennis
- Track and Field
- Watersports
- Yachting/Boating

Travel
- Agencies
- Destinations & Accommodation
- Transport

Adult

Now you know.

hitwise
Real-time competitive intelligence

Figure 12.3

The National Gardening Association has landed a #1 position in Google's natural results for "gardening," which makes the association a very attractive advertising venue for garden-related companies.

Figure 12.4

Advertisers can buy up to 10 keywords on the National Gardening Association's web site, in the Buyer's Guide area, starting at $299 per year.

Figure 12.5

In a search for "gardening" within the Buyer's Guide section on the National Gardening Association, here are the first advertisers' listings that were displayed.

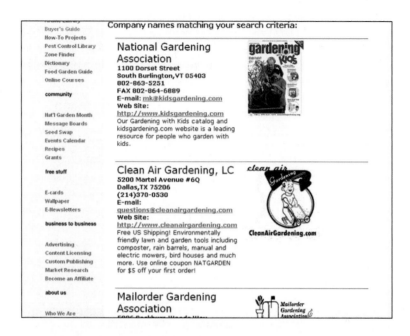

Benefit from Their Marketing Expenditures

Amazon.com champions more than 900,000 affiliates who drive traffic to merchant products on Amazon.com's web site. Could your products be sold there? If so, become an Amazon.com merchant to reap the benefit of Amazon.com's marketing efforts. In addition to their extensive affiliate network, Amazon.com buys media ads across the Internet. Current Amazon.com merchants may have already found themselves competing against this giant, or the affiliates, for keyword buys on general search engines. If it isn't cost-effective to beat them, then join them. Conserve your budget by teaming up with vertical market search engines, like Amazon.com, that spend their marketing dollars for you.

Straight keyword buys aren't available on Amazon.com as they are on other vertical market sites. According to their web page on Paid Placements (http://www.amazon.com/exec/obidos/subst/misc/co-op/small-vendor-info.html), Amazon.com serves an advertiser's product listing to customers most likely to buy that product based on past purchases. It's possible to assume that if titles and descriptions of products are evaluated, then relevant keywords in these areas could help increase the number of times an advertiser's product appears to shoppers.

Don't worry. There are plenty of vertical market search engines that do sell keywords. And many of these are executing online and offline media buys to the tune of thousands, or even millions, of dollars. Pick partners who are investing in their sites...and their advertisers.

Chapter 13

International Search Engines

Does your company conduct business in international markets? If your answer is "yes," know that search engine advertising is becoming an easier and less expensive Internet marketing tactic to reach this audience. The field of international search is quite young; companies quick to execute keyword advertising are still finding limited competition and great prices.

Making this process easier is the handful of U.S. search engines that are expanding their reach into foreign countries, allowing American-based companies to easily market overseas by extending their current keyword buy through U.S. channels. This is a blessing for marketers. No expensive calls overseas, or deciphering language and cultural communication differences. No hassles dealing with multiple foreign currency rates and contracts. Ah, the ability to market internationally is becoming nearly instantaneous and painless.

Don't rule out home-grown international search engines, however. Yahoo! France is a good way to reach the French, but understandably, "les Français" are going to be loyal to their own search engines like Wanadoo (www.wanadoo.fr), shown in Figure 13.1. Even though American goods are desirable overseas, U.S. companies need to make an effort to identify with local residents. This effort begins by advertising on the search engines where international shoppers hang out.

Figure 13.1

Reach international shoppers by marketing on their domestic search engines. Wanadoo, for example, is a favorite among the French.

Important

Working with a country-specific or internationally based marketing agency is recommended if you decide to launch a full-scale marketing campaign.

Before U.S. companies jump into the international search engine game, they should be aware of the significant differences that exist when marketing to an international audience. Simply because search engines make it easier to do so, doesn't mean success is guaranteed. The following tips lend insight into a few of the anticipated challenges along this journey.

Tips for International Marketing

Parlez-vous français? Sprechen Sie Deustche? Promoting a U.S. business on international search engines isn't solely about using the appropriate language. Referencement.com, an international search engine marketing agency based in France, shares a few tips on how to achieve success with the European audience. These may very well apply to other continents as well, including Asia and Latin America.

Sell Brand over Price

Perhaps Americans have had several years of shopping online and are comfortable with the buying process. Or, maybe it's part of our culture to "find the best deal" wherever we shop. This is not to say that international shoppers aren't seeking good prices on the web, but apparently, it's not their number one concern—or at least when U.S. companies are competing with domestic brands. American companies with well-recognized brands can achieve success, but the first secret is to market their famous names instead of price.

Soften the Promotional Pitch

When it comes to business, Americans are quick to discuss proposals and associated fees. A relationship between two companies begins once the contract is signed. When I worked in France, I observed that developing a relationship preceded any business transaction. If other countries operate like the French, then I can see how the American style of business can seem aggressive.

Referencement.com recommends that U.S. companies can forge a relationship-style approach to marketing by providing more information and softening their "buy now" rhetoric. History, quality, ratings, testimonials, and benefits are strong buying incentives to use that don't appear pushy. A promotional offer shouldn't be used as the main selling point, but it can certainly close the deal.

Think Localization, Not Translation

Using a foreign language in your search engine listings and on your respective landing pages isn't enough to win over global customers. There are idiomatic expressions that automated translation tools don't address. Additionally, new photos might need to be commissioned showing that culture's lifestyle, not an American one. These differences in language and images, if overlooked, can be unsettling, if not offensive, to the local consumers. All of the creative components of a search engine campaign—from ad listing to landing page—should be tailored to a particular regional audience. U.S. companies that then go even further and offer an international sales or customer service office become more appealing than a U.S. competitor who appears, and is, so far removed from their international customers.

U.S. companies with international marketing divisions are well acquainted with these challenges, as well as a myriad of others. American marketers who are ready to step into this arena for the first time, and are comfortable with the aforementioned challenges, are probably now wondering "On which international search engines should I start?"

International Search Engine Popularity

Interest in U.S. search engine marketing has contributed to an expansion of research in this area. International search engines haven't received the same kind of press as their U.S. counterparts...yet. Although fewer American companies sell products or services beyond U.S. borders, numerous big brands as well as specialized boutiques are interested. As such, expect more information on international search to become available. Use the Hitwise charts in Figure 13.2 for ideas of which popular international search engines may work for your business.

Figure 13.2

The following charts from Hitwise show the Top 10 most popular search engines in October 2003 for Internet users in Australia, Hong Kong, New Zealand, Singapore, and the United Kingdom.

Real-time competitive intelligence

Australia

Rank	Name - [Show Domain]	Market Share	SEP. 2003	AUG. 2003
1.	Google Australia	23.71%	1	1
2.	Yahoo!	9.89%	2	2
3.	Google	6.35%	3	3
4.	Yahoo! Australia & New Zealand	6.25%	4	4
5.	MSN	4.98%	5	5
6.	ninemsn Search	4.94%	6	6
7.	MSN Search	4.64%	7	7
8.	Yahoo! Search	3.98%	8	8
9.	Yahoo! Australia Search	2.92%	9	10
10.	My Yahoo!	1.86%	10	11

Hong Kong

Rank	Name - [Show Domain]	Market Share	2003 SEP	2003 AUG
1.	Yahoo! Hong Kong	41.27%	1	1
2.	Yahoo! Hong Kong Search	9.53%	2	2
3.	MSN Hong Kong	8.62%	3	3
4.	Yahoo! Hong Kong Directory	5.36%	4	4
5.	Yahoo!	4.24%	5	5
△ 6.	Google HK	3.05%	6	6
▽ 7.	MSN Taiwan	2.61%	7	7
8.	MSN	1.72%	8	8
9.	Yahoo! Search	1.33%	9	9
10.	Google	1.28%	11	11

Real-time competitive intelligence

New Zealand

Rank	Name - [Show Domain]	Market Share	SEP, 2003	AUG, 2003
1.	Google NZ	22.20%	1	1
2.	Yahoo!	7.87%	2	2
3.	MSN	5.96%	3	3
4.	Google	5.79%	4	4
5.	xtramsn Search	4.53%	5	5
6.	MSN Search	4.22%	6	6
7.	Sina China	3.30%	7	7
8.	Yahoo! Search	2.62%	8	8
9.	Yahoo! China	1.92%	9	10
10.	Yahoo! Australia & New Zealand	1.66%	10	12

Singapore

Rank	Name - [Show Domain]	Market Share	SEP, 2003	AUG, 2003
1.	Yahoo!	20.33%	1	1
2.	MSN Singapore Homepage	12.99%	2	2
3.	Yahoo! Singapore Homepage	11.50%	3	3
4.	Yahoo! Search	8.03%	4	4
5.	MSN	6.06%	5	6
6.	Google Singapore	5.95%	6	5
7.	Yahoo! Singapore Search	4.41%	7	9
8.	MSN Search	4.28%	8	7
9.	My Yahoo!	2.00%	9	8
10.	Google	1.61%	10	12

United Kingdom

	Rank	Name - [Show Domain]	Market Share	SEP, 2003	AUG, 2003
	1.	MSN UK	18.76%	1	1
	2.	Google	13.79%	2	2
	3.	Google UK	10.25%	3	3
	4.	Freeserve	9.06%	4	4
	5.	Yahoo!	6.25%	5	5
	6.	MSN.co.uk Search	5.91%	6	6
	7.	Yahoo! UK & Ireland	5.01%	7	7
△	8.	Ask Jeeves UK	2.64%	9	9
▽	9.	MSN	2.44%	8	8
	10.	Yahoo! UK & Ireland Search	2.06%	10	11

Going forward, advertisers can look to Pay-For-Placement (PFP) search engines as a one-stop international marketing solution. Espotting, for example, powers 850 million queries a month across Europe. Their key distribution partners in Europe include Yahoo! Europe, Lycos, UK Plus, Tiscali, Web.de, and O2. As this book goes to print, a merger between Epsotting and FindWhat.com is under negotiation. Should it go forward, advertisers can look to a new entity that will power 2.25 billion queries a month across 11 countries including the United States, the United Kingdom, France, Germany, Spain, Italy, Sweden, Denmark, Norway, Ireland, and Switzerland.

Important

At the end of 2003, Google launched regional targeting as an AdWords feature (https://adwords. google.com/select/faq/ reg_faq.html). Instead of specifying only the countries where advertisers' ads will appear, individual states and regions can be selected as well.

Country-specific PFP search engines will likely pop up, too. It'll be so much easier for companies to market on one search engine that provides search results to a site distribution network focused on one country's users.

Whether you're marketing in the United States or abroad, regional targeting is coming to a search engine near you. This new capability promises to direct consumers in the geographic markets you serve to your web site.

Part IV

Conclusion

The common thread among comparison shopping, vertical markets, and international search engines is the ability for marketers to buy keywords. Specialized search engines are emerging as a similar, but separate, marketing channel within the search industry. Although relatively unknown, they're poised for explosive growth. Successful programs cultivated by the traditional search engines are being coupled with the specialized engines' own technological advancements. This combination benefits early adopters who don't yet face massive competition.

If any of these specialized search engines fit your business, join now. Enjoy low rates while optimizing your campaigns to maximize your profitability. You'll be well-prepared to attract fresh customers among a swelling sea of competitors.

Visit www.searchenginesales.com for updates and links to many of the resources mentioned in this book.

PART V

Tracking Your Return on Investment

Part V

Introduction

Here's the part you've been waiting for: *Show me the money!* Once your paid listings are live, you can monitor your sales in real time and your associated costs almost as fast.

More ROI tracking tools exist today than ever before to help marketers execute highly profitable campaigns. The benefits of these solutions extend beyond search engine advertising. The solutions described in this section are designed to support general e-commerce and e-marketing initiatives. Marketers accomplish two objectives for the price of one.

Chapter 14

Before You Start Advertising...

Don't submit your ad listings yet.

As soon as you embark on your search engine journey, it's less efficient to radically alter the direction of your ship's course. It's possible, but you'll reach your destination sooner, with less effort and expense, by mapping out a tentative route and packing all the necessary supplies. A little planning saves a lot of time and money.

Return to Chapter 2,"Marketing Campaign Foundation," for a refresher. Specifically, review your call to action list as you read how to determine your return on investment (ROI) and set a cost-per-acquisition (CPA) goal for each action on your list. You'll then be happy to learn what new tracking tools leading search engines currently offer for free to their advertisers. Tracking your search engine ROI just got a whole lot better.

What Is ROI?

Return on investment (ROI) is the profit made from the advertising money you spent. At a super basic level, if you spend $5,000 on search engine advertising and generate $15,000 in new sales, that's a darn good return on your advertising dollars, right? Your ultimate goal, however, is to *increase the total volume of sales at the lowest cost per customer.* Assessing a deeper level of profitability enables you to reallocate ad budgets and efforts across the search engines, your product line, and even the campaign components for each product.

Figuring out your ROI isn't hard. You'll need access to the following data for your analysis. (For simplicity's sake, I address the ROI of one product throughout this chapter. You'll likely sell multiple products, or possibly services.)

- **Ad Cost:** The amount of money you spend during a specific timeframe (many marketers run weekly or monthly ROI reports). This data is provided by the search engines.

- **Clicks:** The number of visits from your paid listings. This data is provided by the search engines.

- **Product Price:** The retail price of a product. You have this data.

- **Number of Sales:** The number of completed orders from your paid listings for that product. This data is generated by your e-commerce solution.

- **Revenue:** The dollar amount generated from completed orders from paid listings for that product. This data is generated by your e-commerce solution.

All you need now is to do a little math. Follow the simple formulas below using the data you identified above.

- **Ad Profit:** The amount of money you earned after advertising costs:

Revenue − Ad Cost

- **CPA:** The amount of money you spent to get each sale:

$$\frac{\text{Ad Cost}}{\text{Number of Sales}}$$

- **ROI:** The profitability based on a percentage:

$$\frac{\text{Ad Profit}}{\text{Ad Cost}} \times 100$$

Let's look at an example. Pretend a company sells a $15 product. The company spent $500 on one search engine advertising campaign and received 2,000 clicks. If 1% of these visits produced sales, then this campaign wasn't profitable. At a 5% conversion rate, it was:

Unprofitable ROI	Profitable ROI
Ad Cost: $500	Ad Cost: $500
Clicks: 2,000	Clicks: 2,000
Product Price: $15	Product Price: $15
Number of Sales (1% conversion): 20	Number of Sales (5% conversion): 100
Revenue: $300	Revenue: $1,500
Ad Profit: –$200	Ad Profit: $1,000
CPA: $25	CPA: $5
ROI: –40%	ROI: 200%

This example assumes a company is selling only one product. An ROI report should be created by search engine, product, and associated keywords per product. The spreadsheet in Figure 14.1 shows a more comprehensive ROI report.

Ideally, you'll include ad listings (titles and descriptions) and landing pages if you're testing more than one per product or keyword. Notice that I've set up the campaign to organize the campaigns by search engine. You could instead organize it by product or keywords.

Tip

Create your ROI report in Microsoft's Excel program and automate the formulas. Each time you run a report, you'll enter your basic ad and sales information and the calculations will instantly generate the ROI data.

Figure 14.1

Sample ROI spreadsheet organized by search engine, then product, and the associated keywords.

ROI Spreadsheet

Search Engine	Product	Keywords	Ad Cost	Clicks	Product Price	Number of Sales	Revenue	Ad Profit	CPA	ROI

Set a Customer Acquisition Cost Goal

Search engine advertising attracts new customers. However, it increases your sales to a limited extent. That's because a finite number of people seek your product or service. If there are 10,000 searches for "home aquarium tanks," you can't make additional people perform searches for that phrase. If you buy this phrase, your text link can only appear a maximum of 10,000 times, and no more. The good news is that you can work to lower your customer acquisition cost, which can significantly increase your overall ROI. Setting CPA goals helps you accomplish three main tasks:

- Immediately identify and delete (or modify) the search engines, products, and campaign components that are weakening your overall ROI.

- Forecast potential ROI before you launch a new search engine ad campaign.

- Negotiate CPA deals for Fixed Placement search engine programs or other Internet marketing campaigns.

The easiest way to set your customer acquisition cost is to use your retail product price. Using the example from the previous section, let's say your company sells a $15 product. A profit margin is typically included. If you spend $15 on advertising, you need to acquire at least one new customer at $15 to break even. Therefore, $15 is your customer acquisition cost maximum. More than likely, you'll strive to earn a larger profit. Perhaps you initially set a CPA target at $12 then.

Obviously, this is a simplistic way of figuring out your customer acquisition cost. It'll at least help you plan and track an initial campaign. Be aware of other factors that affect your customer cost, such as:

- **The lifetime value of a customer:** Does your business generate revenue from long-term relationships with customers? If not, think about how to grow business from your existing client base (the 80/20 rule of marketing: 80% of your revenue comes from 20% of your customer base). For example, an auto dealer knows the sales cycle doesn't end with the purchase of a vehicle. Car accessories, extended warranties, and financing services are all additional revenue opportunities.

You may assume that to sell a $15 product, you must acquire a customer for $15 or less. But if on the average your customers make a minimum of three purchases at $15 each over their lifetime of being your customer, then you can acquire a new customer at $45 or less. The bigger your CPA number, the easier it is to find advertising programs that deliver results under this amount.

- **The profit margin:** Most products and services have production or labor costs. If your $15 sale gives you only $1 of "pure profit," then acquiring new customers at $15 each is certainly not ideal.

  However, if you use the profit margin as your customer acquisition cost, search engine advertising might not be profitable for you. In general, it's highly unlikely that paid listings would yield new customers at $1 each. Clicks at $1 each? Yes. New sales at $1 each? No. Without a doubt, using the profit margin as your cost per customer acquisition is a good, yet aggressive goal. Consider working toward it over the course of your advertising campaign.

Consider how these two factors impact your customer acquisition costs. Initially, you might track your results by total ad profit instead because it's less time consuming. That works. When you're ready to take your campaigns to the next level of efficiency, then start evaluating your CPA data. Work toward increasing your profitability as well as sales volume.

My examples here focus on product sales. Of course, ROI and CPA analysis apply to services. Additionally, this analysis is an important part of nonrevenue-generating calls to action as well. For instance, if one of your objectives is to increase subscriptions to your e-zine, then set your CPA goal to anything you want and still track your ROI. I bought paid listings on Overture to increase my own newsletter subscriber list. By modifying the keywords in my campaign, I cut my CPA from a few dollars to under $1 per subscriber. Paid listings work for transactions that don't immediately produce sales, too.

Test Before You Invest

Test your search engine advertising plan before investing your entire budget. For less than $100, you can launch campaigns on Pay-For-Placement (PFP) programs including Google ($5), Overture ($50), or FindWhat.com ($25). Your ad listings will be live within days of submitting them, as opposed to paid inclusion programs, which can take weeks or months to achieve improvement in your organic rankings.

Now don't assume that the minimum investment will last very long. If you open an account for $50 and your keywords are $10 per click, you could be lucky to get 20 minutes of search engine fame before your account is depleted. Then again, if your keywords are mere pennies per click and not highly searched by consumers, you could score top positions all month long and barely spend that $50 deposit.

Do you want a general idea of your potential monthly click fees? Run a search for your keywords using Overture's Search Term Suggestion Tool. Write down the number of searches per term. Next, run a search in Overture for the same keywords, and then click on the View Advertisers' Max Bids link in the upper-right corner of the results page (Figure 14.2).

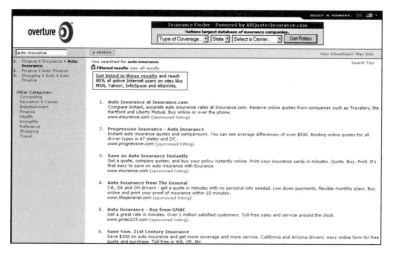

Figure 14.2
To view sponsors' bids on Overture, run a keyword search, click the "View Advertisers' Max Bids" link, and enter the security code displayed.

Once you enter the security code number presented, you'll be able to see what advertisers are willing to pay per click for their positions (Figure 14.3).

Figure 14.3

The sponsors' max bids are revealed by Overture. Here's an example for the phrase "auto insurance."

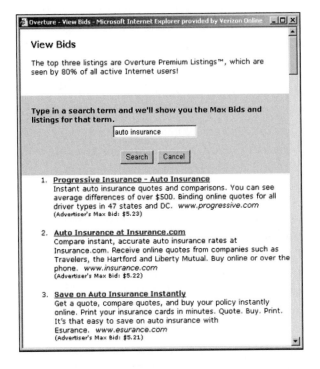

Choose the position you want knowing you'll need to bid a penny above the current position holder. Unfortunately, the big unknown is your click-through rate. Try 1–5% as a reasonable rate for a top-three position on generic keywords (branded keywords are usually higher), or use your average rate from other online media campaigns. Multiply the click rate percentage by the estimated search volume for each of your keywords. Then multiply your estimated clicks by your position bid per keyword. These are very rough estimates, but at least you'll know if your ad expenditures will be closer to $500 or $50,000 per month.

Where should you run a test campaign? PFP is your best choice for achieving top keyword positions within days. Plus, it's easy for any level of marketer to tweak his campaign components to impact his performance. I mention Google, Overture, and FindWhat.com throughout this book because these are today's leaders in PFP. Each has an expansive search distribution network enabling your listings to appear on other sites instantaneously. They also offer helpful management tools to their advertisers.

Search Engine Click-Through Reports

Search engines that offer paid placement or paid inclusion programs provide click-through reports (as shown in Figure 14.4) to their advertisers free of charge. You can log in anytime and check the number of impressions, clicks, click-through rates, and click fees for each keyword in your campaign. (Not all Submit URL inclusion programs offer detailed reporting by keyword.)

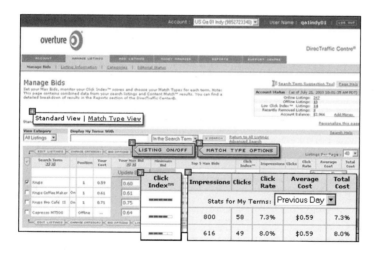

Figure 14.4
Sample click-through report from Overture.

Click-through reports don't reveal your ad profitability. However, if you don't yet have an ROI tracking system to monitor sales data by search engine, product, and campaign components, then a click-through report is equivalent to illuminating the dark alley of marketing with a match. It's better than pure darkness, but without a lantern you'll hit a few wall edges and potholes along the way.

Important

If you don't use the automatic budget renewal feature on PFP engines, once your account is depleted of funds, your ad listings are dropped. Setting a fixed maximum budget is a good idea to prevent surprise spending spikes; just periodically ensure there are sufficient funds in your account to keep it active.

You can use click-through reports to immediately spot problems with your campaign: keywords that were rejected during the submission process or deleted due to poor click-through performance.

In addition to performance issues, use click-through reports to keep an eye on your budget. Monitor your fees the first few days of a new campaign to gauge your monthly expenses and see how the actual costs compare to what you, or your media representative, estimated. Routinely check reports on long-term campaigns as well. One of my e-zine subscribers shared that he wasted $4,000 on one PFP program over a weekend because he wasn't monitoring it. Ouch. Without an ROI bid management system in place (see Chapter 19, "Bid Management Tools"), it's critical to constantly monitor your advertising expenses. Traffic or bids frequently spike without warning.

Search Engine Conversion Tracking

One of the most exciting developments from search engines in 2003 was free conversion tracking for their advertisers. PFP program owners led the way, with FindWhat.com hitting the market first (Figure 14.5). Overture and Google followed, as have others I'm sure. No more excuses for advertisers to not track their paid listings by total sales and profitability. How long will it be free? Who knows. Let's keep our fingers crossed that the answer is "always."

Figure 14.5

Sample conversion tracking report provided by FindWhat.com to their advertisers.

KEYWORD COST REPORT, 4/1/2003 - 4/8/2003								
Keyword	Keyword Cost	Clicks	Average Cost	Page Views	Conv	Conv. Pct.	Rev.	ROI
Film	$24.39	271	$0.090	373	9	3.32%	$35.00	143.50%
Cinema	$0.78	13	$0.060	13	1	7.69%	$5.00	641.03%
SUBTOTAL	$25.17	284	$0.089	386	10	3.52%	$40.00	158.92%

AdAnalyzer™ Data

Once you've signed up for an account, you'll copy and paste the piece of HTML code the search engine generates onto a page of your web site (usually the sales or other transaction confirmation page). A Webmaster can do this within minutes. Not to worry if you are running more than one ROI tracking program that works in this fashion. It's not a problem to place several pieces of code on the same web page.

There is a drawback. Each search engine offers conversion tracking exclusively to their advertisers. It's significantly more efficient to run one ROI tracking solution if you're executing campaigns on multiple search engines. This probably isn't a concern for first-time marketers, or for those concentrating on a limited number of search engines. In the long run, however, a third-party ROI tracking solution is best.

Important

At the end of 2003, Overture launched Marketing Console, an online performance-tracking product for marketers. ROI data can be tracked across multiple Internet channels.

Chapter 15

ROI Tracking Tips

It doesn't matter whether you develop an in-house return on investment (ROI) tracking solution or utilize one from a third party. As long as you can track your paid listing sales, then "it's all good." Which should you choose? Well, entrepreneurs and companies without a programming team can save considerable time, money, and frustration by leasing or purchasing one of the types of ROI solutions discussed in this section. Numerous companies choose to run both. It's a good option. The premade ROI tracking solutions (from the search engines or tracking specialists) collect a substantial amount of marketing data that can be compared to the sales data from e-commerce solutions in-house programmers have designed.

Regardless of the ROI tracking solution you choose, you can get the most out of your data by following a few steps. Keep these tips, and the conversion issues discussed here, in the back of your mind as you select, and then implement a solution.

Get Deep with Your Data

You spend a notable amount of time researching keywords, writing titles and descriptions, plus designing landing pages. Each component independently impacts your bottom line. As such, it's important to evaluate the performance of each piece of your paid listing campaign.

A top-level tracking view would be similar to the example I gave in the last chapter: $15,000 in sales from $5,000 in ad costs. A deep or granular level of tracking reveals profit and loss by specific components. Perhaps the $15,000 in sales resulted from five keywords that equaled $3,000 of the total ad cost. The remaining 10 keywords used $2,000 of the budget and delivered zero sales. What would you do? Cut those 10 keywords and save $2,000 of waste. This example barely breaks the surface of the detailed level of data at your fingertips. Dig deep to find gold.

Routine Campaign Analysis

It can't be said too often: Evaluate and re-evaluate your paid listing campaigns. Search engines' ad programs change. Online consumer searching and shopping behaviors change. Before you become aware of what the change is, you might very well witness its impact on your business in your ROI reports. That's one reason why you, or your Internet marketing agency, should run routine campaign analysis. Although the exact schedule is up to you, suggested benchmarks for analysis include:

- **Daily (short term: monitor the following types of activities during the first few days of launch):** Addition of search engines/keywords/products, revision of a promotional offer in the ad listing or landing page, or a feature change by a search engine or your ROI tracking solution provider

- **Weekly:** Quick system check on listing performance (traffic, sales, CPA, and ROI numbers), troubleshoot nonperforming listings, and update ad listing copy as necessary

- **Monthly:** Deep ROI analysis (by search engine, products, and campaign components per product), evaluate monthly fluctuations (delete search engines, products, or keywords if two months or more of unprofitable performance), add new products and keywords, and modify ad listing copy to keep it fresh

- **Quarterly:** Evaluate quarterly fluctuations and forecast the upcoming quarter based on past history along with seasonal market considerations

Double-Check Your ROI Reports

This recommendation is primarily for marketers who use a third-party solution, or several, plus their own internal sales data. One agency I worked for ran both external and internal reporting systems for paid listings. When our data showed a 30% discrepancy in orders from what the third-party vendor was reporting, we knew there was a problem. This story points out a sad reality: Data from different reporting systems almost never matches. I've experienced this when comparing search engine click-through reports to web traffic analytics reports, and even two web analytics reports from competing vendors.

What's an acceptable reporting discrepancy number? A couple of industry experts agree that up to a 10% discrepancy is normal. That's probably because on the web, tools count in myriad ways, and don't count or double count site visitors and associated sales.

Both deep data tracking and routine campaign analysis assist with this issue. You'll be able to catch anomalies in discrepancy patterns. Perhaps your internal sales report and third-party ROI report are consistently off by 5–7%, but suddenly you notice a 10% incongruity. The random fluctuation suggests an error with what's being, or not being, counted.

Conversion Issues

The Internet is a data analyst's dream. A wide range of online marketing efforts can be tracked from ad view, to ad click, to final transaction. Logging detailed data about the customers' travels to the checkout line is no trouble at all either, including the time of day or the path taken once at the web site.

Whether you're using ROI tracking reports to assess your paid listings or other Internet programs, remember that just because online purchases can immediately result from these promotional efforts doesn't mean they always do. Don't be hasty in cutting nonperforming parts of your advertising campaigns. Your ROI solution isn't always accounting for deferred or offline conversions.

Deferred Conversions

Important

In his book *E-Commerce User Experience*, Jakob Nielsen gives several examples of why people put items in a shopping cart but don't buy at that time. Consumers might use the shopping cart to find out how much they'll have to pay, or leave the site to comparison shop. Their browser may crash during the transaction, or perhaps shoppers are interrupted.

When a customer clicks your paid listing to visit your site, doesn't buy at that time, but returns sometime later to make a purchase, that's considered a deferred conversion. Your ad still generated, or at a minimum contributed to, that sale.

How does your ROI tracking solution handle deferred conversions? As you move forward with your research on choosing a vendor, ask candidates this question. Their default may be 24 hours or 30 days. Upon request, it can be possible to extend the deferred conversion tracking setting. Generally, 30 days is a fair timeframe, although 60 days isn't a bad idea. Search engine advertisers might be surprised at how many sales they've missed if their solution isn't yet tracking this. The discovery of delayed revenue could breathe new life into the campaigns you thought were dead.

Offline Conversions

This topic concerns stores with an offline presence. For instance, Sears could use paid listings to promote a discount on hardware tools. How are the customers who gather discount information from the web site and then buy from their local Sears store counted? They're probably not, unless the company has an online/offline coupon redemption program. Again, paid listings were responsible for, or contributed to, these sales but aren't being given credit.

An online/offline coupon redemption program is one way to ensure that your search engines investment is justified. Another way is to direct sales to the online checkout counter. Internet-only specials or free shipping are appealing incentives. Or, email customers a coupon that can be redeemed offline after they've made an online purchase. Refer back to Chapter 4, "Copywriting Tips to Improve Your Click-Through Rate," to look at ideas that might work for you.

> **Important**
>
> An online/offline coupon program allows Internet promotions to be redeemed at an offline retail store. CoolSavings and Valpak offer this type of coupon service to advertisers.

Your Solution Options

Search engine marketers today are lucky because we have a variety of tools to improve the profitability of our campaigns...but a majority of these aren't free. With an increase in the number of pay-to-play programs and in the bid prices on Pay-For-Placement (PFP) search engines in particular, marketers need cost-saving strategies.

I wrote the ROI tracking section to present solutions that provide companies with marketing features that extend beyond search engine advertising. Here's how I've categorized them:

- **Small Business E-Commerce:** Combines the ability to manage an online store and promote it in one system.

- **Affiliate Programs:** Manage the affiliates who promote your products or services for a commission fee.

- **Web Analytics:** Collect web site traffic data, from how visitors found the site to an end transaction, and the paths in between.

- **Bid Management Tools:** Automatically adjust your bids and positions on PFP search engines.

- **Internet Marketing Agencies:** Act as an extension of your marketing team; they use a variety of tools to execute your search engine and other promotional programs.

With any luck, you're already using one of these solutions for another focus and you'll learn how to apply it to your search engine analysis. Or, you're researching one of these types of solutions and will now add search engine tracking to your evaluation criteria.

An entire book could be dedicated to each solution discussed in the upcoming chapters. In the interest of getting you started with your ad campaigns as soon as possible, I've provided you with a program overview, likely main strengths and weaknesses, as well as examples of solution providers. Explore your options within the solution category that interests you. In the end, any ROI tracking program you choose is better than not having one at all.

Chapter 16

Small Business E-Commerce Solutions

Do you want a one-stop shop for your marketing and selling needs? You might already be using an e-commerce system that offers, or will soon, Internet marketing features that include an ad-tracking component. It's a convenient solution for entrepreneurs looking to manage and promote an online store.

1ShoppingCart.com (Figure 16.1) and Yahoo! Small Business Merchant Solutions (Figure 16.2) are examples of e-commerce solutions geared for growing companies. These screen captures show which package level includes the ad-tracking feature (visit their web sites for complete program information).

Figure 16.1

1ShoppingCart.com's e-commerce solutions start at $19.99 per month. An ad-tracking feature is offered at the level one option.

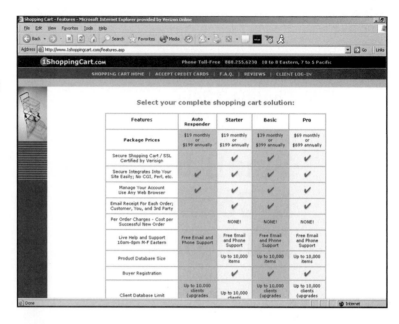

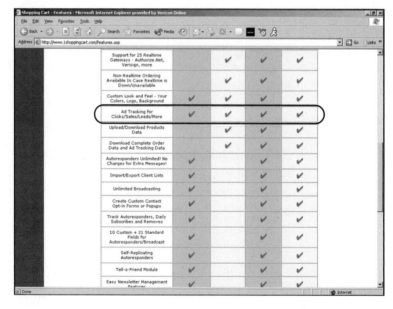

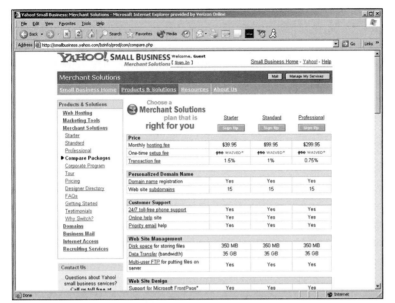

Figure 16.2

Yahoo!'s e-commerce solutions start at $39.95 per month. A trackable links feature is offered at the level two option; it's for revenue-sharing programs but could be used to track ad campaigns. A discount on an optional ad performance tracking service is also offered.

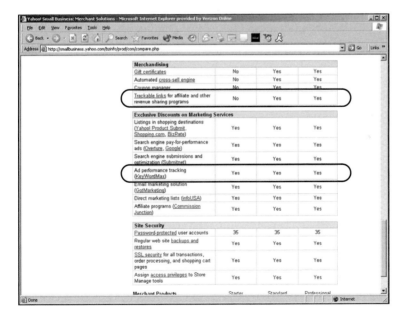

Advantages of E-Commerce Systems

An all-in-one solution has its advantages, especially for small business managers who prefer not to outsource their search engine marketing efforts, or lack the resources to set up sophisticated tracking systems in-house.

E-Commerce Plus E-Marketing

It's convenient to operate an online store and promote it all from within one system. E-marketing features can include coupons, refer-a-friend, newsletter, affiliate, and ad-tracking management. An ad-tracking tool can be used to monitor sales from virtually any online marketing effort. If you can include a link from a banner ad, email, or search engine listing to your web site, then you can track the resulting orders. In your e-commerce system, all you do is create a campaign name (for your reference) and set the destination landing page. Your system should generate a unique tracking URL that you'll use for your paid placement or paid inclusion campaigns.

Uh-oh. Only one link has been generated, right? Well, you'll need to generate a different tracking URL for each campaign component you want to monitor. I suggest that first-time Internet marketers start with the following:

- By search engine (for example, Ask Jeeves)
- By groups of keywords (for example, an auto insurance company could name one campaign "insurance," which would track "auto insurance," "auto insurance quote," and "car insurance" under one tracking URL

This allows you to evaluate campaign performance by each search engine and by groups of keywords. Ready to take your advertising campaigns to a higher level of performance? If so, go deeper with your analysis. Generate different tracking URLs for the following:

- By search engine
- By groups or individual keywords

- By ad listing (separate title and description if you create different ones for testing purposes)

- By landing pages (you can set up different ones for the same product for testing purposes)

Let's use the car insurance company as an example. Pretend the company wants to track one search engine and keyword group as identified earlier. Then, they want to test two different ad listings and landing pages. This firm would set up four campaigns, which would generate four tracking URLs:

Ask Jeeves, Insurance, Ad 1, Landing 1

Ask Jeeves, Insurance, Ad 1, Landing 2

Ask Jeeves, Insurance, Ad 2, Landing 1

Ask Jeeves, Insurance, Ad 2, Landing 2

Name each tracking URL anything you want. Each e-commerce system has different limits on character length; if you're faced with a low limit, abbreviate your names or use codes to keep them short. The tracking URL that's generated won't display this information; it's for your reference when you check the performance of each ad.

Because I use an e-commerce solution (1ShoppingCart.com), I can show you how this process works. Let's say my first tracking URL is for the keyword phrase "search engine tips" on Ask Jeeves. Perhaps I'll test two versions of my ad listings and two landing pages (the home page for this example, although a custom landing page would be better). I could name the first ad listing and associated landing page:

Ask Jeeves, search engine tips, Ad 1, Home 1

Figure 16.3 shows how I could create a tracking link using this method in 1ShoppingCart.com. Figure 16.4 shows the URL that's generated. I'd use this as the destination URL for the first listing in Ask Jeeves. When clicked, it would send consumers to the home page of my book web site (www.searchenginesales.com).

Tip

Use a tracking URL when promoting your products and services in your own e-zine. You'll learn what promotional copy and which offers get the best response from your subscribers. Use this information to develop new offers for them, as well for your other marketing campaigns.

Figure 16.3
Generating a tracking URL using an e-commerce solution such as 1ShoppingCart.com typically requires only a campaign name and destination URL.

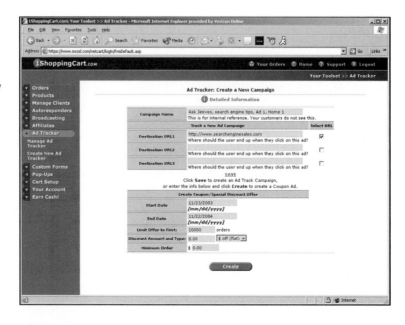

Figure 16.4
A unique tracking URL is created for each listing you set up.

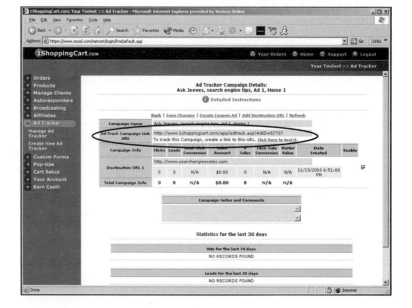

Easy Setup for Non-Techies

I confess that I'd rather throw a computer out the window than fix it. I lack patience for learning about hardware or software. My time is spent teaching, writing, or executing my clients' search engine marketing campaigns. When it's time for me to send out my monthly e-zine or launch a paid listing campaign, for example, I want the process to be quick and painless. Can you relate?

Well, merchant solutions are a good match for nontechnical marketers, like me. Numerous business owners tell me that they're swamped directing daily business operations. Yet, they are responsible for marketing their company. Solutions by 1ShoppingCart.com and Yahoo! enable site owners to easily track incoming orders from their search engine campaigns without doing any additional programming work. Other tracking programs require integration of at least a few lines of code into their web site. This step is already taken care of in combined e-commerce/e-marketing solutions. That makes me, and other non-techies, quite happy.

Low Cost

For less than $100 per month, entrepreneurs can run an online store plus promote it to new and existing customers through a variety of programs. And unlike with other return on investment (ROI) programs mentioned in this section (with the exception of web analytics), it doesn't matter how much money you spend on search engine advertising, or how much traffic you get. The monthly fee remains the same. Other ROI tracking solutions charge additional fees, which means you'll need to include this number when budgeting for your search engine campaigns.

There can be a transaction fee in addition to a solution leasing fee, but it's relatively small. It's better to pay a reasonable sales transaction fee than to spend additional money for clicks that don't convert.

Marketing Perks and Discounts

Users of Yahoo!'s Merchant Solutions score bonus marketing opportunities. These customers are included in Yahoo! Shopping and can save 20% on marketing costs for all categories. Yahoo! merchants are offered discounts on shopping destination listings, Pay-For-Placement (PFP) search engines, search engine submissions, and email marketing services provided by third parties.

The trend of e-commerce providers partnering with third-party marketing vendors will continue. It's a great enticement for new merchants to leverage low-cost technology and services by essentially joining a network of partners.

Entrepreneurs aren't the only beneficiary of these solutions. Plenty of large-scale corporations use an e-commerce solution that's designed primarily for small businesses. Corporations might have an in-house custom solution plus a Yahoo! store with a few of their top-selling items, or excess inventory. Why would they do this? To get access to the marketing perks. A few years ago, only Yahoo! merchants could enhance their store visibility by advertising in Yahoo! Shopping.

Challenges of E-Commerce Solutions

As great as small business e-commerce solutions are, they're not without their flaws. If your sole reason for leasing a solution is to track your search engine marketing campaigns, it's not robust enough to be your number one choice.

Time-Consuming to Track Search Engine Advertising

Did you notice how four tracking URLs were generated in the auto insurance example? Only one search engine and keyword group were considered. How many search engines are in your media plan? 2? 5? 15? How many keywords are you buying? 10? 500? 1,000? When you track each variation separately, you'll be generating and monitoring a bucket load of tracking URLs. At some point you really should assess your campaigns at a granular level, or you won't catch the pieces that are dragging down your overall ROI. Referring to the auto insurance example, perhaps "auto insurance quote" is wildly profitable while "car insurance" is bleeding money. If these keywords are grouped under one tracking URL, the advertiser wouldn't know to cut one word. It wouldn't be wise to cancel the entire campaign.

E-commerce solutions won't maintain bid positions on PFP search engines either. It's possible to update particular search engines hourly. Your watchful eye on your positions, or use of a bid management tool, is necessary.

Nor is there a report that displays your cost-per-order from search engines. This task of comparing your search engine spending reports to your ad-tracking ones is time-consuming.

E-Commerce Sites Aren't Search-Engine Friendly

E-commerce sites are mostly dynamic. What did you learn in Part III about dynamic web pages? A majority are not indexable by the search engines, not even by Google if there are more than two variables in the URL.

Review various sites using e-commerce solutions (check out Yahoo! Merchant Solutions or 1ShoppingCart.com's client lists, for example). Click on product or service links within merchants' sites to study the URLs. You'll notice how sometimes the root domain of the URL changes to a different one, which may be a problem. A web designer skilled in search engine optimization (SEO) can work with these solutions in a way that won't obstruct potential organic rankings. For example, instead of linking to a newsletter sign-up page that redirects to the e-commerce solution's server, keep the newsletter content page on your site and include sign-up fields on that page. Once people hit a "submit" button, then the transaction occurs via the e-commerce provider.

Be aware if your e-commerce solution generates a site template. A *template* enables you to cut and paste copy into a web interface to create and modify site pages. No programming is required. This is very affordable because marketers simply work with preconfigured site designs. It's a breeze to create a web site, although a custom "look and feel" is somewhat limited. Make sure you look at the URLs that are generated with a template program. Ones with multiple variables in the URL (look for symbols such as &, %, and =) are problems. Ones with two variables or less are usually fine.

Important

If you're using an e-commerce solution, refer to the section in Chapter 10, "Web Site Optimization," for optimization tips. Or, refer to Shari Thurow's book, *Search Engine Visibility*, for more advanced workarounds for dynamic web pages.

Tip

If you hire a web developer who can customize the shopping cart URL structure and page design, then the site will probably get better search engine visibility.

Lack of Customer Support

Yahoo! offers 24/7 phone support to their small business solution merchants. That's extremely helpful. 1ShoppingCart.com provides phone support Monday through Friday, 10 A.M. to 8 P.M. Eastern standard time, which is good, but can be frustrating if technical problems occur on the weekends or in the wee hours of the night.

Because e-commerce solution providers offer varying degrees of assistance, review their customer support hours and ask potential vendors questions about how accounts are served. Here are a few suggestions:

- How many of their customer support members service how many clients?

- What's the average response time to an email inquiry?

- Does a live person answer customer support calls, or if questions are sent to voicemail, what's the average response time for a callback?

These are just a few questions you could ask to get a sense of which e-commerce solution providers run responsive technical support teams. Feel free to use these questions in conversations with other ROI tracking solution providers, too.

Chapter 17

Affiliate Programs

Welcome to performance-based marketing. An affiliate program provides merchants with an online sales force that's paid a commission only for the products or services they sell. Affiliates use a variety of Internet marketing tactics to drive sales to merchants' web sites. An additional benefit to search engine marketers is that the same technology that tracks their affiliates' sales can be used to track their paid listings.

Be Free and Commission Junction are examples of well-recognized Application Service Providers (ASPs) in this industry who boast a large, built-in affiliate network. Merchants who enlist one of these providers will unleash a marketing-savvy team on the Internet immediately. As shown in Figures 17.1 and 17.2, both support an array of services designed to increase performance-based sales.

Figure 17.1
Be Free's additional services include search engine marketing and an automated merchandising assistant that serves real-time product recommendations.

Figure 17.2
Commission Junction's additional services include agency and channel partnerships.

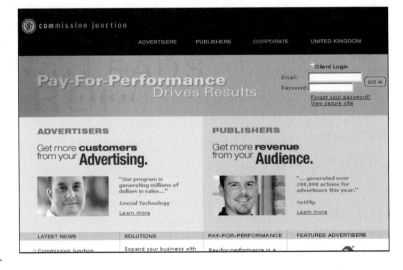

Important

In December 2003, ValueClick completed its acquisition of Commission Junction, which will be combined with its Be Free affiliate marketing subsidiary.

Advantages of Affiliate Programs

Undoubtedly, marketers planning to launch an affiliate program see a benefit that's much bigger than simply tracking paid listings. Fortunately, a few vendors are spearheading enhancements in this area as well.

Instantly Generate a Savvy Marketing Channel

Work with an affiliate network provider, and you'll tap into thousands of commission-based salespeople who are eager to deliver sales. Affiliates know how to work the Internet. From January through October 2003, for example, Commission Junction affiliates delivered more than 5.1 million verified sales to advertisers.

Top-producing affiliates are executing paid placement and paid inclusion campaigns. Does your strategy allow these efforts? If so, you've basically hired a team of search engine marketers who will work on a cost-per-acquisition (CPA) basis. Your affiliates will perform the keyword analysis, write ad listing copy, develop landing pages, and monitor the results so that you don't have to. (Don't assume that having affiliates perform these services is in your best interest. Read Chapter 23, "Managing Your Affiliates," first to determine the strategy that's right for you.)

It's easy for affiliates to join a network (the application process for Commission Junction was painless for me). Therefore, when you select prospective affiliates, or when they contact you, invite them to join the network you've selected. These networks handle commission processing, fraud detection, and other tasks related to managing affiliates, which removes one more administrative headache from your plate.

Evolving Support for Paid Listings

There's even better news for companies employing affiliate programs: Technology providers are beginning to incorporate search engine advertising resources as part of their solution.

Be Free sells an optional search engine marketing service, including both paid inclusion and Pay-For-Placement (PFP). Then there's My Affiliate Program, which offers an optional pay-per-click (PPC) Track module, where clients can manage their own paid listing campaigns. Clients enter a list of keywords into PPC Track, which creates a unique tracking URL for each phrase. My Affiliate Program generates a search engine–friendly file for marketers to log in to their search engine account and upload the new URLs and associated keywords.

Until affiliate program providers develop a paid listing tracking extension of their service, you can utilize their existing technology, if allowed. (However, it's more cumbersome than using an e-commerce solution that has an ad tracking feature.) I'm proposing three levels of tracking, depending on your time and interest in getting deep with your data. If your program requires contact data for each affiliate, the advanced tracking option is going to be a nightmare to set up. You'll be forced to enter contact data over and over again.

Basic Tracking

Set up each search engine as an affiliate and combine all keywords under that affiliate name.

Intermediate Tracking

Divide your keywords into relevant groups. For example, an insurance broker could lump "auto insurance" terms together and "homeowner insurance" terms into another group. Name an affiliate based on the search engine plus keyword group. Campaigns on Ask Jeeves could be called "Ask Jeeves, Auto" and "Ask Jeeves, Home." Or, create a naming convention that makes sense to you.

Advanced Tracking

Set up each affiliate as a specific part of your paid listing campaigns. For example, the insurance broker mentioned in the previous section could create "Ask Jeeves, Auto, Ad 1, Landing 1" as one affiliate. Here again are your optional tracking levels (from Chapter 16, "Small Business E-Commerce Solutions"):

- By search engine

- By groups or individual keywords

- By ad listing (separate title and description if you create different ones for testing purposes)

- By landing pages (you can set up different ones for the same product for testing purposes)

Set your commission fees to zero if your affiliate program supports this data entry.

Challenges of Affiliate Programs

I've alluded to a few challenges of using affiliate programs for search engine return on investment (ROI) tracking: the issues of same-channel conflict from your affiliates and the time required for setup. A few others warrant your attention, too.

Expensive Program Fees

Well-known affiliate management programs offering an ASP model are quite pricey. Yes, the value of tapping into an affiliate sales team and the account management is well worth the cost. However, are entrepreneurs willing to cough up a few thousand dollars for a setup fee? I doubt it. Add that cost to the ASP's monthly minimums, annual renewal fees, and transaction fees, and this is the worst ROI tracking tool choice if it's only being used for search engine advertising. Perhaps more ASPs will follow Be Free's example and offer optional search engine services (or tools) on a per-click or per-click plus revenue-sharing basis.

That being said, there's an alternative to the large-scale affiliate network service providers. Amen, right? Go for affiliate program software. For less than $1,000 you can buy software from My Affiliate Program, AffiliateShop, and AssocTRAC. There are no annual renewal or transaction fees either. Software programs generally don't supply a network of gung-ho affiliates to you, but that might be ok. For a fairly low investment, you'll own a program to grow your own affiliate team while having the ability to track the sales from your paid listings.

No Ownership of Your Affiliates

Do you own your affiliates? You'd better ask this question before you sign up with an affiliate network.

For example, the Be Free or Commission Junction affiliates belong to those networks. If as an advertiser you leave, you either can't or won't be able to take those affiliates to a new system you use. A couple of affiliate network providers prohibit this practice altogether. Others might send out an email alerting your affiliates that you're moving to a new platform, but keep in mind that those affiliates are often loyal to the network provider. Unless they're making a lot of money for and from you, they'll likely continue marketing the merchants in the network. Those affiliates have plenty of business opportunities to choose from.

Yes, you can personally woo your top-performing affiliates to your new system, but the network owners frown upon this big time. However, Marty Fahncke, professional revenue developer for FawnKey & Associates, shared that the network he used wasn't happy about him taking his best affiliates with him to a new system, but because he still continued to generate $100,000 per month through the old network, that provider whined more than they did yell.

Chapter 18

Web Analytics

From which web sites did visitors click a link to reach yours? What pages did they access the most and least on your site? On which page did they exit your site without completing a transaction? These are simply a smattering of questions web analytics answer. Web analytics reports shed light on web site visitor patterns, enabling marketers to improve their conversions and lower customer acquisition costs.

Various Internet marketing programs, including search engine positioning, drive traffic to your site. A portion of those visitors will become buyers. What are the prospects doing? No other return on investment (ROI) tracking will lend as much insight into this question as web analytics. WebSideStory's HitBox product line and NetIQ's WebTrends line are long-standing examples of web analytics solutions (see Figures 18.1 and 18.2).

Figure 18.1

This sample HitBox Commerce report shows keywords or ad groups related to the number of orders, revenue amount, number of customers, and number of items, to name a few factors.

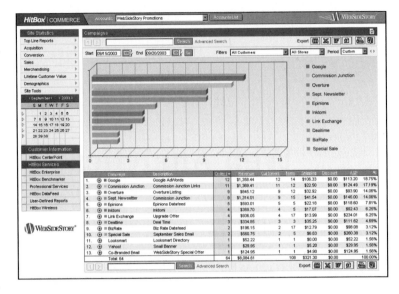

Figure 18.2

This sample screen capture from WebTrends Reporting Series, Enterprise Edition, shows the purchase conversion funnel success/drop-off based on phrases visitors used from paid listings. (Organic listings can be added to this report, or viewed separately.)

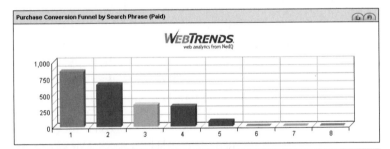

Search Phrase	Purchase Conversion Funnel	Visits	Step Conversion Rate
■1. wireless phone service	Cart View	147	-
	Cart Add	60	40.82%
	Started Checkout	42	70.00%
	Cart Complete	11	26.19%
	Other	N/A	N/A
■2. wireless phones	Cart View	126	-
	Cart Add	48	38.10%
	Started Checkout	43	89.58%
	Cart Complete	7	16.28%
	Other	N/A	N/A
■3. wireless phone plan	Cart View	61	-
	Cart Add	22	36.07%
	Started Checkout	15	68.18%
	Cart Complete	1	6.67%
	Other	N/A	N/A

Advantages of Web Analytics

Web analytics comes close to being the top choice for a paid listing ROI tracking solution. Because it's critical for assessing all Internet marketing efforts, web analytics may become part of your marketing foundation even before you give it extra points for the search engine advertising component.

Data That Improves Site Conversions

Without web analytics, marketers are clueless about how their site serves, or doesn't serve, their site visitors. This information is the Holy Grail of understanding online customers.

Whereas other ROI tracking solutions count the number of paid listing clicks and resulting sales, they miss the customers' travels within the web site. Worse yet, they don't identify shopping abandonment patterns. Web analytics logs all of this data and more. How can this information help marketers? Let's look at a couple of basic scenarios.

Web Analytics Data	Marketers' Potential Responses
Most popular entry pages	On these pages, do the following: • Place product offers, rotate weekly • Promote online store • Offer free subscription to the e-zine • Sell advertising • Include toll-free phone number • Remind visitors to bookmark these pages
Most popular exit pages	On these pages, do the following: • Promote "limited time" offer • Offer coupon in exchange for email address • Launch exit pop-up survey asking why their needs weren't met (multiple choice)
Visits by day of the week	On these pages, do the following: • Replace offers on the least-visited day • Ramp up sales pitch in web page marketing copy daily until most-popular day • On days following the most popular one, promote "liquidation" or "last chance" sale • Increase Pay-For-Placement positions on search engines during strong-performing days, lower positions on poor-performing days • Buy sponsorships in content-related e-zines that email 24–48 hours before best sales days

Think of the insight you'll gain with web analytics. You'll see where your customers are going and what they're doing in your online store or sales office. You'll even see how they landed on your site, which gives you ideas for possible marketing partnerships, or helps you evaluate current ones. Add a splash of site design and copywriting creativity to your analysis, and you'll figure out how to get a greater number of your site visitors to buy. That'll lower your customer acquisition costs across all of your marketing campaigns.

Drill into Search Engine Marketing

Important

Daypart targeting is the ability to market to consumers during a specified time of the day.

E-commerce solutions provide limited search engine marketing data, if any. Affiliate programs aren't set up to conveniently track it at all, although marketers could tweak them to do so. Web analytics, on the other hand, scores superior marks in this area. These solutions were created to drill deep into web site data. As an example, see ClickTracks' campaign tracking capabilities as related to search engines.

ClickTracks 4.0 Campaign Tracking

Reporting by campaign (search engine and general marketing):

- Number of purchasing visitors*
- Conversion rates*
- The revenue generated by each campaign*
- The number of visitors each campaign brought to the site
- Cost per visitor and total cost
- Revenue per purchasing visitor and per visitor*

(*features only available in ClickTracks Professional 4.0)

Reporting by keyword (organic and pay-per-click listings)

- Total visitors
- Percentage of visitors
- Cost of visitors from pay-per-click campaigns
- Average cost of pay-per-click visitors
- Average time on site
- Percentage of short visits

Not to be outdone, Urchin recently released a campaign tracking module, an optional add-on to their main software product. This module enables marketers to track click fraud activity and daypart targeting, among other search engine-specific actions. Both the ClickTracks and Urchin examples represent the tip of the iceberg in terms of what search engine-specific data is available.

All Companies Can Participate

All companies, large and small, can afford web analytics. Solution providers present a variety of software or services to meet marketers' data analysis needs. There are versions of HitBox, Web-Trends, and ClickTracks that start at less than $50 per month. Referring traffic from search engines is included in the small business versions, but not all offer ROI tracking. Find out the reporting details from the product information on providers' web sites. It's helpful when vendors, such as ClickTracks, show a product comparison chart to help marketers determine the best solution for their business (Figure 18.3).

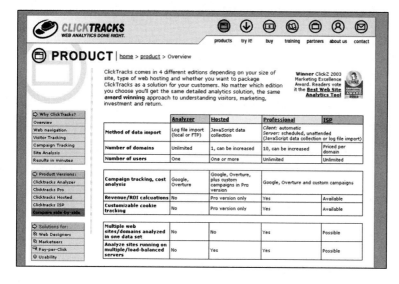

Figure 18.3
ClickTracks presents a side-by-side comparison chart of their web analytics tools to help marketers choose the edition that's right for them.

A great way for small business to get site statistics reports for free, or at a low fee, is to host their web sites with Internet service providers (ISPs) who have purchased a web analytics multi-user license. For example, NTT/Verio and Earthlink include Urchin reports with their hosting service.

This brings up an important point: *Ask your current ISP if traffic statistics are included in your hosting agreement.* Storing the data for these reports takes up server space, so unless you ask, these reports generally aren't made available. One simple email or phone call can change that—at no additional charge. E-commerce solution providers, including Yahoo!, might offer statistics as part of their merchant solutions, too.

Challenges of Web Analytics

One of the initial challenges of web analytics is figuring out which web analytics vendor, and version of their solution, to choose. Beyond that, the detailed data on search engine marketing is great, but site statistical products or services don't compare to tools that specifically manage and track paid listings.

No Management of Paid Listings

Web analytics outperforms several other ROI solutions by tracking detailed traffic and revenue data from search engine marketing. Yet it falls short when it comes to the management of paid listings. Let's look at GO TOAST's summary benefits for their basic product, BidManager:

- ROI Tracking reports your return on investment for your pay-per-click search terms.

- Rules-Based Bidding gives you total control over tailoring your bidding parameters and preferences, with 13 rules to choose from.

- Keyword MasterList vastly simplifies the management of listing titles, descriptions, and URLs, and facilitates propagation of all of your listings across many engines.

- Automatic monitoring of your pay-per-click search term bids 2×, 6×, 12×, 24×, or 48× per day.

- Detailed HTML email status updates.

- Independent third-party verification of your bid status and position.

- Scheduling tools for whenever you want your keyword bids to be reviewed.

- Automatic minimum and maximum keyword cost bid management.

- Price gap elimination between you and your competition.

- Manage all your keywords through one user-friendly interface.

- Select and pay for only the keywords you want or need to manage.

- Extensive time savings as GO TOAST checks the status of your terms so you don't have to.

- No hassles from software downloads or constant upgrades. No need for your own dedicated Internet connection to monitor your words 24×7×365.

- Integrated support for Overture Auto Bidding.

There's no interface within web analytics to set up or modify Pay-For-Placement (PFP) listings, as there is with bid management tool providers such as GO TOAST. There's also no way to add or delete paid inclusion listings. To be fair, neither e-commerce nor affiliate programs do this either. Therefore, this challenge applies to all three.

It won't surprise me when web analytics providers begin offering paid inclusion services as an optional service, which they'll likely outsource to an inclusion partner. As we're seeing other ROI tracking vendors create partnerships with search engines or search engine service providers, the same will happen within web analytics. These services might be in place but just aren't yet publicly promoted in marketing materials.

A marriage between a bid management tool company and web analytics company appears to be harmonious. The first continuously optimizes paid listing campaigns, while the latter can be utilized to double-check the performance of paid listings, free organic rankings, and all other online marketing efforts.

Not Quite Perfect Reporting for Paid Listings

Let's face it, the tools designed to improve paid listing campaigns supply the best reports. Bid management tools (discussed in the next chapter) get much deeper with search engine advertising data than most web analytics solutions.

Additionally, bid management programs generally have more options to run a variety of reports. Often, your web analytics report is preconfigured to certain parameters. Your Webmaster can redefine these parameters, but in most cases, only one format of report will be generated each time it's run. Again, if your sole focus is optimizing your paid listings, then bid management tools are the optimal management and reporting solution.

Chapter 19

Bid Management Tools

Bid management tools automatically adjust advertisers' bids and positions on Pay-For-Placement (PFP) search engines. A few vendors track Trusted Feed listings as well.

If you invest in a bid management tool, choose one that's authorized to manage the search engines in your marketing plan. (Being an *authorized vendor* means that the search engines allow the tool direct access to their ad-serving technology, which is required for the tool to work properly.) A good place to start your research is with Overture's list of approved third-party vendors because, more than likely, Overture is in your plan. As of this publication, the following are Overture-approved bidding tool companies:

- BidRank

- Did-it.com

- Dynamic Keyword Bid Maximizer (Apex Pacific)

- Epic Sky

- GO TOAST

- PPC BidTracker (Trellian)

- PPC Pro (PPC Management)

- Send Traffic

- Sure Hits

Important

ASPs that are not on a search engine's approved vendor list can still manage client campaigns by using a tool that is authorized. Select marketing agencies may also provide a bid management service to their clients if they've signed a special agreement directly with the search engines.

As with other return on investment (ROI) tracking solutions, these tools can be purchased as software, or leased as part of a monthly service from an Application Service Provider (ASP). Software is generally less expensive, whereas an ASP model tends to include hands-on assistance with advertisers' campaigns in addition to tool access.

A couple of bid management companies go beyond adjusting listings based on advertisers' desired positions or bids; their technology operates on advertisers' cost-per-acquisition (CPA) goals. Both Did-it.com and GO TOAST (see Figures 19.1 and 19.2) are making a big splash in the search engine marketing community with their ROI bid management programs.

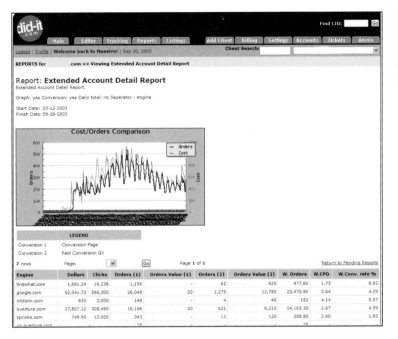

Figure 19.1

A sample Account Detail Report, which shows revenue data by search engine, for Did-it.com's Maestro service.

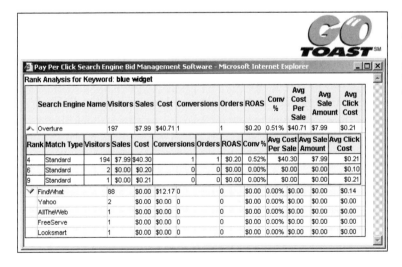

Figure 19.2

A sample Rank Analysis report, which shows revenue data by keyword, for GO TOAST's ProfitBuilder ROI Tracking Tool.

Advantages of Bid Management Tools

ROI bid management tools are by far the optimal choice for a tracking solution for do-it-yourself marketers. Why? Because they're exclusively designed for search engine advertising. These tools enable marketers to micromanage their paid listings while reducing the hours needed to improve their performance.

Paid Placement and Paid Inclusion Integration

Not only are their tools specific to paid listings, but some bid management firms help launch advertisers' campaigns on both PFP and Trusted Feed programs. Marketers specify the search engines to be included in their campaigns. Then, bid companies might assist with any or all parts of the campaign setup: keyword analysis, ad listing copywriting, and URL generation tracking (and web page optimization for Trusted Feed because remember, inclusion programs are for crawler-based search engines). This is in addition to optimizing the listings by adjusting bids (and subsequently your positions).

Early Notification of Paid Listing Errors

Smile if this has happened to you—you're running a keyword search in the search engines and spot your ad listing, or your client's. You know that it's not an expensive term so you click the ad listing to check it out. Um, it's a broken link. Or, it's pointing to the wrong landing page. Ok, you're not actually smiling; you're totally freaking out. How long has this been going on? How many wasted clicks did you, or your clients, pay for? Your stomach is turning like you're on the spinning tea cup ride at Disneyland. All is not well.

Sure, search engines might catch a broken link and send you an automated email identifying the problem listing. But unless you're checking an ROI report constantly, looking for good and bad spikes in CPA numbers, a paid listing error might go unnoticed for weeks. If you don't run an ROI reporting system in-house, a bid management tool with this feature enables you to spot anomalies immediately. Better still, if there's a broken link or other issue, a bid maximizing tool lowers the position of your listing because it won't be converting. You won't be burning cash paying for that #1 position. This is a solid cost-savings benefit for marketers who only periodically verify their campaign performance.

Tip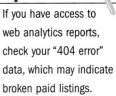
If you have access to web analytics reports, check your "404 error" data, which may indicate broken paid listings.

When I worked at an agency that enlisted Did-it.com's services, my Did-it.com representative emailed me after he noticed one of my client's weekend sales had plummeted. With a little investigation, I discovered that the client moved their web site to another agency a few days earlier. The tracking code wasn't in their new site's sales confirmation page; that's why no sales were being counted. Nobody at the agency I worked for was aware that this client planned to leave; the personal alert from Did-it.com revealed this. Sometimes, it takes both man and machine to detect advertising (and business) blunders.

Automated Bid Management Based on CPA Targets

What's the number one reason to hire a bid management solution with ROI optimization? Their solution adjusts your listings based on CPA goals. No search engine marketing campaign should be evaluated based on the number of clicks or the CPC rate. That's all rubbish. Unless you exclusively sell advertising on your web site and simply need "eyeballs," then your search engine marketing goal has little to do with traffic. It's about attaining new customers at the lowest cost-per-customer.

Would you like to buy keywords based on your customer acquisition cost targets? Well, you can. Using services offered by Did-it.com and GO TOAST, for example, you can set $15 as the most you're willing to pay in search engine fees for a sale. The bid and associated position for each ad listing will be increased or decreased based on the sales performance.

Keep in mind, though, that you might have to increase your CPA maximum if your position ends up being significantly lower than your competitors'. If your per-order goals are not high enough, your listing won't win a top spot...or the bulk of the traffic. If $15 places you at position #11, perhaps increasing your allowable CPA to $20 means that your listing jumps into a Top 10 spot, delivering more traffic and subsequent sales. Don't increase your per-order goal if it's not profitable. Simply be aware that if you set an aggressive CPA number, your competition may force you to re-evaluate it.

Challenges of Bid Management Tools

Were you thinking that if this is the best solution then it's trouble-free? I wish that were the case. Unfortunately, because bid management systems (with or without an ROI optimization feature) make it delightfully easier to micromanage paid listings, there's more data to watch.

Management of Bid Management Tools Required

It seems counter-intuitive. You're choosing a bid management tool to eliminate your time updating bids manually. Tools that maximize listings based on your ROI targets should alleviate your stress of achieving profitable sales too, right? These tools do help. Nevertheless, there are plenty of details that demand your watchful eye. Writing from personal experience, avoid a few future surprises by being aware of the potential problems listed in the following sections.

Inaccuracy of Search Engine Data

Does your bid management tool report search engine data in real-time? Ask them, and routinely compare their report to those from search engines. You might need to wait a few days before you report the number of clicks, sales, and associated click fees to your boss, or clients, because you'll miss updated data.

Nonremoval of Nonperforming Listings

What happens if your listings have already been demoted to the lowest possible bids on PFP search engines and they're still losing money? What if you're paying a low, fixed click fee for Trusted Feed listings that don't convert? Bid software won't remove listings for you, nor will all ROI bid management firms. Ask how this is handled and how you're alerted. Don't assume your listings can't drain your pocketbook if they're in the lowest-paying spot.

Hiccups Caused by Search Engine Changes

Bid management software owners frequently have to download newer versions, or experience usability problems for several hours with their current version, when search engines make changes to their ad-serving technology.

Clients of ROI bid management firms aren't free from problems either; their listings may be temporarily stuck in unprofitable positions.

For marketers who spend thousands of dollars per day and must adjust their bids constantly, these setbacks can be costly.

Are your bids or CPA targets outdated? Your bids or CPA targets could have mysteriously reverted to your previous numbers, or a system default number. Potential technological glitches coupled with human error mandate that marketers routinely review the various components of their campaigns to catch recent or longstanding errors.

Can't Yet Track All Online Marketing Efforts

If you are a do-it-yourself search engine marketer, a bid management tool is my first choice for a search engine ROI tracking solution. This technology could easily be applied to tracking other marketing campaigns, including email, banner ads, and content sponsorships. Unfortunately, it's not yet a complete online marketing ROI tracking solution.

A few of the solutions mentioned in this book have the capability to track other online marketing efforts. But at this time, no other solution can effectively manage PFP and Trusted Feed as well as the bid management tools do; more specifically, they can't do it as well as the firms that optimize campaigns based on ROI goals.

It's disappointing that there isn't an extension within most bid management tools to track other Internet marketing efforts. A few firms are venturing into this space: GO TOAST, Send Traffic, and Sure Hits, to name a few. Other bid management tool vendors will likely soon offer a general conversion tracking tool as an integrated part of their bid management software or service. Or, it could be sold as a stand-alone item. If you're already using a bid management tool, inquire about this option and delivery timeline from your vendor.

Costs Can Be Difficult to Estimate

Bid management is a more difficult pricing model to evaluate as compared to other ROI solutions because there are so many options within this category.

Software purchase prices are easy to determine; at a few hundred dollars this option is very affordable, even for budding entrepreneurs. A few software vendors—such as PPC Management (PPC Pro) and BidRank—offer an ROI tracking feature. These software products don't update bids based on ROI performance, but at least advertisers can see their campaign profitability at a granular level, and then use the software to manually improve their results as often as possible.

Confusion enters the scene when it comes to bid management firms' costs. These Application Service Providers might charge a percentage of the total keyword media cost, a flat monthly fee, a per-click rate, a per-keyword rate, or any combination of these. These prices can seem expensive to new advertisers. Theoretically, the firms that optimize paid listings for maximum profitability by using CPA targets, such as Did-it.com or GO TOAST, should easily cover their own service fees in the higher profits they'll provide. Collect costs from multiple vendors to determine which appears to be the most cost-effective for your business. And if you represent a company with a lot of paid listing traffic potential or an agency that works with multiple clients, remember to negotiate!

Chapter 20

Internet Marketing Agencies

Are you a bit overwhelmed by your ROI tracking tool options? Luckily, there's a "hands-free" alternative if you want it. Work with an Internet marketing agency. Let them implement a range of tools (or use yours) to monitor and then refine your search engine campaigns. You can supervise.

Advertising.com and Performics (see Figures 20.1 and 20.2) are two examples of agencies that offer search engine marketing as one of several services. I chose these agencies because they represent a rarity in this field: They offer a cost-per-acquisition (CPA) pricing model instead of a flat rate or media commission fee. It's not always the best among the three choices, but this no-risk opportunity is unquestionably appealing to companies that prioritize a performance guarantee.

Figure 20.1
Advertising.com offers search engine, email, web, and promotional marketing on a CPA basis.

Figure 20.2
Performics offers search engine, affiliate, and email marketing on a CPA basis.

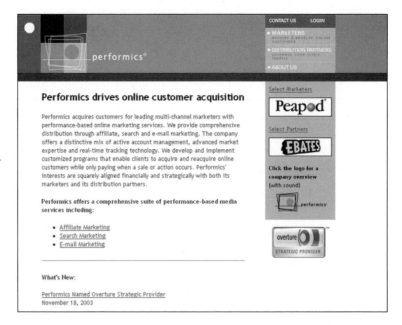

Tip

Ask agencies you're interviewing to define search engine marketing. Do they handle paid placement (Fixed Placement and Pay-For-Placement)? Do they manage paid inclusion (Submit URL and Trusted Feed), along with site optimization, which is a necessary foundation to achieve success through inclusion programs?

I've worked at two agencies and now run my own, but I'm not sold on the agency model for everyone. I also train marketers on how to execute their own campaigns because I believe those with the interest and dedication can reap similar success as achieved by agencies.

Advantages of Internet Marketing Agencies

One advantage of agencies has already been revealed: *Agencies do the work for you.* Companies that can afford to outsource receive the gifts of time and an experienced marketing team. That's an attractive combination. The following sections list a few other benefits to consider.

Fast Time to Market

Is search engine marketing your sole focus? Probably not. Small business owners are consumed by daily operations; marketing directors of corporations juggle various online and offline promotions at once. Internet agencies present over-committed marketers assistance with part or all of their online campaigns. Equipped with tools and strategic action plans, agencies turbo-boost web site visibility in a relatively short timeframe.

This isn't to say that agencies wave their magic wands to get instant listings in the search engines. Keywords have to be researched, ad copy written, landing pages designed, and tracking URLs generated for paid placement. Plus, ad listings require approval by search engine editors before they are "live."

For paid inclusion, each web site page that'll be submitted to the search engines for possible organic rankings must be optimized. Rankings are not guaranteed through inclusion programs, and if achieved, these pages typically require continuous optimization to combat competitors and changes in search engines' ranking methodologies (see Figure 20.3 for the location of paid placement versus organic listings). Still, Internet marketing agencies can expedite these processes.

Some agencies specialize in search engine marketing. Firms including Bruce Clay, Grantastic Designs, and iProspect, all well-rated in the industry, do nothing but eat, sleep, and dream about search engines. Traditional marketing agencies can execute search engine advertising more effectively than site optimization, because the former is somewhat similar to their media buying process. However, even within paid placement or paid inclusion programs, the ever-changing rules require a team of search engine negotiation, copy-writing, programming, and ROI specialists. Search engine-centric agencies tend to be better equipped with proven tools and expertise.

Figure 20.3
The "Sponsored Links" on Google are paid placement programs. The main search results are organic listings that can be influenced by optimization efforts. (Google is one of the few search engines that offers a free Submit URL program.)

Organic listings

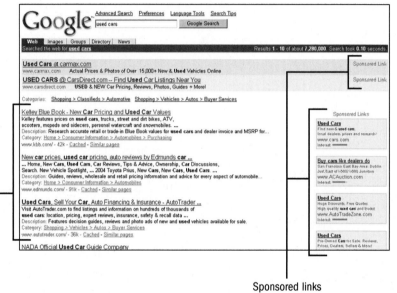

Sponsored links

Campaign Analysis and Recommendations Included

Software is an important piece of a marketer's toolbox, but it doesn't replace human analysis. Agencies certainly rely on a suite of tools to manage your paid listings. Plus, agencies, Internet marketing specialists, and search engine companies leverage these tools to provide you with customized campaign recommendations. Their suggestions are based on detailed analysis of your ROI data, market research, and customer behavior profiling, plus creative copywriting specific to your business.

It's often beneficial for an agency to assess a company's web site strategy. Outside analysts can create customer-focused campaigns more easily than company marketers who are "too close" to their work. Agencies have also developed winning formulas. They act as a car driver, while the clients act as the driver's navigator. Agencies handle the "hands-on" responsibilities of the road trip while clients provide the end destination goal and assistance with directions. Teamwork is essential.

Comprehensive Online Marketing Services

Full-service Internet marketing agencies handle all aspects of your promotional campaigns, from media planning/buying to creative design to ROI analysis. Agencies may even outsource particular services to industry specialists, so there's a chance you'll be hiring the best teams for each marketing channel, while communicating and writing a check to one. Although not all agencies are readily willing to reveal their technology partners, do ask if you're curious about who'll be working on your campaigns. A star network of expert partners could be available.

Challenges of Internet Marketing Agencies

Turning everything over to an Internet marketing or search engine marketing agency might sound like the best solution. Let others micromanage paid listings for you, right? As you may have guessed, this isn't always an affordable option. Nor is it the right option for companies with the capability or desire to proactively direct their own strategies.

Cost-Prohibitive for Small Businesses

The concept of Internet agencies working on a CPA basis must sound like a dream come true. What's the catch? Well, there are two.

First of all, agencies that consider CPA deals are looking for a high sales volume and hefty commission per sale. Companies with strong brand names and a history of solid online sales are good matches for CPA agencies. Entrepreneurs are out of luck.

Second, CPA models can be more expensive than others. For one client account I managed while at a direct response television (DRTV) agency, $800 in search engine fees yielded nearly $40,000 in sales in one month. At the time, search engine advertising was a free program to the clients; they paid their own search engine fees. A 20–30% CPA fee, for example, paid to another agency or affiliates, would have equaled $8,000 to $12,000 in commission fees instead of the $800 in search engine fees. That's a pretty big incentive to manage your campaigns in-house and keep the extra profits, yes?

Flat fee or media commission-based agencies aren't affordable for all small business owners either. Reputable search engine firms require several thousand dollars per month as a contract minimum, with six-month or one-year commitments required.

Thankfully, small business marketers can access a variety of free resources on this topic (see the Resources section in this book). In addition, plenty of tools (and seminars) now exist to help them execute cost-effective campaigns with greater ease and knowledge. Many of the tools are mentioned in this book. Microsoft bCentral offers a suite of online marketing tools including search engine marketing, web analytics, email marketing, and banner ads for less than $500 a year. This isn't a "hands-free" option, but it can help you ramp up your business to meet your revenue goals as well as attract the interest of agencies.

Tip

Changing paid listing tools is a hassle. Therefore, ask agency representatives what'll happen if you decide to manage your own campaigns, or switch agencies. Are the tools and search engine accounts in your company's name? Or does all of the work disappear if you terminate a relationship with an agency? Prepare yourself for this option before you need it.

Minimal Control Over Strategies, Tools, and Industry Contacts

Agencies bring their own resources to the table. These serve as the platform for the agencies' expertise and current procedures. This is a double-edged sword. Agencies' toolsets give them their marketing strength, but therefore, their clients are generally locked into their system. This isn't true of all agencies. But before you forge a relationship with an interactive agency, learn about their strategies and tools because their solution is likely to become yours.

Want a Yahoo! directory editor's phone number? How about the contact information for the opt-in mailing lists your agency is using? No way. Media sales representatives and search engine techies are protected celebrities to a great many agencies. Those relationships took years to build. Once again, you're committing to the agency's network, and if you leave, all of the resources used for your campaigns usually remain in their secret vault.

To continue to grow your own expertise in-house, refer to the Resources section in the back of this book. You'll find informational hubs that I and other search engine marketers turn to in continuing our education in this evolving industry.

Last in Line

Although agency clients are given a team of marketers to work on their campaigns, it's not on an exclusive basis. Agency representatives are responsible for multiple clients whose campaigns are in prelaunch, launch, tracking, or refinement mode. Large corporate accounts typically receive greater attention because they have numerous campaigns running. Agency clients, large or small, can occasionally feel neglected.

Help your account receive continued excellent service by reviewing agencies' reports and scheduling routine conference calls. A web agency I worked for frequently scored new accounts because these clients had received outstanding initial service from their previous agency, but then it declined as the company grew, or new clients came aboard. If weeks or months go by without contact from your agency, touch base with your account manager if you feel forgotten.

Part V

Conclusion

Do-it-yourself search engine advertisers have a variety of options for managing their paid listings: e-commerce solutions, affiliate programs, web analytics, or bid management tools. The first three options support additional online marketing initiatives, whereas the last makes automated optimization of return on investment (ROI) goals possible. Often, marketers use more than one solution because each possesses different strengths. Then again, a significant number of corporations outsource the daily management of search engine advertising (and optimization) altogether to agencies, either those with a general Internet focus or search engine specialists. The agencies utilize a suite of tools to achieve maximum profitability for their clients.

Whether marketers execute their own campaigns or supervise an agency's efforts, the key is to increase their volume of sales at the lowest per-customer cost. Routine campaign analysis is necessary to identify and resolve weak points within each campaign. A systematic evaluation process also helps marketers discover the winning combinations that can be used to improve their overall campaign performance.

Visit www.searchenginesales.com for updates and links to many of the resources mentioned in this book.

 **PART VI**

Protecting Your Profits

Introduction

A return on investment (ROI) tracking solution identifies the profitability of your campaign components by search engine, keyword, title, description, and landing page. Unfortunately, it can't reveal the business tactics that drain your advertising budget.

Competitors are the primary profit killers. You're responsible for policing any of their activities that attack your campaigns. But don't overlook your external sales force—you could be fighting an increasingly expensive battle against your own company. The earlier you put protective policies in place, the sooner you'll repair holes in your purse.

Chapter 21

Watch Out for Click Fraud

People who have no intention of buying from you but who purposely click your ad listings to waste your money are engaging in click fraud. Some companies aren't really impacted. But for others, this sort of search engine sabotage is quietly draining their advertising budget—wasting thousands of dollars each month. Are you an unknowing victim of click fraud?

If you're in a highly-competitive industry and your keywords are several dollars or more per click, chances are your competitors are intentionally clicking your ads. Malicious clicks on Pay-For-Placement (PFP) search engines at $0.50, $1, or more quickly amount to significant waste. Even clicks on Trusted Feed listings, which are priced at a fixed cost-per-click rate, add up. Your competitors aren't the only perpetrators either.

Many search engines offer a revenue-sharing incentive to their search distribution partners for displaying their search results. Because the distribution partners get paid when web site listings are clicked, there's an incentive for them to send clicks your way without caring if they convert. It's unsettling to know that in the past unethical distribution partners have offered their site visitors a per-click commission to click ad listings. Or, they've clicked the listings themselves. Today, these blatant activities are usually caught by the search engines and the partnerships are subsequently terminated. On occasion, though, an unethical distribution partner slides through the fraud filters.

Resolving click fraud requires active participation by both search engines and advertisers. Together, ad profits can be better protected.

Safeguards Search Engines Can and Can't Offer

The search engines realize that if your campaigns don't make money, you'll stop advertising. They're aware that your ROI takes a nose dive if you're paying for clicks from competitors who hit your listings a hundred times; therefore, additional clicks from these types of activities are not counted. Automated robot or spider activities aren't fraudulent, but are fortunately also considered invalid clicks for which advertisers don't pay.

In an effort to shield their advertisers from unfair profit loss, search engines have implemented click protection systems to remove fraudulent, or invalid, clicks from your accounts. Overture, a leader in sharing information with the public on click fraud, notes that each click is evaluated along 20–50 different data points every day (http://www.overture.com/d/USm/ac/su/faq_as.jhtml). Sample data points evaluated include:

- IP address
- User session information

- User cookie information

- The network to which an IP belongs

- The user's browser information

- The search term requested by the user

- The time of the click

- The rank of the advertiser's listing

- The bid of the advertiser's listing

- The time of the search

- The time of the click

Google also reports how they actively monitor for click abuse or robot activity and remove these clicks from your reports and billing statements (https://adwords.google.com/select/faq/guidelines.html#3).

Even with search engines taking an active role policing click fraud, not all of it is caught. Because malicious clickers aren't addressed by search engines, this activity isn't deterred either.

Once upon a time, there was a CEO of a lead generation company whom I'll call Bob. Every day, Bob would click a portion of his Top 10 competitors' listings on PFP search engines. He'd click the listings once from his home, then from his office. And he'd click listings from his laptop while traveling. His strategy was simple: by clicking his competitors' keywords they eventually depleted their ad budgets and dropped out of the top positions for a short time until they added more money to their accounts. Bob, paying much less for a lower position, jumped into a Top 3 spot. He scored a premium position for a low amount. Because he randomly clicked select keywords from different locations, his competitors might have paid for a portion of his fraudulent behavior as well. Bad Bob. This story of Bob, the Evil Clicker, demonstrates why companies need to patrol their own campaigns. The search engines won't catch every fraudulent click from competitors who employ sneaky tactics. Besides, perpetrators' behavior needs to be deterred.

Identifying Click Fraud Patterns

In Part V, "Tracking Your Return on Investment," I discussed how to track the various components of your paid listing campaigns: search engine, keyword, ad listing, and landing page. Assigning a unique tracking code to every listing helps you determine the ROI of each ad component. Furthermore, this enables you to spot unusual fluctuations in your campaigns that could indicate click fraud activity. Although you can identify suspicious click fraud behavior by relying on raw log activity shown in your web analytics reports, you cannot effectively attribute such activity to "questionable" clicks without having tracking URLs in place.

Look for anomalies per search engine and per keyword by studying the following data:

- Average daily clicks

- Average page views per click

- Average conversion rate per keyword, per click

If possible, monitor:

- Click trends by hour

- Click trends by day

- Click averages based on specific positions

Abnormal behavior could include:

Important

An increase in advertising efforts or media attention could contribute to traffic surges from paid listings. And web site modifications can influence visitor behavior. Evaluate other possible factors before you assume there's click fraud activity.

- Spikes in click volume for specific terms

- Click increases plus atypical visitor behavior (zero conversions, zero page views, and off-peak click times or dates)

- More than one competitor dropping out of a top position during times of suspicious activity, while one competitor remains seemingly untouched (remember the story of Bob, the Evil Clicker)

These are the patterns Jessie Stricchiola, now president of the search engine marketing firm Alchemist Media, Inc., monitored while she managed a large paid listing campaign for a nationwide law firm. She had worked closely with the firm's in-house PHP programmer to develop a tracking system that would track all click data, independent of cookie and IP address (known as *session tracking*). Each keyword had its own unique tracking URL that was given to the search engines that stored click data, including keyword and the specific engine source in the database. She studied the click patterns and in one instance was able to associate click fraud activity with specific IP addresses. Between FindWhat.com and Overture, Stricchiola tracked nearly $10,000 of click fraud within 30 days.

Outsource your ROI tracking efforts if setting up a home-grown system seems too time-consuming. A few third-party tracking vendors even incorporate a form of click monitoring. But you might want a program that's dedicated for this type of reporting. Thankfully, a click fraud service made its debut in the summer of 2003, and it seems promising.

WhosClickingWho? is an independent pay-per-click (PPC) auditing service designed to gather information on all visitor clicks to a web site via all major PPC search engines: Overture, FindWhat.com, Sprinks, 7Search, ah-ha.com, ePilot, GoClick, LookSmart, Google AdWords, and all of their affiliates. WhosClickingWho? compiles and generates the following data:

- Who is hitting your site from multiple pay-per-click search engines.

- Uniquely identify each PPC visitor via IP address and unique identifier string, enabling you to detect most AOL, Prodigy, and even dial-up abusers who have multiple IPs.

- Generate custom reports detailing who has clicked on your site from PPCs two, three, four, five, or even six times, allowing you to identify potential PPC abusers quickly.

- Download your reports or email them with comments.

Figure 21.1 shows how repeat visitors are identified by their IP addresses through WhosClickingWho?.

Figure 21.1
WhosClickingWho? is a pay-per-click auditing service designed to track and report click fraud activity.

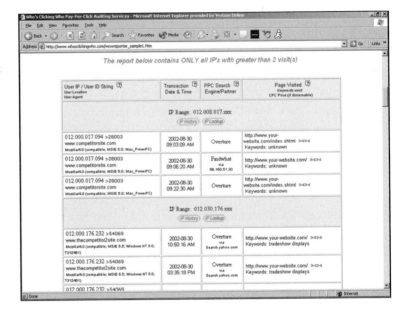

Deter Fraudulent Clickers

My favorite part of the WhosClickingWho? service is the Click-Minder pop-up that appears on the computer screens of people who have clicked five times from a PPC search engine (see Figure 21.2). Although you can customize the warning message, start with polite copy. Many web users aren't aware that sponsored listings are ads. The click-happy consumers are simply checking out your business a few times before buying. Instead of bookmarking your site, a percentage of them return to search engines to find your site again. They don't know you're charged for their clicks on your ad listings.

Figure 21.2
Sample pop-up message offered by WhosClickingWho? to deter repeat click activity from the same person.

A "cease and desist" letter works wonders. Much to her surprise, Stricchiola discovered that her law firm's prominent click fraud perpetrator was another law firm, one that specialized in Internet fraud issues! A letter sent from her law firm to the competing law firm abruptly halted the fraudulent click behavior.

Deborah Wilcox, a partner with the Cleveland office of the law firm of Baker & Hostetler LLP, offers the following as a sample cease and desist letter to address click fraud. Wilcox recommends sending the letter by email and certified mail; ask for a return receipt for the mailing. Replace "Company" with the name of your company, and customize the other elements of this letter with your information.

Deborah A. Wilcox
Phone Number: (216) 861-7864
Email: dwilcox@bakerlaw.com

Date

Name
Address

Re: Click Fraud

Dear Sir or Madam:

Baker & Hostetler LLP represents Company with respect to, among other matters, the enforcement of its intellectual property and e-commerce rights.

Company has purchased various online advertising. We have recent evidence that your company is clicking on our client's ad listings with the sole purpose and unlawful intent to increase ad costs to our client and harm its business. This is "click fraud" and constitutes trespass, tortious interference with contract, fraud, and unfair competition, among other things.

In addition to seeking injunctive relief prohibiting your further infringing actions, our client may seek damages and its attorney's fees. On behalf of our client, we therefore demand that your company immediately and permanently cease any and all fraudulent clicking on our client's ad listings. You must immediately provide written confirmation of your compliance with our demands.

---

continues

continued

> We trust that you will understand the concern of our client about the violation of its rights and that you will fully cooperate with us. You must direct your written response to my attention by no later than [date] to avoid the necessity of our taking further legal action.
>
> This letter is written without prejudice to any of our client's legal rights or remedies, all of which are hereby expressly reserved.
>
> Very truly yours,
> Deborah A. Wilcox
>
> Cc: Search Engines

When it comes to the search engines deterring fraudulent activity, Google wins a "gold star" thanks to its ad-serving technology. A top position on Google's AdWords is granted to an advertiser with a high maximum bid amount *plus* strong click-through popularity. The malicious clicking incentive is lessened because you'll jump above your perpetrators' listings if they click your ads. Point for you, minus one for them.

Reporting Evidence to Resolve Past and Future Incidents

You've possibly noticed in your search engine click-through reports that you've received a number of clicks without being charged for them. When the search engines identify fraudulent or invalid clicks, they remove these from their billing system. However, it's then your responsibility to catch any fraudulent activity they miss. With the proper documentation, you can seek a credit or refund.

With evidence of click fraud in hand, Stricchiola negotiated a credit from both FindWhat.com and Overture. Auditing tools, such as WhosClickingWho?, may make it easier for advertisers to collect and present click fraud cases to the search engines.

Per-click costs will continue to rise for paid listings. You can squeeze every penny out of your profit margins by paying attention to problem areas like click fraud and then resolving any discrepancies directly with the search engines.

Chapter 22

Trademark Infringement

Competitors might click paid listings in an attempt to waste advertisers' marketing budgets. To add insult to injury, the brazen ones attack advertisers head on by bidding on advertisers' trademarks and redirecting traffic to their own web sites.

Trademark owners who are not already aware of this problem are going to soon get a shocking wake-up call. Many still aren't marketing their branded terms on the search engines, let alone policing the space for their competitors. While trademark owners sleep their customers are being wooed away.

Savvy trademark owners have and continue to engage in the trademark protection battle. With an increasing number of complaints from big brand owners, and growing media exposure, the search engines are responding. They're posting trademark (and copyright) infringement complaint procedures on their web sites, and most remove competitors' ad listings of trademark owners who report infringement.

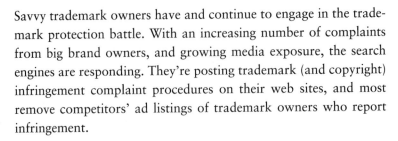

Important

Because I'm not a lawyer, I can't offer legal counsel on trademark issues. Please use this chapter as an educational resource, and then consult an attorney if you need legal representation or advice.

Are search engines proactively monitoring the trademark space? Not generally. For one thing, they can't. It's not their job or within their resources to research and manage company trademarks. And think about it. Search engines make more money with a greater number of advertisers who increase their bids. If trademark owners don't complain, search engines and competitors quietly profit.

Trademark owners, it's time to make some noise.

Filing a Complaint with the Search Engines

Important

A trademark is a word, phrase, symbol, or design that identifies the owner of the marked item. Company, product/ service, or domain names that are registered with the U.S. Patent and Trademark Office will likely be easier to protect.

Run a query in search engines for your trademarks; include your company name, products, services, and slogans. Start on Google and Overture because their paid listing results appear on numerous search engines and content sites. Are competitors bidding on your trademarks?

Before you fire off an email to your search engine media representative, you'll need proper documentation to resolve this in a timely manner. Even with the required data identified in the following bullets, it took me anywhere from a few days to over a month to receive responses from the various search engines' legal departments regarding my first client case. Regardless of how many times you report trademark infringement, be sure to include the following information in each letter to prevent any hold-ups.

- Your contact information: your name, company name, mailing address, phone number, email address

- The trademark(s) on which the claim is based, plus the registration information, if available

- Description of the trademark violation (i.e., the bidding on the trademark, or the use of a trademark in the ad listing copy)

- The company name(s) and URL(s) associated with the trademark violation

- Status of your communication with the trademark violator(s)

If you don't have your trademark registration number handy, you can get it from the U.S. Patent and Trademark Office (http://www.uspto.gov), assuming you filed for a federal registration in the United States. You can use the "SEARCH Trademarks" feature to access your registration information as well as preliminarily check the availability of a trademark you'd like to file (Figure 22.1).

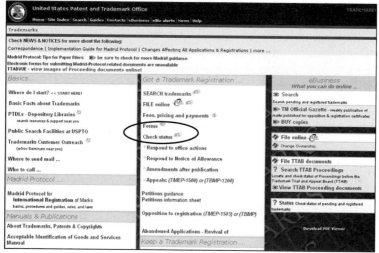

Figure 22.1
To retrieve your federal trademark registration number or check trademark availability, go to the "SEARCH Trademarks" area of the U.S. Patent and Trademark Office web site.

This is the core set of requirements search engines expect in a trademark infringement complaint. Because each search engine varies, review their policies to tailor your complaint accordingly (visit the book site at www.searchenginesales.com for the URLs). For example, you'll probably be required to include the legal statement they've created that asserts you're the trademark owner. You'll also need to find out if the complaint letter needs to be mailed, faxed, or emailed to their legal department.

Important

Agencies or lawyers representing trademark owners need to include their contact information plus a statement noting that they're authorized to represent the trademark owners.

Cease and Desist Letter

You'll notice that a handful of search engines request that you contact trademark violators before you ask them to evaluate the matter. Of course, the search engines prefer that you handle this situation directly with your competitors and not involve them at all. And this is often possible.

A cease and desist letter from your attorney gets the immediate attention of your trademark violators. The letter identifies the issue and the solution needed to avoid the next step—a lawsuit.

Deborah Wilcox, a partner with the Cleveland office of the law firm of Baker & Hostetler LLP, says that 90% of this type of trademark infringement is stopped by having legal counsel send a cease and desist letter and follow up as necessary to resolve the matter short of litigation. Wilcox has offered the following letter as an example (its impact is arguably stronger when it comes from a law firm if you don't have a well-recognized company name with an internal legal department). Just as with a click fraud cease and desist letter described in Chapter 21, "Watch Out for Click Fraud," send a trademark violation letter by email and certified mail. Remember to customize this sample letter with your information.

> Deborah A. Wilcox
> Phone Number: (216) 861-7864
> Email: dwilcox@bakerlaw.com
>
> Date
>
> Name
> Address
>
> Re: Violation of Trademark Rights
>
> Dear Sir or Madam:
>
> Baker & Hostetler LLP represents Company with respect to, among other matters, the enforcement of its intellectual property rights. [Describe Company's Trademark rights.]

It has recently come to our attention that your company is using the Company Trademark to lead consumers to your competing web site. Your purchase of the Company Trademark as a search engine keyword is a blatant attempt to "spam" the search engine into bringing up your web site when the Company Trademark is entered in a search. You have no rights in the Company Trademark and such unauthorized activity constitutes trademark infringement, false advertising, dilution of the Company mark, and unfair competition, among other things, in violation of the federal Lanham Act and state laws.

In addition to seeking injunctive relief prohibiting your further infringing actions pursuant to 15 U.S.C. § 1117, our client may seek damages and attorney's fees. The amount of these monetary damages may be tripled by the court pursuant to the same section of the United States Code.

On behalf of our client, we therefore demand that your company immediately and permanently cease any and all uses of the Company Trademark, including the purchase of the Trademark as a keyword. We also demand that you immediately notify all search engines to cease linking the web sites operated by your company with the Company Trademark. We likewise will send copies of this letter to the relevant search engines. You must immediately provide written confirmation of your compliance with our demands.

We trust that you will understand the concern of our client about the infringement of its rights and that you will fully cooperate with us. You must direct your written response to my attention by no later than [date] to avoid the necessity of our taking further legal action.

This letter is written without prejudice to any of our client's legal rights or remedies, all of which are hereby expressly reserved.

Very truly yours,
Deborah A. Wilcox

cc: Search Engines

Attach a copy of this letter to your complaint for the search engines; they may respond faster seeing that you're attempting to resolve the matter directly with the trademark violators. Sending a cease and desist letter directly to the violators hopefully prevents future occurrences, whereas going to a search engine first might address current listings but new ad listings posted by the same violator could slip by in the future.

It's a good idea to send a strong message to search engines and competitors by issuing trademark infringement complaints and legal letters in one directive. Periodic monitoring of the search engine space is strongly recommended. Companies such as Cyveillance and NameProtect can help monitor the use of your trademarks across the web if this is a tedious, ongoing battle for your company.

Legal Loopholes

Much to the dismay of brand holders, there's no current law making it illegal to bid on another company's trademark terms on the search engines. That's why advertisers must waste precious time filing infringement complaints, cease and desist letters, and occasionally even lawsuits against violators or search engines. New laws are needed to prevent future occurrences where reasonably possible.

In February 2002, Mark Nutritionals filed lawsuits for alleged trademark infringement and unfair competition against AltaVista, FindWhat.com, Kanoodle, and Overture (*Mark Nutritionals v. Overture*). The company's weight loss product "Body Solutions" web site listing was positioned below competing sites that also bid on this keyword phrase. Unfortunately, later that year Mark Nutritionals filed for bankruptcy, and the Federal Trade Commission ordered an injunction against the company's product for false claims. Where does that leave trademark owners? In legal limbo. At least there's limited relief through the aforementioned actions.

The reason I wrote "limited relief" is because there are a few other ways in which competitors can bid on your trademarks.

The Keyword-Matching Technology

One problem is the keyword-matching technology of search engines like Google, and now Overture. Both allow you to appear in results for only your specified keyword phrase ("exact match"), phrases with words that are added before or after your exact phrase ("phrase match"), or phrases with words that are added anywhere within your exact phrase, even often reversing the order of your words ("broad match"). Here's an example:

Exact Match: used cars

Phrase Match: used cars, Ford used cars, used cars Ford

Broad Match: used cars, cars used, Ford used cars, new and used cars, new and used Ford cars

Google advertisers' campaigns are set to broad match as the default (see Figure 22.2). Overture's are set to exact match, which they call *standard match*. Whether an advertiser on either search engine chooses their matching option or it's served by default, phrase and broad match could include trademark terms.

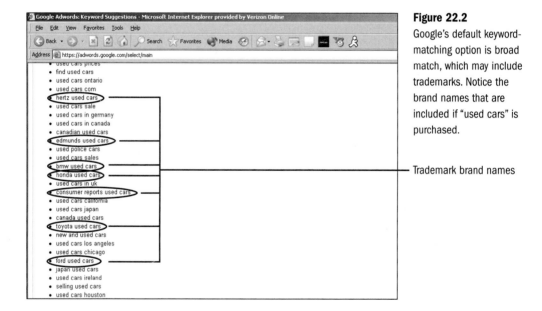

Figure 22.2
Google's default keyword-matching option is broad match, which may include trademarks. Notice the brand names that are included if "used cars" is purchased.

Trademark brand names

In this example, you see how broad match pairs trademark and generic terms automatically. The keyword tools of the search engines using this technology even suggest that these phrases be purchased. This could spell legal trouble for search engines. But for now, it gives them the ability to sidestep an infringement complaint for phrases that include both kinds of keywords. "The technology does it, we can't do anything" is essentially their answer. This is the response I received from Google for one of my client accounts. Interestingly enough, in July 2003 eBay moved to block Google advertisers from using phrases that included their trademark: eBay selling, eBay power seller, and eBay management software, for instance. Did eBay have the clout to elicit a different response from Google?

Although the details of eBay's letter weren't disclosed, when I wrote this section I couldn't find ad listings on Google AdWords for these phrases that openly promoted an eBay-related product or service. If Google removed these ads when they claimed they couldn't for my client, then this demonstrates another problem that I've experienced and had confirmed by a couple of trademark owners: *inconsistent policy enforcement*. This isn't just a Google problem; others are guilty of playing favorites as well.

Comparison Pages

Although only a couple of search engines offer a broad-match feature, inconsistent policy enforcement is often exercised in the treatment of comparison pages.

If a competitor bids on your trademarks and builds a landing page that compares your products or services to his, occasionally search engines let this slide under their editorial guidelines. A comparison page used in this way appears to be legal under current comparative advertising laws, so long as the comparison is truthful and the use of the competitor's trademarks does not create a likelihood of consumer confusion as to source or sponsorship. So according to Overture, comparison advertising (as well as fair use and free speech) support their policy, which allows bidding on competitors' trademarks if comparison landing pages are used:

Important

The URLs of the major search engines that address trademark and copyright infringement can be found at www.searchenginesales.com

> "In cases in which an advertiser has bid on a term that may be the trademark of another, Overture allows the bids only if the advertiser presents content on its web site that (a) refers to the trademark or its owner or related product in a permissible nominative manner without creating a likelihood of consumer confusion (for example, comparative advertising, sale of a product bearing the trademark, or commentary about the trademark owner or its product) or (b) uses the term in a generic or merely descriptive manner. In addition, the advertiser's listing should disclose the nature of the relevant content."

Based on Overture's language, in your trademark infringement complaint letter to Overture you would need to point out how your competitor's landing page is *not editorially relevant* to the keyword or ad listing. If you prove how this ad listing *is an attempt to confuse consumers*, Overture (and other search engines) will carefully consider this compelling argument. As attorney Deborah Wilcox points out, that's because the definition of infringement is "use of another's mark that is likely to cause confusion, or to cause mistake, or to deceive as to source, affiliation, sponsorship, origin, or approval. If the comparative advertisement is untruthful or crosses the line by causing a likelihood of consumer confusion, the fair use defense might not apply." Work that definition to your protection.

International Law Leading the Way

In August 2003, handbag maker Louis Vuitton filed a lawsuit against Google and its French subsidiary for trademark infringement. The filing itself isn't monumental news. The fact that in an October 2003 court ruling in France, French firms Viaticum and Luteciel sued Google's French subsidiary for trademark violation and collectively won $89,000 in damages *is* significant. A legal precedent, even if overseas, has been set.

New laws addressing trademark infringement in the search engine advertising market are coming. However, it will take time to determine how comparative advertising, First Amendment (free speech) rights, fair use provisions, false advertising, dilution of company marks, unfair competition, the Lanham Act, and other laws or issues apply to the use of trademarks on the Internet. In the meantime, brand owners can enlist the help of a legal team and the search engines in protecting their trademarks from competitors.

The money big brands are losing to competitors is nothing compared to what many are losing to their own affiliates. If managed properly, an affiliate program is truly performance-based marketing at its finest. But without supervision, trademark owners are simply nurturing an expanding ring of profit killers.

Chapter 23

Managing Your Affiliates

Search engines are generally sympathetic and fairly responsive to trademark infringement complaints against competitors. Want them to remove your affiliates' listings? Forget it. Affiliates are an extension of your sales force; therefore, it's your job to manage how they promote your business.

An affiliate program is potentially a merchant's best friend. Unlike a majority of online marketing programs, this one is solely performance based. Companies, or individuals, sign up as your affiliates to market your products or services and receive a commission fee on each sale. Their sales are monitored by a unique tracking URL you provide to them. No sales? No commission fee. Affiliates might promote your products via a testimonial in their own e-zine, through banner ads on their web site, or by purchasing keywords on search engines.

Unfortunately, a number of affiliates use various types of spam to lure in customers at little cost. Merchants who are connected to these unethical affiliates are at risk for having their web sites shut down by Internet service providers (ISPs). Additionally, merchants could experience brand dilution and damage customer loyalty. But that's a chapter unto itself. With regard to search engine advertising, big brands must create an affiliate strategy because many are losing massive profits to their marketing partners. How much is "massive?" I'm talking about the loss of millions of dollars.

The Amazing Success of Trademarks

Conversion rates for trademark terms are high—extremely high. In the direct response television (DRTV) advertising industry, for example, an estimated 20% of consumers who watch the commercial for an "As Seen on TV" product and type the product name into a search engine click the web site listing that appears. Then, an estimated 20% of those web site visitors buy the product. That's impressive! REVShare Corporation, a cost-per-acquisition TV media broker, achieved these conversion rates for their top DRTV product clients whose web sites REVShare managed. These conversion rates held true *until* the DRTV advertisers' wholesalers or affiliates jumped into the search engine space.

Almost instantly, per-click fees spiked and conversion rates plummeted for As Seen on TV product advertisers, once their affiliates or wholesalers bought the trademark terms. DRTV product manufacturers who sold products to only a handful of wholesalers suddenly found themselves competing with dozens of each wholesaler's affiliates who then promoted a lower retail price. Sales and valuable customer contact data were redirected to wholesalers instead of the parent company (see Figure 23.1 as an example of competition from wholesalers and affiliates).

In an effort to educate the direct response industry, REVShare has created an information site on search engine marketing channel conflict at http://www.DRTVReport.com, and offers a free Cannibalization Calculator so DRTV product advertisers can see how much money they could be making on the search engines (Figure 23.2).

Figure 23.1

In a search for their product line "aerobed" on Google, the Aero Products International web site (www.thinkaero.com) doesn't appear as a top sponsored link or organic ranking for their own brand. The positions instead are occupied by third-party companies that are promoting the products at discounted prices.

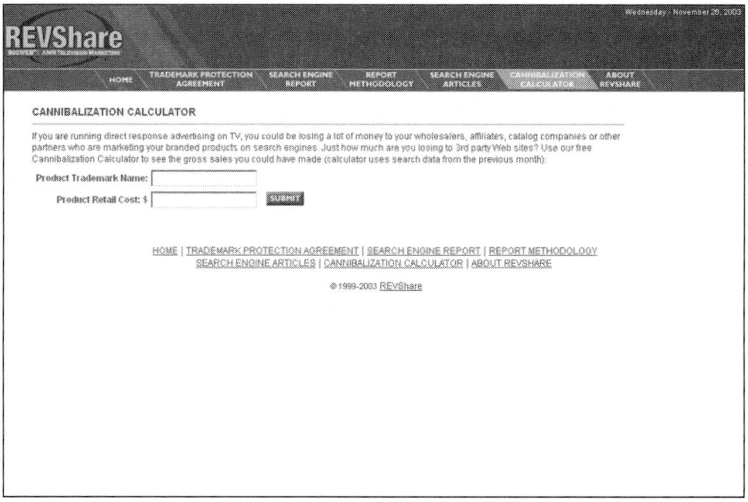

Figure 23.2

On REVShare's DRTVReport site, TV product advertisers can type in their product name and retail price to see their estimated gross sales from search engines.

The conversion rates for each industry and every company vary. Nevertheless, REVShare's research reveals that same-channel competition by companies' own marketing partners caused significant profit loss. And the heat is getting turned up. More online and offline partners are discovering the lucrative results of trademark advertising. Marketing partners aren't just affiliates; they include:

- Wholesalers
- Retail stores
- Catalog companies
- Marketing agencies
- Comparison shopping engines
- Online auction sites

Unfortunately, once you sell a product, you can't control how it's marketed. This means wholesalers or retail stores can buy your trademarks and then redirect sales to their sites by promoting discounted prices. You have greater control over your marketing partners such as affiliates or shopping engines because these companies market your product but refer the sales to you. Normally, this group uses tracking URLs that you control and can subsequently deactivate.

You can ask your marketing partners to sign a trademark protection agreement, which restricts them from marketing your trademarks on the search engines. Be prepared for kicking, screaming, and whining. Your current partners who are already generating huge amounts of cash will be most unhappy. Unfortunately, if wholesalers or retail outlets won't stop this practice, then your only option is to discontinue selling products to them. But this distribution channel could represent too much revenue for you to pull their accounts over this issue.

Most affiliate or other marketing partnerships, on the other hand, can be terminated immediately for noncompliance with your search engine marketing policies. This assumes you want to enforce one. Do you? As I mentioned, affiliates are an incredibly powerful sales force. They certainly fueled the growth of Amazon.com, whose network consists of more than 900,000 affiliates, and is growing.

Regardless of where your search engine marketing or affiliate programs are currently, it's time to design a strategy that best supports your business.

Create an Affiliate Strategy

Determine which affiliate search engine marketing policy fits your company's needs. You have three options:

1. Allow affiliates to manage all search engine marketing.

2. Prohibit affiliates from any search engine marketing.

3. Restrict the marketing of branded keywords, but allow generic keywords.

A couple of factors will influence your decision:

- Your competitive landscape

- Your affiliate commission payout

The greater the competition for your keywords, the more time-consuming it is to manage advertising and optimization campaigns. Hard-working affiliates achieve premium positions for the merchants they represent. Why not let them run all of your search engine marketing and pay them strictly for sales? If they're aggressively marketing generic terms and not exclusively scoring easy sales from your trademarks, they're certainly earning their keep. You can supervise their overall efforts but let them focus on the daily tasks. One less marketing program you need to worry about.

On the other hand, if you prefer to execute your own search engine campaigns, you will be competing with your affiliates for organic rankings and having to continually pay more for Pay-For-Placement (PFP) positions. Perhaps the competitive arena for generic terms is a challenge you welcome. Furthermore, if you're the brand holder, there should be no competition for your trademark terms. Are the profit margins on search engine sales worth running campaigns in-house, or outsourcing to one search engine firm for a fixed fee? A well-branded company might use an affiliate program to reach new customers via e-zines or content sponsorships, but prohibit the search engine space they can dominate fairly easily and cost-effectively.

Is there a happy medium? Kind of. Merchants can prohibit affiliates from marketing their branded keywords, while allowing them to fight for coveted generic terms. Competent affiliates will rise to this challenge and deliver new customers...if the price is right. Don't expect affiliates to rush into your program if you remove the easy trademark sale from their grasp and then only offer a 10% commission fee on a $10 item. More importantly, be prepared to constantly monitor your branded keywords to terminate relationships with affiliates who violate your trademark protection agreement. All in all, if you're willing to police and market your trademarks, then this option might be a profitable deal for both you and your affiliates.

Trademark Protection Agreement

If you decide to prohibit your affiliates or other marketing partners from marketing your trademarks in the search engines, review the following excerpt from REVShare's Trademark Protection Agreement as an example. This agreement addresses optimization and advertising tactics. Revise the specific restrictions herein based on your company's business strategy. An attorney can help you customize an agreement plus add the necessary provisions.

TRADEMARK PROTECTION AGREEMENT

This Trademark Protection Agreement ("Agreement") is entered into as of _____ 2004, by and between _____ ("Buyer") and _____ ("Seller"), with reference to the following facts:

RECITALS:

A.   Seller advertises, markets, sells, and distributes products (the "Products") under the trademarks (the "Marks") described on Exhibit A hereto directly and through authorized distributors to the public.

B.   Seller has entered into an agreement with Buyer, which authorizes and licenses Buyer to advertise, market, sell, and distribute the Products and to exploit the Marks in connection thereto.

C.   Buyer acknowledges that (a) the Marks are owned by and constitute value property of Seller; (b) that Seller has the right to restrict, limit, and otherwise control use of the Marks; and (c) that certain abuses exist in the market which undermine the integrity and value of the Marks and the Products, specifically in the use of the Marks or some variation thereof in connection with the marketing of the Products through the Internet without Seller's consent which have the effect of directing traffic from Seller's business.

Now, therefore, in consideration of the above recitals and other valuable consideration, the receipt and sufficiency of which is hereby acknowledged, the parties agree as follows:

1. **Restrictions.** Buyer shall not advertise, offer, market, distribute, or sell the Products or exploit the Marks in any manner on or through Internet Search Engines or Directories except as expressly provided in this Agreement. Buyer agrees to the restrictions, prohibitions, and terms set forth in this Agreement are reasonable and not to engage in any of the prohibited tactics set forth below.

2. **Prohibitions Apply to All Sales of Products.** Buyer agrees that all of the restrictions set forth in this Agreement apply to all sales of Products or the use of the Marks in connection with the advertising, promotion, or marketing of the Products, including Products previously purchased from Seller, whether delivered or not, and all Products which Buyer is permitted to sell under any currently existing agreement(s), or in the future under this, or any other agreement with Seller. With respect to Buyer's existing rights to sell Products, Buyer agrees to fully comply with all of the terms of this Agreement forthwith, but in no event later than thirty (30) days following the execution hereof. (TIME IS OF THE ESSENCE!)

3. **Restriction on Use of Trademarks in Meta Tags.** Buyer may not include any Product trademark, or similar variations, in the meta tags of any web site HTML code. This includes the meta title, meta keywords, or meta description.

4. **Restrictions on Use of Trademark Terms on Search Engines.** Buyer may not purchase, obtain, or use any keywords from Search Engines so as to redirect traffic to the Buyer's web Site or any other web Site whereby the Marks, or any variation thereof, is used as either a keyword and/or included in any ad copy, titles, or descriptions. Use of any keywords, including but not limited to, the singular/plural form of the Marks, misspellings, or other variations of the Marks, or any variation thereof, is prohibited. Buyer may not purchase the Marks, or any variations thereof, for use in text links, banner ads, pop-up ads, or any other type of ad that could be associated with a keyword campaign.

5. **Domain Names.** Buyer may not purchase or obtain additional domain names (URLs) with any part of the Marks, or any variations thereof, included as part of the address. Ownership of all domain names Buyer currently uses, including the Marks, and all variations

thereof, must be transferred to Seller's name through a domain name registrar company of Seller's choice. Said transfer must occur no later than thirty (30) days following the execution of this Agreement.

6. **Outsourcing to Online Marketing Firms.** Buyer may not outsource Search Engine marketing efforts to any third party. If Buyer is currently marketing Seller's trademarked Products on Search Engines, Buyer is required to immediately implement and abide by all of the terms, restrictions, and prohibitions set forth in this Agreement. Buyer shall contact each Search Engine, or third party agency, and revise all ad copy, titles, descriptions, keywords, URL's, text links, and advertisements, including all meta tags (meta titles, meta keywords, and meta descriptions), to comply with the terms of this Agreement. Buyer agrees to be in full compliance with all of the terms of this Agreement not later than thirty (30) days following the execution of this Agreement. (TIME IS OF THE ESSENCE!)

7. **Partial List of Prohibited Search Engines.** The restrictions and prohibitions set forth in this Agreement apply to all Search Engines used by U.S. residents, including but not limited to:

a. About.com	l. iWon
b. AllTheWeb/FAST	m. InfoSpace
c. AltaVista	n. LookSmart
d. Ah-ha	o. Lycos
e. America Online	p. MSN
f. Ask Jeeves	q. Netscape
g. Excite	r. Open Directory
h. FindWhat	s. Overture
i. Google	t. Teoma
j. HotBot	u. Yahoo!
k. Kanoodle	

As a partial exception to the foregoing, provided Buyer is permitted to sell the Products outside the United States, Buyer is exempt from complying with the restrictions and terms of this Agreement with respect only to Search Engines that do not primarily target a U.S. audience, e.g., "uk.yahoo.com".

8. **Permitted Resale.** Provided Buyer has the right to resell the Products to any entity or party other than the ultimate end user customer ("Reseller") under written Agreement with Seller, Buyer may only sell Product to any such Reseller provided that prior to any such sale or distribution, or agreement of sale or distribution, Buyer shall obtain

the execution by such Reseller of this Agreement, which shall be incorporated in and become a part of all agreements for such sale or distribution by and between Buyer and Reseller. Additionally, included in the Agreement shall be the express statement and agreement by Buyer and Reseller that Seller is a third party beneficiary of the Agreement.

9.   **Notices.** All notices, demands, approvals, and other communications provided for herein shall be in writing and be delivered to counsel for the parties by postage prepaid U.S. mail, facsimile (only if confirmed within 24 hours by mail or by overnight air courier), overnight air courier, personal delivery, or registered or certified U.S. mail with return receipt requested to the appropriate party at its address as follows:

Buyer:

_____

_____

_____

(Fax) _____

Seller:

_____

_____

_____

(Fax) _____

If You're an Affiliate: The Gold Rush Is On!

The joy of being an affiliate is that you're not responsible for developing, packaging, and shipping products or services. Hurray! Your focus is limited to marketing. Yes, you're taking a risk promoting merchants without upfront payment, but the financial payoffs can be huge. I've known affiliates who've generated well over $10,000 per month in commission fees, a significant amount of which came from search engine marketing.

All of the techniques in this book are critical to helping you dramatically increase your affiliate commissions. Are you wondering why I'm so harsh on affiliates in this chapter? Well, I believe trademark owners with strong brand name recognition have already invested millions of dollars igniting market demand for their products. They have the right to protect their profits resulting from trademark marketing.

Not to my surprise, I heard that an apparel manufacturer cut their entire affiliate program because several affiliates continually violated their agreement by marketing trademarks on search engines. Now, no affiliates enjoy working for this company. Further cutbacks are coming. However, programs won't disappear altogether as long as affiliates are team players (I also participate in affiliate programs, as a merchant and affiliate). I'd like these true marketing partners to continue earning generous income for their efforts.

Branded companies may start hand selecting a few affiliates who will be well rewarded for their supportive, not combative, efforts. There will also be new opportunities to work with small and medium-sized businesses investing only in performance-driven marketing. This is the perfect time for honorable affiliates to take center stage. In an effort to support the existence of affiliate programs while growing your personal income as an affiliate, here are a few recommendations:

- **Build a good content site:** Don't build doorway pages for the search engines. These pages would simply link to merchants without providing any valuable content to web users. This clutters up search engines with junk pages, infuriates consumers who won't buy anything from them anyway, and will quickly end your program with the merchants who spot these. Design an attractive, information-rich site for consumers, then integrate merchant links into your site. Your conversion rates will be better and merchants will be happy. Market generic, yet related, keywords in the search engines to drive relevant traffic to your site.

- **Support the brand, don't duplicate it:** Web pages with content that has been duplicated from merchant sites are red flags to algorithm-based search engines. It's regarded as a spam tactic. The duplicate or original pages can be deleted from the search engines' databases. Use original content to prevent this from occurring and to show merchants you're not just mimicking their sites.

- **Maximize income by joining multiple programs:** Find merchants that offer affiliate programs related to the same theme. Build a content site around a topic that promotes an array of merchants; for example, a health spa site could link to merchants who sell health or spa magazines, bath products, massage gifts, home hot tubs, resort vacations, and travel books. Start with the keyword research tools in Chapter 3, "Choosing Keywords for Maximum Performance," to find popular topics. You have unlimited options! Consider joining an affiliate network such as Be Free or Commission Junction to instantly connect with a wide range of merchants. Also check out http://www.associateprograms.com for a directory that lists thousands of merchants with affiliate programs.

- **Contact companies without an affiliate program:** Once you've established a track record of selling products for merchants, hand select the companies you'd like to promote, even if they don't appear to offer an affiliate program. There's a chance they're working with a small number of top producers. Sell your experience, and you might join their elite sales force. There'll be more of the commission pie to split among fewer affiliates.

- **Be first, or be better:** Savvy affiliates are all over the search engines. The ones who get there first to promote a product or service score a high percentage of the sales. Once others join in, consumers are given a greater selection of online stores. Therefore, if you enter the game late, differentiate the offer proposed in your ad listings from those of other affiliates.

Affiliates and merchants can turn to the Internet Affiliate Marketing Association (http://www.iafma.org) as a resource on revenue-sharing ethics and standards. This organization is promoting self-regulation as a way to expand this industry while benefiting affiliates, merchants, and consumers. By working together, merchants reach new customers on a pay-per-performance basis, while their affiliates earn potentially unlimited income for their efforts.

Part VI

Conclusion

Maximizing your return on investment
from paid listings requires attention to the business tactics, both inside and outside of your company, that can quietly drain your profits.

Study your campaign reports for unusual dips in conversion rates, which could indicate click fraud behavior. Document these patterns for potential discussions with search engine representatives as well as the perpetrators.

Also monitor ad listings that appear for your trademarks. If you're a victim of trademark infringement by competitors, consult an attorney and follow the search engines' complaint procedures. Additionally, develop a business strategy that addresses your affiliates' roles in your search engine marketing plan that will maximize revenue for both parties.

Search engine advertising is a cost-effective method of generating web site traffic, leads, and sales. Leverage existing tools to help you manage effective campaigns. Then invest creativity and routine evaluation to continually improve your profitability.

Visit www.searchenginesales.com for updates and links to many of the resources mentioned in this book.

◾ **Resources**

The following resources are ones that I refer to when managing clients' campaigns, teaching seminars, or writing articles on search engine marketing. A majority of the search engines and industry vendors mentioned in this book also offer free newsletters.

There are additional resources that don't specifically focus on search engines, but can help you with your campaigns. I've included resources on related topics such as web usability, online copywriting, and customer acquisition/retention.

Web Sites

ClickZ

http://www.clickz.com

Experienced marketers can read and subscribe to a variety of marketing columns: email, advertising technology, customer relationships, search engine marketing, and a few others. Each column contains articles from a variety of industry experts.

CNET News.com

http://news.com.com

This news site covers technology and its impact on enterprise computing, e-business, finance, communications, personal technology, and entertainment. Search engines' significant business deals and financial reviews can be found here.

eMarketer

http://www.emarketer.com

If you appreciate Internet statistics, then subscribe to eMarketer's free daily newsletter. Information specific to search engines is frequently included among the research studies, charts, and interviews.

Entrepreneur Media Inc.

http://www.entrepreneur.com

Business owners and managers looking to grow their companies can turn to *Entrepreneur* magazine and the extensive resources on the Entrepreneur.com site. Both cover Internet marketing topics, including search engines, periodically.

GrokDotCom

http://www.futurenowinc.com

This free, twice-monthly newsletter focuses on improving conversion rates from subscriptions, sweepstake entries, phone inquires, and other sales efforts. The tips can usually be applied to search engine advertising.

High Rankings Advisor

http://www.highrankings.com

This is a free, weekly e-zine published by Jill Whalen that focuses on search engine optimization. Each issue contains her detailed responses to readers' specific questions about their own optimization efforts.

Internet Retailer

http://www.internetretailer.com

Companies engaged in multi-channel marketing can read related articles from the current *Internet Retailer* magazine issue, plus search industry news updates from the web site. The online Buyer's Guide helps companies connect with vendors within specific retailing categories.

Pay Per Click Analyst

http://www.payperclickanalyst.com

Pay Per Click Analyst offers the latest news about the top pay-per-click search engines. This site contains product and service reviews plus articles from a variety of paid listing experts. You can receive monthly industry updates via email.

Microsoft's bCentral

http://www.bcentral.com

Small business web solutions, news, and how-to advice can be found on this site. There's a free weekly newsletter with tips, product information, and special offers for running a business.

Nielsen/NetRatings

http://www.netratings.com

NetRatings provides Internet and digital media measurement and analysis, offering technology-driven Internet information solutions to companies. Check their press releases for new research, and their Top Rankings for updates in the Internet industry.

Search Engine Watch

http://www.searchenginewatch.com

Undoubtedly, this is the educational hub for all levels of search engine marketers, both optimizers and advertisers. Created by Danny Sullivan, this site offers an extensive library of articles and several newsletter subscription options. It's a comprehensive collection of search engine news, tips, business deals, guest articles, and other industry updates.

SearchDay

http://www.searchenginewatch.com/searchday

SearchDay is a free daily newsletter from Search Engine Watch featuring web search news, reviews, tools, tips, and search engine headlines from across the web. For those marketers who can't wait to receive the Search Engine Watch newsletters, subscribe to this publication, too.

Webmaster World

http://www.webmasterworld.com

This is an online forum for advanced web professionals to share experiences, ask questions, post tips, and discuss industry rumors. There are separate forums for the worlds of search engines, marketing, and Webmasters.

Books

Don't Make Me Think: A Common Sense Approach to Web Usability
Steve Krug
New Riders Publishing
http://www.stevekrug.com

By revealing how people use web sites, Steve Krug explains how companies can reduce online visitor confusion and frustration. This book describes simple approaches and exercises for team members responsible for their company's web site: designers, programmers, project managers, and marketers. Readers are also taught how to run their own usability tests and evaluate the results. Krug's examples are entertaining as well as educational.

The Invisible Web: Uncovering Information Sources the Search Engines Can't See

Chris Sherman and Gary Price

CyberAge Books

http://www.invisible-web.net

Most search engines can't crawl valuable information that is stored inside a web site's database. This means that free content offered by libraries, universities, organizations, and businesses may never be found by online searchers. This book describes how to find and use hidden web resources. The authors include informational resources by particular categories to assist a wide range of searchers.

Net Words: Creating High-Impact Online Copy

Nick Usborne

McGraw-Hill

http://www.nickusborne.com

This book explains how to write effective copy for web sites, online newsletters, and email campaigns. Nick Usborne discusses why online copywriting is different from standard copywriting, and how marketers can use words to set them apart from their competitors, increase online sales, and improve customer service as well as customer loyalty. In addition to providing examples of good and bad copy to demonstrate his points, he offers a 10-step starting point for overwhelmed copywriters.

Search Engine Visibility

Shari Thurow

New Riders Publishing

http://www.searchenginesbook.com

This book is a guide for creating a web site that appeals to the site's visitors, and helps users find the site in the search engines and directories. It teaches designers, programmers, and online marketers the foundation of a successful search engine optimization strategy. Shari Thurow's book can be used as a roadmap for developing new web sites, or it can be used as a reference guide for web sites that already exist, but with modification can boost their visibility in search engines.

The Unusually Useful Web Book
June Cohen
New Riders Publishing
www.newriders.com

As a reference guide and a do-it-yourself workbook, June Cohen's book outlines the principles of successful web sites. She covers the site development process in four phases: planning, designing, building, and maintaining. Additionally, project leaders can turn to Cohen's "Managing a Web Project and Team" chapter to keep their team on schedule and within budget. Lessons from nearly 50 web veterans are included in this book, providing valuable ideas to large and small companies.

Glossary

above the fold

The portion of a web page that consumers can see on their computer monitor without scrolling.

ad copy

The words used in an ad listing.

ad listing

Includes the title and description that are displayed for the keyword(s) purchased.

ad profit

The amount of money generated from an advertising campaign after the advertising costs are subtracted from the resulting revenue.

ad sponsor

The advertiser who has purchased an ad. In search engine advertising, it's the advertiser who has purchased a listing in the search results.

affiliate

An individual or company that markets a merchant's products or services and is paid only a sales commission fee.

affiliate program

A program that allows other companies, or individuals, to market a company's products or services for a commission fee per item sold.

algorithm

A mathematical formula used by search engines to determine a web site page's ranking in the search results.

alternative text

Text placed inside the image source tag of HTML code. This text is shown when images can't be displayed. It's often viewable by rolling the computer mouse over an image. Also known as *alt tag*.

ASP

Abbreviation for Application Service Provider. An ASP leases their product or service generally for a less-expensive recurring fee than selling it at a one-time cost.

bid gap

The amount of money between two advertisers who are competing for top positions on Pay-For-Placement search engine programs.

bid management tool

Third-party companies that manage advertisers' ad listings on pay-per-click (PPC) search engines. PPC can include Pay-For-Placement and Trusted Feed programs.

brand

The collective consumer concept of a company. Elements such as names, slogans, logos, and URLs are part of brand identification, but they are not "the brand."

brand awareness

The expansion of a company's brand in the marketplace.

branded keyword

Names, trademarks, slogans, and URLs are considered branded keywords if they are associated with a particular company.

browser

The software used to view web pages. A browser is generally provided by an Internet service provider (ISP) to their clients who sign up for Internet access. Microsoft Internet Explorer (IE) and America Online (AOL) are common browsers. Both Microsoft and America Online are ISPs that offer their own browsers to their Internet access clients.

call to action

An activity requested of a consumer. Examples include buying a product, completing a survey, or subscribing to an online newsletter.

campaign components

Campaign components specific to search engine advertising include keywords, listing titles, listing descriptions, and landing pages.

cease and desist letter

This type of letter requests that a company stop the activity mentioned in the letter to prevent legal action.

click fraud

The act of purposely clicking ad listings without intending to buy from the advertiser.

click-through

The action of a consumer viewing a link and clicking on it to visit a web page.

click-through rate (CTR)

The percentage of clicks on a link out of the number of times it was displayed.

comparison page

A web page that compares two competing products or services. In search engine advertising, it's used as a landing page to enable a company to buy or bid on the trademark keyword of a competitor.

comparison shopping engine

A search engine that enables consumers to find, compare, and buy products within one shopping environment.

contextual advertising

A program in which advertisers' paid listings appear on web sites containing content relevant to the listings. A keyword search isn't required for the listings to appear. Approved web site publishers insert code into their web pages to allow the search engine's technology to determine which ads to serve, based on content relevancy.

conversion

A completed call to action. Typically, a lead or sale.

conversion rate

The number of site visits (click-throughs) that result in a sale or other call to action.

CPA

Abbreviation for cost-per-acquisition, also referred to as *cost-per-action*. It's the fee paid to an advertising vendor for each lead or sale generated (or another call to action).

CPC

Abbreviation for cost-per-click. It's the fee paid to an advertising vendor for each click on a link that sends consumers to an advertiser's web page.

CPM

Abbreviation for cost per thousand. It's the fee paid to an advertising vendor for every 1,000 times an ad is displayed (*impressions*).

daypart targeting

The ability to run an ad campaign by specific times of the day.

deferred conversion

Occurs when a customer visits a site and doesn't buy at that time, but returns later to make a purchase.

destination page

See *landing page*.

direct path

The link provided along with an ad that sends consumers to a relevant web page within the site.

directory

A collection of web sites that are organized by topic category and are included in a specific category (or categories) after being reviewed by a human editor. Examples include www.dmoz.org, Business.com, and Yahoo!.

domain name

The name that identifies a web site (e.g., company.com). Also referred to as a *URL*.

doorway page

Generally refers to a web page that is created for the sole purpose of achieving high organic listings in the search engines. This page offers little or no value to consumers, and therefore is considered spam. Also known as *gateway, attraction, envelope, directory information pages (DIPs)*, and *hallway pages*.

dynamic page

A page that is generated by a database. This type of page typically contains characters such as ?, =, %, + in the URL. Also called a *dynamic URL*.

e-commerce solution

A program that includes a variety of tools for managing an online store. These solutions may be purchased or leased, and may include other features such as web site hosting or e-marketing tools.

Fixed Placement

In relationship to search engine advertising, a specific ad listing position can be purchased for a keyword, for a set fee. Fee structures are based on a negotiated CPM, CPC, or CPA rate. Fixed Placement is a paid placement program.

generic keyword

A general keyword that describes a company and their products or services. A generic term applies to more than one company; it is not exclusive to one company's brand.

HTML

Abbreviation for Hypertext Markup Language. It's a text formatting system for developing web pages, including text, images, animation, and page layout design elements.

hypertext link

Text in a web site that takes consumers to another web page when clicked. It's a word or set of words inside an anchor tag. Also called *hyperlink*.

inbound link

A hypertext link that points from an external web site to the marketer's site.

ISP

Abbreviation for Internet service provider. An ISP provides Internet access and often web site hosting services.

JavaScript

A scripting language developed by Netscape and used by web designers to create interactive web pages.

keyword

A word or set of words (phrase) that consumers type into a search engine to find relevant web pages.

keyword density

The number of times a keyword or phrase appears within a web page divided by the total number of words on that page.

landing page

The web page a consumer arrives at once a link is clicked. Also referred to as a *destination page, destination URL,* or *target URL.*

link popularity

An important element search engines consider in ranking web pages in the natural search results area. It incorporates both the number and quality of relevant inbound links to a company's web site.

meta tag

Information within the HTML code of a web page that provides information about the page. Common meta tags are the title, keyword, and description tags.

natural listing

The listing of a web page in the search results produced by algorithm-based (or crawler-based) search engines. Paid inclusion programs can help web sites appear for a natural listing, also called an *organic listing*.

organic listing

See *natural listing*.

page copy

The visible words on a web site page.

paid inclusion

A program where marketers pay a fee to submit a web page to a search engine or directory's database. Top rankings are not guaranteed. Submit URL and Trusted Feed are paid inclusion programs.

paid listings

A web page listing that's a result of paying a paid inclusion or paid placement fee. This phrase generally refers to the search engines that offer pay-per-click pricing.

paid placement

A program where marketers pay a fee for a specified position, for a specified keyword. Fixed Placement and Pay-For-Placement are paid placement programs.

PFP

Abbreviation for Pay-For-Placement. Advertisers determine their own per-click fee based on what they are willing to pay for each keyword. Ad listing positions are typically awarded to the highest bidder. Pay-For-Placement is a paid placement program.

PPC

Abbreviation for pay-per-click. In search engine advertising, it's a pricing model that typically refers to Pay-For-Placement (paid placement) and often includes Trusted Feed (paid inclusion) programs.

query

A request for specific information from a database.

ranking

The position of a web page in the search results. "Ranking" generally refers to organic or natural listings achieved through site optimization plus inclusion efforts; specific positions can't be determined as with paid placement.

regional targeting

The ability to market to a specific geographic region by country, state, city, or ZIP code.

ROI

Abbreviation for return on investment. ROI focuses on the profitability of an advertising campaign. An ROI formula by percentage is: ad profit divided by the ad cost times 100.

search distribution partners

Search engine and content sites that display the natural or sponsored search results (or both) of a search engine.

search engine

Software that searches a database of web site pages to find and then return page matches to the keyword query.

search engine advertising

The process of paying money to search engines or directories to enhance a site's position; paid placement and paid inclusion programs are included.

search engine marketing

Includes both advertising and optimization efforts to achieve high visibility of a web site for relevant keywords. Also referred to as *search engine positioning* or *search engine promotion*.

SEO

Abbreviation for search engine optimization. The process of designing the web site to attract search engine spiders and improve a site's ranking for relevant keywords within a search engine's database. This process includes search engine and directory submission, which can require an inclusion fee.

spam

Any activity designed to trick the search engines into giving a site a higher ranking. Common tactics include hiding keywords as white text on a white page background, submitting a web page to a search engine daily, and building doorway pages.

spider

Software used by a search engine to find and retrieve web pages to include in its database (also called *index*).

static web page

An HTML page, as opposed to a dynamic page, which is generated by a database. Also known as a *flat page*.

submission

The process of registering a web site, usually a specific page (URL) within the site, with search engines and directories.

Submit URL

This program, offered by some search engines, allows a company to submit their web site pages to be included in the search engine's database and pay a per-page fee. Submit URL is a paid inclusion program in which web page review is guaranteed, but rankings are not. Sometimes referred to as *Add URL, Direct Submit,* or *Site Submit.*

target market

The intended audience of a marketer's efforts. Demographic and psychograpic information are typically included in assessing a target market.

tracking URL

A specific URL with code that identifies information about the resulting clicks. The referring search engine, keyword, ad listing, and landing page can be included in a tracking URL. Tracking URLs can be created in-house or automatically generated by an ROI tracking solution. These URLs must be given to the search engines in order for resulting clicks and/or sales to be tracked.

trademark

Words, phrases, symbols, or designs that identify an owner of the items marked.

trademark infringement

This occurs when a company uses the trademark of another company, which may result in confusion or deception of consumers.

Trusted Feed

This program is offered by some search engines, and allows a company to submit their web site pages to be included in the search engine's database, and pay a per-click fee. Trusted Feed is a paid inclusion program in which web page review is guaranteed, but rankings are not. Also referred to as *Direct*, *Data*, or *XML Feed*.

URL

Abbreviation for uniform (or universal) resource locator. A URL is the location of a file on the Internet, which may include a web document, a web page, or an image file.

USP

Abbreviation for unique selling point. A differentiating factor that makes a company and their product or service better than a competitor's.

vertical market search engine

A search engine that focuses on a particular topic. A niche content site that contains a site-based search function could be considered a vertical market search engine.

visibility

The position of a web page in search engines or directories.

visit

Each time a consumer arrives at a web page. A unique visitor can account for multiple visits to a web page. Unless click fraud is present, search engines that charge for click-throughs include all visits, not just clicks from unique visitors.

web analytics

A tool that collects data on web site user behavior.

web ring

A collection of sites that exclusively link from one to another, without linking to any sites outside of this group. A web ring is considered spam.

word stemming

The ability for a search engine to include the root of words.

Chapter 1, excerpted from

Search Engine
Visibility

Shari Thurow

0-7357-1256-5

Search Engine Visibility is about designing,
writing, and creating a web site primarily for your site's
visitors, and helping them find what they are searching for via the major search engines, directories, and
industry-related sites. This book teaches developers,
designers, programmers, and online marketers what
pitfalls to avoid from the beginning so they can provide
their clients with more effective site designs.

part 1

Before You Build

Introduction

Search engine optimization (SEO) is a powerful online marketing strategy. When done correctly, millions of online searchers can find your site among millions of top search results.

Many web site owners consider SEO as an afterthought—after a site has already been built. If you are about to create a new site or redesign an existing one, understanding how the search engines work, how your target audience searches, and how best to design your site from the onset can save your company thousands of dollars in time and expenses.

Why Search Engine Visibility Is Important

Search engines and directories are the main way Internet users discover web sites. Various resources confirm this statement, and the percentages generally range from 42 percent of Internet users to 86 percent.

A January 2001 study conducted by NPD Group, a research organization specializing in consumer purchasing and behavior, tested the impact of search engine listings and banner advertisements across a variety of web sites to determine which marketing medium was more effective. In each situation, search engine listings came out on top. They found consumers are five times more likely to purchase your products or services after finding a web site through a search engine rather than through a banner advertisement.

Jupiter Media Metrix, another Internet research firm, determined that 28 percent of consumers go to a search engine and type the product name as a search query when they are looking for a product to purchase online.

Search engines and directories average over 300 million searches per day. Therefore, regardless of whether the percentage value is as low as 28 percent or as high as 86 percent, millions of searches are performed every day. Properly preparing your web site for search engine visibility increases the probability that web searchers will visit your site.

Additionally, think about your own personal experience. Where do you go to search for information about a company or a product on the web? Where do you go to find a site whose web address you do not know or cannot remember? In these cases, you probably use a search engine or directory to find the information.

Web searchers are not random visitors. When searchers enter a series of words into a search engine query, they are actively searching out a specific product or service. Thus, the traffic your site receives from the search engines is already targeted. In other words, web searchers are self-qualified prospects for your business.

Of course, search engines are not the only way in which people discover web sites. People may find a web address in offline sources such as print, television, or radio. They might click a link to a web site in an email document or a banner advertisement. Word of mouth (referral marketing) also is a popular method of bringing visitors to sites. In addition, people locate sites by clicking links from one site to another, commonly known as surfing the web.

Because millions of people use the search engines and directories to discover web sites, maximizing your site's search engine visibility can be a powerful and cost-effective part of an online marketing plan. A properly performed search engine marketing campaign can provide a tremendous, long-term return on investment (ROI).

Understanding the Search Services

Search services can generally be categorized into two types of sources: directories and search engines. Many people confuse the two terms, often referring to Yahoo! as a search engine. (Yahoo! is a directory.)

The reason for the confusion is understandable. People see a Search button on a web site and assume that when they click the button, they are using a search engine. Both Yahoo! and Google have search boxes, as shown in Figure 1.1.

The search services use two main sources to obtain their listings. The first type of search service is called a directory, and a directory uses human editors to manually place web sites or web pages into specific categories. A directory is commonly called a "human-based" search engine.

The other type of search service is called a search engine, and a search engine uses special software robots, called *spiders* or *crawlers*, to retrieve information from web pages. This type of search service is called a "spider-based" or "crawler-based" search engine.

Figure 1.1

Although both Yahoo! and Google enable people to search, the information they provide in their search results is different.

Many search services are a hybrid of a search engine and a directory. A hybrid search service usually gets most of its listings from one source; thus, hybrid search services are classified according to the main source used. If a hybrid search service gets its primary results from a directory and its secondary results from a search engine, the search service is generally classified as a directory.

MSN Search is classified as a directory. Its primary results come from the LookSmart database, and its secondary (fall-through) results currently come from Inktomi, a search engine.

Most search engine marketers label both search engines and directories as "search engines," even though search engines and directories have unique characteristics. Web site owners need to understand the differences between the two terms because the strategies for getting listed well in search engines are quite different from the strategies for getting listed well in directories.

Search Engines

What differentiates a search engine from a directory is that the directory databases consist of sites that have been added by human editors. Search engine databases are compiled through the use of special software robots, called spiders, to retrieve information from web pages.

Search engines perform three basic tasks:

- Search engine *spiders* find and fetch web pages, a process called crawling or spidering, and build lists of words and phrases found on each web page.

- Search engines keep an index (or database) of the words and phrases they find on each web page they are able to crawl. The part of the search engine that places the web pages into the database is called an *indexer*.

- Search engines then enable end users to search for keywords and keyword phrases found in their indices. Search engines try to match the words typed in a search query with the web page that is most likely to have the information for which end users are searching. This part of the search engine is called the *query processor*.

How do search engines begin finding web pages? The usual starting points are lists of heavily used servers from major Internet service providers (ISPs), such as America Online, and the most frequently visited web sites, such as Yahoo!, the Open Directory, LookSmart, and other major directories. Search engine spiders will begin crawling these popular sites, indexing the words on every single page of a site and following every link found within a site. This is one of the major reasons it is important for a web site to be listed in the major directories.

What Is a URL?

A uniform resource locator (URL) is an address referring to the location of a file on the Internet. In terms of search engine marketing, it is the address of an individual web page element or web document on the Internet.

Many people believe a URL is the same as a domain name or home page, but this is not so. Every web document and web graphic image on a web site has a URL. The syntax of a URL consists of three elements:

- The protocol, or the communication language, that the URL uses.
- The domain name, or the exclusive name, that identifies a web site.
- The pathname of the file to be retrieved, usually related to the pathname of a file on the server. The file can contain any type of data, but only certain files, usually an HTML document or a graphic image, are interpreted directly by most browsers.

For example, the URL for a home page is commonly written as follows: http://www.companyname.com/index.html.

- The http:// is the protocol (Hypertext Transfer Protocol).
- The www.companyname.com is the domain name.
- The index.html is the pathname. In this example, it is a Hypertext Markup Language (HTML) document named index.

The URL for an About Us page for a company called TranquiliTeas is commonly written as this: http://www.tranquiliteasorganic.com/about.html.

- The http:// is the protocol.
- The www.tranquiliteasorganic.com is the domain name.
- The about.html is the path name.

As a general rule of thumb, whenever you see Add URL or Submit URL to the search engines, remember that every web page has a unique URL.

Figure 1.2 outlines the search engine crawling process for a single web page.

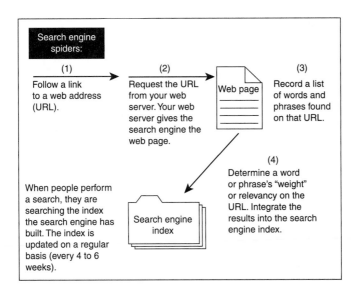

Figure 1.2
How search engines crawl
web pages.

Because search engine spiders are continuously crawling the web, their indices are constantly receiving new and updated data. Search engines regularly update their indices about every four to six weeks.

The search engine index contains full-text indices of web pages. Thus, when you perform a search query on a search engine, you are actually searching this full-text index of retrieved web pages, not the web itself.

To determine the most relevant URL for a search query, most search engines take the text information on a web page and assign a "weight" to the individual words and phrases on that page. An engine might give more "weight" to the number of times that a word appears on a page. An engine might assign more "weight" to words that appear in the title tags, meta tags, and subheadings. An engine might assign more "weight" to words that appear at the top of a document. This assigning of "weight" to a set of words on a web page is part of a search engine's algorithm, which is a mathematical formula that determines how web pages are ranked. Every search engine has a different formula for assigning "weight" to the words and phrases in its index.

Search engine algorithms are kept highly confidential and change almost every day. Thus, no search engine optimization expert can ever claim to know an exact search engine algorithm at a specified point in time.

Submission Forms Versus Natural Spidering

Search engines also add web pages through submission forms, generally labeled as Add URL or Submit URL. The Submit URL form enables web site owners to notify the search engines of a web page's existence and its URL.

Unfortunately, unethical search engine marketers (called spammers) created automated submission tools that bombard submission forms with thousands of URLs. These URLs point to poorly written and constructed web pages that are of no use to a web site owner's target audience.

Most of the major search engines state that 95 percent of submissions made through the Add URL form are considered spam.

Because of the overwhelming spam problems, submitting a web page through an Add URL form does not guarantee that the search engines will accept your web page. Therefore, it is generally more beneficial for web pages to be discovered by a search engine spider during its normal crawling process.

However, a search engine optimization expert can do the following:

- Ensure that targeted words and phrases are placed in a strategic manner on the web pages, no matter what the current algorithms are.

- Ensure that spiders are able to access the web pages.

The key to understanding search engine optimization is comprehending Figure 1.2. Why? Because search engine spiders are always going to index text on web pages, and they are always going to find web pages by crawling links from web page to web page, from web site to web site. *Anything that interferes with the process outlined in Figure 1.2 will negatively impact a site's search engine positions.* If a search engine spider is not able to access your web pages, those pages will not rank well. If a search engine can access your web pages but cannot find your targeted keyword phrases on those web pages, those pages also will not rank well.

Pay-for-Inclusion Models

With a pay-for-inclusion model, a search engine includes pages from a web site in its index in exchange for payment. The pay-for-inclusion model is beneficial to search engine marketers and web site owners because (a) they know their web pages will not be dropped from a search engine index, and (b) any new information added to their web pages will be reflected in the search engines very quickly.

This type of program guarantees that your submitted web pages will not be dropped from the search engine index for a specified period of time, generally six months or a year. To keep your guaranteed inclusion in the search engine's index, you must renew your payment.

Submitting web pages in a pay-for-inclusion program does *not* guarantee that the pages will appear in top positions. Thus, it is best that pages submitted through pay-for-inclusion programs be optimized.

Search engine marketers find pay-for-inclusion programs save them considerable time and expense because a web page cannot rank if it is not included in the search engine index. Furthermore, pay-for-inclusion programs enable dynamic web pages to be included in the search engine index without marketers having to implement costly workarounds.

Pay-for-Placement Models

In contrast to pay-for-inclusion models, a pay-for-placement search engine guarantees top positions in exchange for payment. With pay-for-placement search engines, participants bid against each other to obtain top positions for specified keywords or keyword phrases. Typically, the higher the bid, the higher the web page ranks.

Participants are charged every time a person clicks through from the search results to their web sites. This is why pay-for-placement search engines are also referred to as "pay-per-click" search engines. Participants pay each time a person clicks a link to their web site from that search engine.

Many pay-for-placement search engines have excellent distribution networks, and the top two or three positions are often displayed in other search engines and directories. Paid placement advertisements are generally marked on partnered sites as "Featured Listings," "Sponsored Links," and so on.

If no one bids on a particular search term, the free, fall-through results are generally displayed from a search engine partner. For example, currently, the fall-through results for Overture.com come from Inktomi.

Participating in pay-for-placement programs can get expensive. Part 3, "Page Design Workarounds," discusses how to best utilize this type of service.

Search Engine Optimization Strategies

Search engine optimization is the process of designing, writing, coding (in HTML), programming, and scripting your entire web site so that there is a good chance that your web pages will appear at the top of search engine queries for your selected keywords. Optimization is a means of helping your potential customers find your web site.

To get the best overall, long-term search engine visibility, the following components must be present on a web page:

- Text component
- Link component
- Popularity component

All the major search engines (Google, FAST Search, MSN Search, and other Inktomi-based engines) use these components as part of their search engine algorithm. Figure 1.3 illustrates the "ideal" web page that is designed and written for the search engines.

Very few web pages can attain the "ideal" match for all search engine algorithms. In reality, most web pages have different combinations of these components, as illustrated in Figure 1.4.

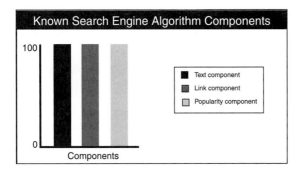

Figure 1.3
Known search engine
algorithm components:
text, link, and popularity.

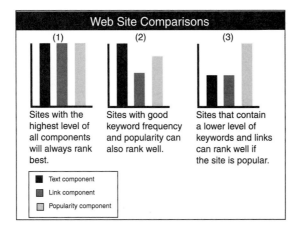

Figure 1.4
Web site comparisons.

Sites perform well in the search engines overall when they have (a) all the components on their web pages and (b) optimal levels of all the components.

Text Component—An Overview

Because the search engines build lists of words and phrases on URLs, it naturally follows that to do well on the search engines, you must place these words on your web pages in the strategic HTML tags.

The most important part of the text component of a search engine algorithm is keyword selection. For your target audience to find your site on the search engines, your pages must contain keyword phrases that match the phrases your target audience is typing into search queries.

After you have determined the best keyword phrases to use on your web pages, you will need to place them within your HTML tags. Different search engines do not place emphasis on the same HTML tags. For example, Inktomi places some emphasis on meta tags; Google ignores meta tags. Thus, to do well on all the search engines, it is best to place keywords in all the HTML tags possible, without keyword stuffing. Then, no matter what the search engine algorithm is, you know that your keywords are optimally placed.

Keywords need to be placed in the following places:

- Title tags

- Visible body text

- Meta tags

- Graphic images (the alternative text)

The title tag and the visible body text are the two most important places to insert keywords because all the search engines index and place significant "weight" on this text.

Keywords in Your Domain Name

Many search engine marketers believe that placing keywords in your domain name and your filenames affect search engine positioning. Some search engine marketers believe that this strategy gives a significant boost whereas others believe that the boost is miniscule.

One reason people believe the position boost is significant is that the words or phrases matching the words you typed in a query are highlighted when you view the search results. This occurrence is called *search-term highlighting* or *term highlighting*.

Search engines and directories might use term highlighting for usability purposes. The process is done dynamically using a highlighting application. This application simply takes your query words and highlights them in the search results for quick reference. Term highlighting merely indicates that query terms were passed through the application. In other words, in search results, just because a word is highlighted in your domain name does not necessarily mean that the domain name received significant boost in search results.

Many other factors determine whether a site will rank, and the three components (text, link, and popularity) have more impact on search engine visibility than using a keyword in a domain name.

Link Component—An Overview

The strategy of placing keyword-rich text in your web pages is useless if the search engine spiders have no way of finding that text. Therefore, the way your pages are linked to each other, and the way your web site is linked to other web sites, does impact your search engine visibility.

Even though search engine spiders are powerful data-gathering programs, HTML coding or scripting can prevent a spider from crawling your pages. Examples of site navigation schemes that can be problematic include the following:

- **Poor HTML coding on all navigation schemes:** Browsers (Netscape and Explorer) can display web pages with sloppy HTML coding; search engine spiders are not as forgiving as browsers.

- **Image maps:** Many search engines do not follow the links inside image maps.

- **Frames:** Google, Inktomi, and Lycos follow links on a framed site, but the manner in which pages display in search results are not ideal.

- **JavaScript:** The major search engines do not follow many of the links, including mouseovers/rollovers, arrays, and navigation menus, embedded inside JavaScript.

- **Dynamic or database-driven web pages:** Pages that are generated through scripts or databases, or that have a ?, &, $, =, +, or % in the URL, pose problems for search engine spiders. URLs with CGI-BIN in them can also be problematic.

- **Flash:** Currently, only Google and FAST Search can follow the links embedded in Flash documents. The others cannot.

Therefore, when designing web pages, be sure to include a navigation scheme so that the spiders have the means to record the words on your web pages. Usually that means having two forms of navigation on a web site: one that pleases your target audience visually and one that the search engines spiders can follow.

For example, let's say that a web site's main navigation scheme is a series of drop-down menus coded with JavaScript. Figure 1.5 illustrates why sites without JavaScript in the navigation scheme consistently rank higher than sites with JavaScript in the navigation scheme.

In Figure 1.5, note that both the text and the popularity component levels are equal in all three graphs. A web page that uses JavaScript in its navigation can rank well in the search engines as long as a spider-friendly navigation scheme (text links, for example) is also present on the web page. However, because some scripts can "trap" a spider (prevent it from indexing the text on a web page), the link component level is lower than a site that does not use JavaScript in its navigation.

Figure 1.5

How a site with JavaScript and a site without JavaScript might rank in the search engines.

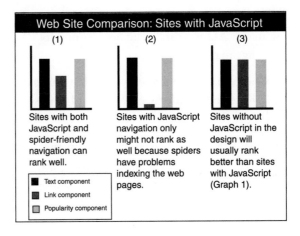

Web Site Comparison: Sites with JavaScript

(1)   (2)   (3)

Sites with both JavaScript and spider-friendly navigation can rank well.

Sites with JavaScript navigation only might not rank as well because spiders have problems indexing the web pages.

Sites without JavaScript in the design will usually rank better than sites with JavaScript (Graph 1).

■ Text component
■ Link component
□ Popularity component

Popularity Component—An Overview

The popularity component of a search engine algorithm consists of two subcomponents:

- Link popularity

- Click-through or click popularity

Attaining an optimal popularity component is not as simple as obtaining as many links as possible to a web site. The quality of the sites linking to your site holds more weight than the quantity of sites linking to your site. Because Yahoo! is one of the most frequently visited sites on the web, a link from Yahoo! to your web site carries far more weight than a link from a smaller, less visited site.

To develop effective link popularity to a site, the site should be listed in the most frequently visited directories. Yahoo!, LookSmart, and the Open Directory are examples of the most frequently visited directories.

More importantly, it can boost your search engine position if a directory that is associated with a search engine lists your site. For example, a site that is listed in LookSmart can be given higher visibility in an MSN Search.

Obtaining links from other sites is not enough to maintain optimal popularity. The major search engines and directories are measuring how often end users are clicking the links to your site and how long they are staying on your site and reading your web pages. They are also measuring how often end users return to your site. All these measurements constitute a site's click-through popularity.

The search engines and directories measure both link popularity (quality and quantity of links) and click-through popularity to determine the overall popularity component of a web site.

If a single page (web page 1) ranks well in the search engines and end users click the links to that web page and browse your site, web page 1's popularity level increases. If a different web page (web page 2) ranks well in the search engines for a different keyword phrase, web page 2's popularity level increases. The total page popularity of your site will increase your overall site's online visibility.

One of the reasons that a site's home page is more important than any other web page is that search engines assign a higher "weight" to it. In all likelihood, the home page is going to be the URL listed in the major directories, and the home page has more links to it from within the web site.

Figure 1.6 illustrates the popularity within a web site. Pages with more links pointing to them have a higher page popularity "weight."

Figure 1.7 illustrates the popularity of a web site, which search engines do not always measure. Search engines measure a web page's popularity; a web site owner also will measure a web site's popularity. Sites with more links pointing to them have a higher site popularity "weight."

Figure 1.6

How search engines measure web page popularity.

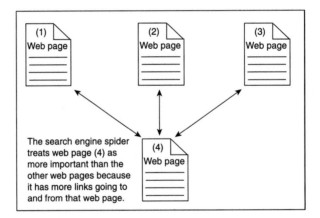

Figure 1.7

How web site owners measure web site popularity.

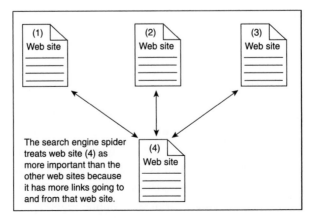

Because popularity consists of multiple subcomponents and these subcomponents are always fluctuating, the popularity measurement is dynamic and cumulative.

All search engine marketing campaigns should begin with the popularity component because all the major search engines measure popularity as a part of their search engine algorithms. The quickest way to achieve an initial, effective popularity component is to have your site listed in what search engines consider reliable sources: the major directories.

Web Directories

Web directories use human editors to create their listings. When you submit a site to be included in a directory, a human editor reviews your site and determines whether to include your site in the directory. Human editors also discover sites on their own through searching or browsing the web.

Every web page (or site) listed in a directory is categorized in some way. The categories are typically hierarchical in nature, branching off into different subcategories. Web searchers can find sites in directories by browsing categories, or they can perform a keyword search for information.

For example, a company that sells "organic teas" might be listed in this Yahoo! category: Business and Economy > Shopping and Services > Food and Drinks > Drinks > Tea > Organic. If we place the categories in a vertical hierarchy, it will look like this:

Business and Economy

        Shopping and Services

                Food and Drinks

                    Drinks

                        Tea

                            Organic

In this example, the top-level category is called "Business and Economy." A subcategory of "Business and Economy" is "Shopping and Services." A subcategory of "Shopping and Services" is "Food and Drinks," and so on. As we move down (drill down) the category structure, notice that the categories get more and more specific.

A company that sells "herbal teas" might be listed in a different Yahoo! category: Business and Economy > Shopping and Services > Food and Drinks > Drinks > Tea > Herbal. Let's place this categorization into a vertical hierarchy:

Business and Economy

    Shopping and Services

        Food and Drinks

            Drinks

                Tea

                    Herbal

A company that sells a variety of teas might be listed in a less specific Yahoo! category:

Business and Economy

    Shopping and Services

        Food and Drinks

            Drinks

                Tea

Directories are structured in this manner to make it easier for their end users to find sites.

Web pages are generally displayed in directories with a Title and a Description. The Title and Description originate either from the directory editors themselves (upon reviewing a site) or are adapted from site owner submissions. It is important to remember that directories do *not* necessarily use the HTML <title> tag or the description contained in your site's meta tags.

Because most web directories tend to be small, directory results are often supplemented with additional results from a search engine partner. These supplemental results are commonly referred to as *fall-through* results. In fact, many people mistakenly believe that their sites are listed in a directory when they are actually appearing in the fall-through results from a search engine.

Directories usually differentiate their directory listings and their fall-through listings. If you perform a keyword search on a directory, the directory results might appear under a heading titled "Web Site Matches" or "Reviewed Web Sites." Sites that are listed in directories generally have a category displayed with them.

When a web directory fails to return any results, fall-through results from a search engine partner are usually presented as the primary results. Fall-through results are typically labeled "Web Page Matches" or something similar.

One way you can tell if your site is listed in a directory is to perform a keyword search on your company name or URL. If you see a "Powered by Google" or "Powered by Inktomi" near your web site listing, then in all likelihood, your site is listed in the search engine fall-through results but not in the directory (see Figure 1.8).

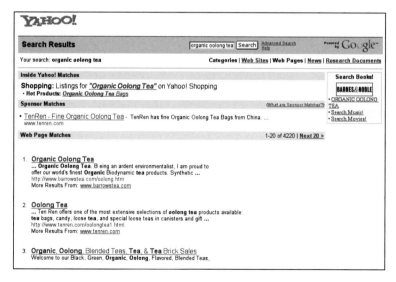

Figure 1.8

The "Powered by Google" image indicates that the search results came from the search engine (Google), not the directory (Yahoo!).

Finally, directories tend to list web sites, not individual web pages. A web site is a collection of web pages that generally focuses on a specific topic. In other words, a web page is part of a web site. A directory is most likely to list only your domain name (www.companyname.com), not individual web pages. In contrast, search engines can list all individual web pages from an entire web site, not just a single home page.

If a particular web page (or set of pages) within a site contains unique, valuable information about a particular topic, that page can be listed in a different directory category. Glossaries and how-to tips are examples of content-rich sections of web sites that can receive additional directory listings.

Paid Submission Programs

A search engine or directory that uses a paid submission program charges a submission fee to process a request to be included in its index. Payment of the submission fee guarantees that your site will be reviewed within a specified period of time (generally 48 hours to 1 week).

If you want to have individual, content-rich web pages included in separate categories, in most cases, you must pay an additional submission fee for another review. Some directories accept content-rich pages without payment, but directory editors generally do not review these pages as quickly as the paid submissions.

The main advantage of paid submission is speed. You know your web site is being reviewed quickly, and, if the editors find your site acceptable, your site is added to the directory database quickly. Furthermore, after your site is added to the directory, the listing gives your site a significant popularity boost in the search engines. Yahoo! is an example of a directory that has a paid submission program.

How Directories Rank Web Sites

When you perform a keyword search in a directory, the search results are displayed in order of importance. Top directory listings are based on the following criteria:

- The directory category

- The web site's title

- The web site's description

If the words you searched for appear in a category name, the category name appears at the top of a directory's search results. For example, if we searched for "organic teas" on Yahoo!, the category that has both the word "organic" and the word "tea" appears at the top of the search results, as shown in Figure 1.9.

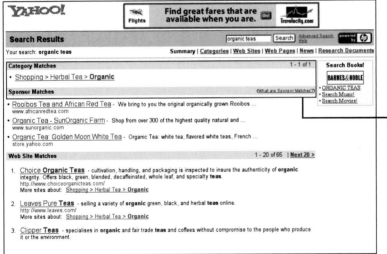

Figure 1.9

Matching category results for the phrase "organic teas" in Yahoo!.

Category match for "organic teas"

Immediately following the category listings are Sponsor Matches, which are pay-for-placement advertisements (see Figure 1.10).

If the words in a search query do not appear in a directory category, the search results display sites that use these words in their titles and descriptions. Figure 1.11 shows the results of scrolling down the Yahoo! search results page.

Sites that have keywords in the category name, title (company name), and description are displayed at the top of the page. Figure 1.11 shows how Yahoo! provides access to some web sites that it feels are directly relevant to the search.

Sites that have keywords in their company name and description appear next, and sites that have only keywords in the description appear after that.

Figure 1.10
Paid advertisements appearing in Yahoo! search results.

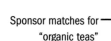
Sponsor matches for "organic teas"

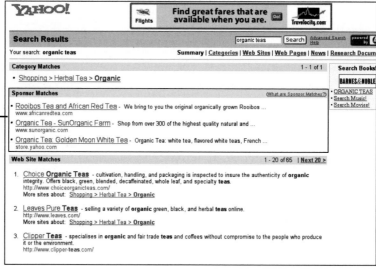

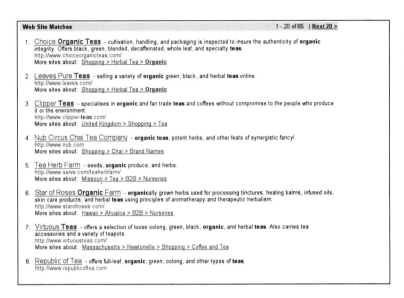

Figure 1.11
Web site matches in
Yahoo! for the phrase
"organic teas."

How Directory Editors Evaluate Web Sites

Directory editors look at a submitted web site to determine (a) whether unique, quality content is present on the web site, and (b) how this content is presented. Great content is the most important element of any web site, and that content needs to be delivered to your target audience in the most effective way possible. Figure 1.12 illustrates the directory submission process.

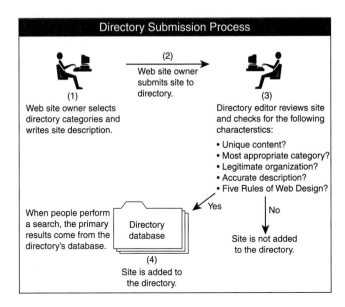

Figure 1.12
How directory editors
evaluate a web site.

Directory editors are looking for particular characteristics before including a site in the directory. We discuss those characteristics next.

Unique Content

Directory editors do not want to place sites with identical information in the same category. Thus, before you submit your site to a directory, check out the other sites in your targeted category. Make sure your site contains unique information so that it will add value to that directory category.

You can point out any unique content to the directory editor using your description or the extra comments field in the submission form.

Most Appropriate Category

To select the most appropriate category (or categories) for your web site, type your selected keywords in the directory search box and study the results. If multiple categories appear, view many of the web sites listed under each category. Your site's actual content must accurately reflect the category or categories you wish to be listed under and be similar to the other sites listed in those categories.

You will probably be listed under the same categories your competitors are listed under, though it is important to understand that from directory editors' perspectives, your site belongs in a category that they deem appropriate, not necessarily in a category in which you believe your target audience is searching.

Legitimate Organization/Company

Editors want legitimate organizations and companies listed in their commercial categories. They do not want a small start-up company that will not be around next year. This would result in a dead link to a URL in the directory.

Having a virtual domain (www.companyname.com) is an indication that you are a legitimate organization or business. Having all your contact information (address, telephone number, fax number, and email address) readily available on your site is also an indication that you have a legitimate business. Directory editors will perform a WHOIS lookup (www.netsol.com/cgi-bin/whois/whois) to see if the information there matches the information you gave in your submission form.

If you have an e-commerce site, directory editors are looking for such items as secure credit card processing (for sites that accept credit cards), a return policy or a money-back guarantee (for sites the sell products), and a physical address, not a post office box.

Accurate Description

The description you submit to directory editors should accurately reflect the content of your web site. Directory editors should be able to determine that the description is accurate just by viewing your home page.

For example, if you sell organic tea on your web site and you specialize in three types of tea (oolong, black, and green teas), those three specialties should be obvious to an editor just by his viewing your home page. Furthermore, if directory editors navigate your site or perform a search on a site search engine, they should easily be able to find the pages that show the items used in your description.

Part 2 of this book, "How to Build Better Web Pages," details how to write effective directory descriptions.

Web Design Rules

The Five Basic Rules of Web Design state that a web site should be:

- Easy to read

- Easy to navigate

- Easy to find

- Consistent in layout and design

- Quick to download

In other words, your web site should be easy to use by your target audience.

To have a web site that your target audience will like and that directory editors will approve, these rules all need to be followed. The most successful web sites generally follow these guidelines. What is good about these rules is that they apply not only to directory submissions but also your target audience.

It is important to understand that these rules are interrelated. For example, let's say that your home page has a #1 position in one of the major search engines for your targeted keywords, and people click the link to your site. If your site designer has placed a considerable amount of graphic images, animations, and scripting on your home page, causing it to download slowly, most people will not wait for that page to download. Thus, a perfectly good #1 search engine position can be wasted if your site designer does not consider download time, or any of the other design rules.

Rule #1: Easy to Read

I hear people say all the time, "Of course my web site is easy to read. I'm looking at it right now and I can read it." It would be great if every single person in your target audience were using the exact same computer screen, the exact same browser, the exact same Internet connection, and the exact same computer you are using. In all likelihood, your target audience is using a variety of different computers, monitors, Internet connections, and browsers.

In fact, no one knows how directory editors are viewing your web site. They might be using a notebook computer. They might be using a dial-up connection or a high-speed connection. They might be using a Macintosh computer. Site designers need to accommodate as many platforms, browsers, and Internet connections as possible.

Thus, as a general rule, before you submit your site to the major directories, every single item on your web pages needs to be legible on both of the major browsers (Netscape and Explorer) and on the two types of computers (PCs and Macintosh).

All HTML text should be legible with the graphic images turned on and the graphic images turned off (for the visually impaired users). That means producing HTML text, background images, and text in graphic images with a high color contrast. (The highest color contrast comes from using black and white.) Your site designer should not use backgrounds that obscure your text or use colors that are hard to read.

Your site designer should not set your text size too small (too hard to read) or too large (it will appear to shout at your visitors). If a site is specifically designed for visually impaired users, the text size should be adjusted accordingly.

All text in graphic images should be legible. High color contrast and font/typeface selection are very important for legibility in graphic images. Generally, producing graphic images that use text in a sans serif ("without feet") typeface results in better legibility. See Figure 1.13 for examples.

Times and **Times New Roman** are serif typefaces.

Arial and **Helvetica** are sans serif typefaces.

Figure 1.13
Serif and sans serif typefaces.

Animations (both GIF and Flash animations) should not move so quickly that your target audience is unable to read them. If your target audience must watch the animation loop three or more times to view the full message, the animation is moving too fast.

When your site design or redesign is in the template stage, view it on different browsers, platforms, and Internet connections. Go to a library or a store (such as Kinko's) that has different computers than you have and view your site. Better yet, have other people view your site (they will probably be more objective) and tell you if everything is legible. Do not rely on your singular, personal perspective to determine your site's legibility.

Rule #2: Easy to Navigate

"Easy to navigate" means your target audience should know where they are at all times when they visit your web site. If they get lost, they should be able to go to a site map, a help section, a site search, or a home page from any page on your site to determine (a) where they are, (b) where they might want to go, and (c) where they have been.

Directory editors are always thinking about your target audience. If professional directory editors, who are generally seasoned web users, are having a difficult time navigating your site, your target audience is likely to have a difficult time navigating your site as well.

All your hyperlinks should be clear to both your target audience and to the directory editors. Graphic images, such as navigation buttons or file tabs, should be clearly labeled and easy to read. Just as indicated in the First Rule of Web Design, your site designer should select the colors, backgrounds, textures, and special effects on your web graphics so that they are legible on the major browsers, computer screens, and platforms.

Colors in your text links should be familiar to your target audience. Blue, underlined text usually indicates an unvisited link and purple/maroon, underlined text usually indicates a visited link. If you elect not to use these default colors, your text links should be emphasized in some other way (bold, a different color, different size, set between small vertical lines, or a combination of these effects).

Your hyperlink colors and effects should always be unique—they should not look the same as any other text on your web pages.

Many site designers like to take the underline out of hyperlinked text to be more creative. If you are designing a site that targets the more experienced web user, this design technique should not be problematic as long as the hyperlinked text is unique. However, if your target audience is not web savvy, it is best to keep the underline on the hyperlinked text.

Some directory editors are volunteer editors, and these editors are generally selected for a particular category because of their expertise. You do not know whether volunteer editors are web savvy. Thus, it is important to select your navigation scheme with great care.

Rule #3: Easy to Find

Rule #3 has multiple meanings. Your web site should be easy to find through the search engines. In addition, the individual products, services, and information that you offer should be easy to find after your target audience arrives at your site.

For maximum online visibility, your web site should be easy to find on the search engines, directories, and popular industry-specific web sites. For example, download.com is an industry-specific site for free software downloads. If your company offers a free demo of a 30-day trial of your software, having a link to your site from download.com can significantly increase your site's traffic. Other popular, industry-specific sites (in the fields of healthcare, finance, manufacturing, and so on) will link to your site.

Internally (within your web site), the products, services, and information you offer on your web pages should be easy to find after your target audience arrives at your site. Generally speaking, your target audience does not want to land on your home page and hunt around for information. People prefer to go directly to the web page that contains the information for which they are searching. If they cannot go directly to the web page(s) containing the specific information, they need to find that information within seven to eight clicks, preferably less. If they have to click more than that, they might get frustrated and leave your web site.

After your target audience finds the page that contains the information for which they are searching, they need to see that information "above the fold," or at the top part of the screen. Even if people can't immediately see your product/service on top of the screen, they need to know that what they are searching for is on a particular web page. People should not have to scroll to verify that the information for which they are searching is available on a web page.

A Frequently Asked Questions (FAQs) page is an example in which web site designers do not use the "above the fold" strategy particularly well (see Figure 1.14). Let's say you place ten questions on your FAQs page, and the information that your target audience is looking for is the answer to Question #4. Suppose your site designer formats your FAQs page in a Question 1–Answer 1, Question 2–Answer 2 format, as shown in Figure 1.14.

Figure 1.14

FAQs page with a Question-Answer, Question-Answer format.

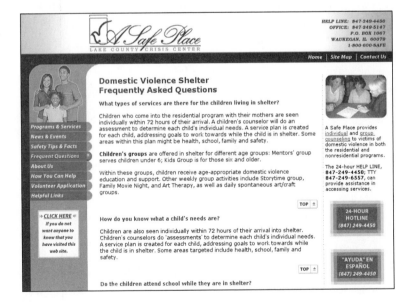

Let's assume that the person viewing this page is a domestic violence victim with children. By looking at the top of this screen, this person is not able to determine whether parent/child interaction is allowed at the shelter. In other words, an answer to an important question might not be available on that web page or site.

However, if all your important questions are placed at the top of your screen, your target audience will know that the answer to a question is available on that web page or site, as shown in Figure 1.15.

All your FAQs pages should be formatted in this manner. Not only is this particular strategy beneficial for reaching your end users, but also it is beneficial because this format is a search engine–friendly layout.

Making your main products and services easy to find is important to directory editors. As stated, if your home page states that your firm specializes in three particular services, those three services need to be obvious on your home page, in terms of graphic images and HTML text. If directory editors, and ultimately your end users, have to hunt around too much to determine what your company specializes in, you did not make your services easy to find.

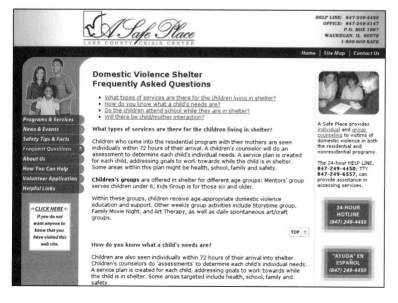

Figure 1.15
A properly formatted FAQs page makes important information about the web page available at the top of the screen.

If the information on your site is password protected or requires some kind of plug-in to get to, directory editors are unable to determine whether your site delivers the information you claim it does. Make sure some of the information available on your web site is not password protected so that directory editors (and your target audience) can see that your site delivers the content that you claim it does.

The last item that should be easy to find is your company's contact information (mailing or physical address, telephone number, fax number, and contact person's email address). Directory editors in particular will search for this information on your web site.

In general, your contact information should be in one of four places:

- A header or footer

- The About Us page or section

- The Contact Us page or section

- A Locations page or section

The most likely place directory editors are looking for your contact information and the correct spelling of your company name is your About Us page. Thus, even if you do provide contact information in other places, it is still a good idea to always place that information in your About Us section—especially if you place your contact information in a footer because many end users do not scroll to the bottom of a web page to view information.

Rule #4: Consistent in Layout and Design

Layout means the use of HTML code, scripting, and white space on your site. This is screen "real estate" where you place your text, graphic images, and navigation schemes. Consistency in layout design helps your target audience navigate your site and feel comfortable doing business with you.

Design means the use of graphic images, the special effects on your graphic images, fonts and typefaces, and the color on your site. Many aspects of the design should be repeated throughout a web site. The fonts, typefaces, and colors used in the main body text, hyperlinks, and headings should be the same on every page of your site.

If you are showing photos of the products you offer, the photo dimensions (length and width) should fall within a short range. Horizontal photos should have the same dimensions and vertical photos should have the same dimensions. If you use a drop shadow on your product photos, you should use drop shadows on all your product photos.

Graphic images and text should never be placed on a web page randomly or arbitrarily. Everything should have a visual connection with other items on a web page. Related items, such as a main navigation scheme and a secondary navigation scheme, should be grouped so that they are seen as a cohesive group rather than as unrelated items.

Making two navigation schemes visually different creates visual contrast but also shows how they are interrelated. For example, a main navigation scheme can be shown at the top of a page using a set of specific colors, and the secondary navigation scheme can open up on the left side of the screen with a different set of colors that blend well with the main navigation.

Figure 1.16 shows an example of a web page that shows visual contrast and connectivity. This is also a well-constructed web page for search engines, directories, and the target audience.

Figure 1.16

Sample of a well-constructed web page.

Subnavigation buttons   Main heading   Subheadings   File tabs

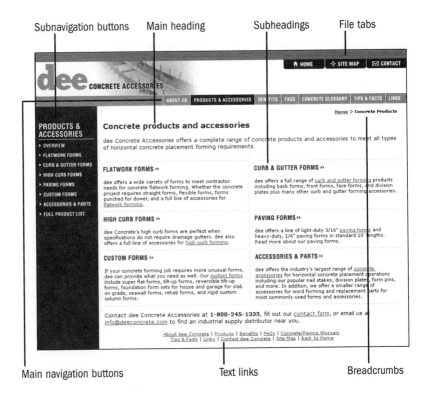

Main navigation buttons   Text links   Breadcrumbs

Note the following in Figure 1.16:

- File tab graphic images link to the home page and site map, in the event the target audience gets lost or needs to reorient themselves. This set of navigation images is in the same place on every web page.

- Main navigation buttons change color when end users are visiting that section of the web site.

- A secondary navigation scheme, or subnavigation, opens up when end users click the link from the main navigation. Text in the subnavigation repeats the text in the main navigation to further indicate that the navigation buttons on the left are a subset of the main navigation.

- Breadcrumbs indicate which page the end users are currently visiting.

- A main heading (which can also be a graphic image) indicates which page the end users are currently visiting.

- Subheadings (graphic images) highlight the main features of this section of the web site. Arrows on the subheadings give a subtle hint that they are hyperlinks.

- Text links at the bottom of the page correspond to the main navigation buttons. These links indicate which pages the target audience has already visited. The hypertext link colors remain similar to a browser's default colors because the target audience is not considered to be as web savvy as people who regularly work on the web.

Rule #5: Quick to Download

Directory editors look for web pages that download very quickly, preferably within 30 seconds on a standard dial-up connection. Of course, there are a few exceptions to this guideline, such as pages that specialize in online video games. Then it is understandable that a web page might take longer to download because plug-ins such as Flash or Shockwave must download first for the game to display.

Most pages do not fall in the "video game" category, so it is best to minimize your pages' download time, particularly your home page. The following are some general guidelines to follow that will decrease your pages' download time:

- **Use animation sparingly:** Animation should be used only to call attention to important sections of your web site. Graphic artists who specialize in animation can safely use animation on their pages as long as they are useful.

- **Follow the KISS rule:** Keep it simple, stupid. You want customers to notice the products, services, and information you offer on your web site, not your pretty site design. If your target audience notices your site design before they notice your content, the design is not effective. A person searching for "accounting software" does not type the words "pretty site design" in a search box when he or she is looking for information about accounting software.

- **Use smaller graphic images, called thumbnails, for product photos:** On your Products pages, a gallery of small photos will download more quickly than full-size photos. Give your target audience the choice to view the larger photos after they show interest.

- **To get a faster download time, always create separate, unique thumbnail-size graphic images from their larger versions:** All graphic images should be resized in graphic image software, not with HTML.

- **Use the same graphic images on multiple pages of your site whenever possible:** Using graphic images consistently also lends to continuity in your presentation. For example, placing your logo on every page of your site (with a hyperlink to your home page) helps with both navigation and branding, and it helps your target audience know whose site they are visiting at all times. The logo image will download only once because it will be saved in the browser's cache. Introducing new graphic images on each page requires time-consuming downloading as a visitor moves around your site.

- **Understand the variety of customers in your target audience:** Different customers will tolerate different download times. If you have graphic design or an online game site, your customers are more likely to wait for pages to download to experience your creative flair. However, if you are selling machine parts to busy manufacturers, ease of access to valuable information should be your primary concern.

Download time is not only important to your target audience. It is also important for search engine visibility. When a search engine spider requests a web page from your server, if the page takes too long to download, or if your server does not give the page to the spider quickly, the search engine might not add the page to the index.

Index

J

JavaScript
as impediment to search engines, 121
placement of, in external files, as best practice, 147

JavaServer Pages (.jsp files), 124

Jupiter Research, 159

K

Kanoodle
ad listings on, as appearing on other search engines, 91
as named in trademark infringement lawsuit, 254
as Pay-For-Placement (PFP) search engine, 90

Keyword Count (keyword density tool), 145

keyword density, 144-146

Keyword Density & Prominence (keyword density tool), 145

Keyword Density Analyzer (Bruce Clay), 145

keyword phrases, 13, 43

keyword rates. *See also* **individual rates**
cost-per-acquisition (CPA), 79, 90, 225-226
cost-per-click (CPC), 79, 90, 129-130
cost-per-thousand (CPM), 79

keywords. *See also* **bidding, on keywords; keywords, branded; keywords, generic**
buying, based on cost-per-acquisition goals, 225-226
of competing companies
as found in source code (meta data), 38-39
as not possible to monitor, 58
density of, on web pages, 144-146
as handled by Fixed Placement programs
exclusivity of, as available, 80-81
rates for, 79-80
as handled by Pay-For-Placement (PFP) programs
costs of competitive keywords, 94

as handled by Submit URL programs
evaluation of, as necessary, 118
secondary keywords, as generated by relevant web site content, 112-113
as handled by vertical market search engines
Amazon.com, as not offering keyword purchasing program, 166-167
eBay, 162-163
National Gardening Association web site, 163, 164-166
hyperlinking of
from ad listing, to web pages, 138-139
via cross-links, within web sites, 119, 142, 146
instead of using "click here," 142
ideas for, as generated by, 82
including, on landing pages, 146
including, in paid listings, 53-55, 97
incorporating, into URLs and file names, 143-144
industry jargon, pros and cons of, 42-43
keyword phrases, 13, 43
keyword universe, 28, 32, 82
long list of, as good first step, 45-46
matching of, by search engine technology, as problematic for trademark owners, 254-256
meta data, as containing, 38-39, 140-141, 147
misspellings of, including, 147
modifying, for each call to action, 26
multiple-word phrases, 43
narrowly focused, as recommended, 32, 43, 146
number of, to use per page, 146
organic listings, as generated by, 38, 109
on plain, text-heavy web sites, as easier to find, 136
purchase of trademarks, as supported by search engines, 255
rates for. *See also* individual rates
cost-per-acquisition (CPA), 79, 90, 225-226
cost-per-click (CPC), 79, 90, 129-130
cost-per-thousand (CPM), 79

L

Visit Peachpit on the Web at www.peachpit.com

- Read the latest articles and download timesaving tipsheets from best-selling authors such as Scott Kelby, Robin Williams, Lynda Weinman, Ted Landau, and more!

- Join the Peachpit Club and save 25% off all your online purchases at peachpit.com every time you shop—plus enjoy free UPS ground shipping within the United States.

- Search through our entire collection of new and upcoming titles by author, ISBN, title, or topic. There's no easier way to find just the book you need.

- Sign up for newsletters offering special Peachpit savings and new book announcements so you're always the first to know about our newest books and killer deals.

- Did you know that Peachpit also publishes books by Apple, New Riders, Adobe Press, Macromedia Press, palmOne Press, and TechTV press? Swing by the Peachpit family section of the site and learn about all our partners and series.

- Got a great idea for a book? Check out our About section to find out how to submit a proposal. You could write our next best-seller!

You'll find all this and more at www.peachpit.com. Stop by and take a look today!

0789723107
Steve Krug
US$35.00

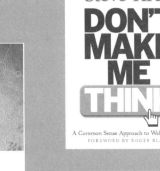

0735712565
Shari Thurow
US$29.99

0735712506
Christina Wodtke
US$29.99

0735711704
Andrew Chak
US$35.00

0735713243
Andrew King
US$39.99

0735712069
June Cohen
US$35.00

VOICES
THAT MATTER™

WWW.NEWRIDERS.COM

Free Pay-Per-Click Advertising Clicks!

Visit http://www.SearchEngineSales.com/Free to
recieve free clicks when you sign up for a new advertising
account with Yahoo! and MIVA (see web page for details).

You'll receive:
- ▲ **$25 credit from Yahoo! Search Marketing**
  (Previously Overture's PPC Program)
- ▲ **$10 credit from MIVA**
  (The new name for FindWhat.com)

DH OwT

659.
144
SED

5000782507

596172.